THE BOOK OF

BOSCASTLE

The Parishes of Forrabury and Minster

THE BOOK OF

BOSCASTLE

The Parishes of Forrabury and Minster

ROD AND ANNE KNIGHT

HALSGROVE

First published in Great Britain in 2004

British Library Cataloguing-in-Publication Data.
A CIP record for this title is available from the British Library.

ISBN 1 84114 325 1

HALSGROVE

Halsgrove House
Lower Moor Way
Tiverton, Devon EX16 6SS
Tel: 01884 243242
Fax: 01884 243325
email: sales@halsgrove.com
website: www.halsgrove.com

Frontispiece photograph: *Smugglers and Tinkers Cottages. The war memorial is just visible on the right-hand side at the entrance to the castle site.*

Contents page photograph: *Daniel Fulford Ward and Sarah Louise Ward.*

Printed and bound in Great Britain by CPI, Bath.

CONTENTS

	Foreword	7
	Acknowledgements	9
	Introduction	10
Chapter 1	***Celts, Churches and Crosses***	11
Chapter 2	***Castles, Knights and Lords of the Manor***	23
Chapter 3	***Piers, Palaces and Pilchard***	39
Chapter 4	***Inns and Pubs***	55
Chapter 5	***Pirates, Smugglers and Wreckers***	69
Chapter 6	***Entertainment***	85
Chapter 7	***Butcher, Baker and Blacksmith***	101
Chapter 8	***Tinker, Tailor, Soldier, Sailor***	125
	Subscribers	154

Postman Bill Hockin in Post Office Lane (or Oxen Road) during Edwardian times.

Foreword

It is a privilege to write a foreword to *The Book of Boscastle*. Over many years people in the village have collected artefacts and photographs, newspapers and paintings, recorded reminiscences, mounted exhibitions, and researched in the Cornwall Record Office and archaeological department, in the Courtney Library in the Royal Institution of Cornwall and in the Cornish Studies Library, culminating in what they call the 'Boscastle Archive'. Congratulations to Rod and Anne Knight, who have drawn on all this information, archaeological, documentary, photographic and anecdotal, to produce a book that illuminates the lives of this hardy community.

As we look down over the romantic little harbour, with its narrow, twisting entrance channel cutting through the rocks, or view the attractive old cottages at the head of the steep valley, we are quite properly reminded that life in the 'good old days' for the people who lived and worked in Boscastle was a constant battle against Nature's harsher elements, the full force of the westerly gales that tear straight off the Atlantic and the waves that crash onto the cliffs. It is good to have this unsentimental record of the community that has had to draw its livelihood from land and sea on this dramatic north coast of Cornwall.

Moira Tangye
Newquay, Cornwall

Flora Dance, 1947. The last dancers leaving High Street.

Boscastle School Recorder Group, 1957. Among those pictured are: *Brian Beer, Basil Snowden, Albert Philp, Gordon Coupe, Tracey Berryman, Alan Ferrett, George Findlay, Pam Hancock, Jean Nicholls, Joyce Hancock, Eunice Honey, Mary Higgins, Wendy Brewer, Trixie Webber, Vivien Hilton, Janet Wakeham, Pauline Martin, Jennifer Ferrett, Kenny Cowling, George Perry, Tacker Wickett, John Sandercock and John Ferrett.*

This picture of the High Street was taken by Richard Webber before the installation of electricity, showing Providence Hotel on the right. The name is just visible on the facing wall.

Acknowledgements

It is the custom in such books to acknowledge the contributions various people have made to the work of the authors, and we now appreciate how absolutely vital these contributions are. Without the help of those who have shared their memories, photographs and family documents we could not have written this book. This volume is their record of Boscastle's past.

We are particularly grateful to Mrs Iris Olde, who spent many hours talking to us and sorting and cataloguing her large photographic collection so that we could identify the people and events. We also owe our thanks to Trixie Webster and her brother Michael Webber for allowing us to reproduce the Richard Webber postcards and photographs. Michael contributed his collection of writings and was responsible for proofreading some of the book, particularly those areas concerning the harbour and shipping. Anne's brother Dr Jon Mills also proofread several chapters involving the Cornish language and music, despite particularly difficult personal circumstances, for which we thank him. Jim Castling may also recognise much of his handiwork as we have leant heavily on his writings from the 'Boscastle Blowhole's Born and Bred' columns. Thank you Jim.

We wouldn't even have got started without the help, advice and support of Moira Tangye whose WEA course set us collecting contributions to the Boscastle Archive, which now contains over 3,000 items of historical information and photographic images. We are very proud that Moira agreed to write the foreword to this book.

Our thanks must also go to: Pamela and Michael Ward, Mrs Ruth Stephens, Mrs Sarah Cooke, Mr and Mrs Julian May, Mr and Mrs Mike Mills, Mrs Yvonne Ayling, Mrs Elizabeth Blamey, Mr and Mrs Stuart Brown, Mrs Sue Scott, Mrs Mary Smee, Miss Carole Vincent, Mr Tim Doubleday, Mrs Odette Rigby-Jones, Mr Andrew Bond, Mrs Monica Bond, Mr and Mrs Roland Buckett, Mr and Mrs Richard Ferrett, Mrs Phyllis Perry, Mrs Eunice Sandercock, Mr Walter Gard, Mr and Mrs Nicky Nicholls, Mr and Mrs Arthur Nicholls, Mr Peter Fleming, Mrs Doreen Hancock, Mrs Margaret Perry, Mrs Vivien Hircock, Mr and Mrs Brian Honey, Mr Dudley Kernick, Mrs Muriel Symons, Mr and Mrs Aubrey Cronin, Mr and Mrs Basil Jose, Mr Richard Wingfield, Mr William Mably, Mrs Jackie Gynn, Revd David Nash, Mr Michael Turner, Mrs Joanna Raymond-Barker, Mr Mark Winnicott, Mrs Babette Scougall, Mrs Marion Ferrett, Mr Stuart Biddick, Mrs Philippa Arthan, Mr Eric Nicholls, Mr Derek Whitmore, Mr and Mrs Dennis Pace, Dr Chris Jarvis, Mr Eric Snowden, Barbara Sandercock, Mr and Mrs Don Henderson, Cdr and Mrs Joe Mills, Dr Jon Mills, Mr Ivor Bright, Mr Arthur Biddick, Mr and Mrs Charles Hancock, Mrs Sue Roundhill, Derek Stedman, Ginny and Heulyn Lewis.

We also wish to thank the following organisations: *The Cornish and Devon Post,* Cornish Studies Library, Courtney Library, National Trust and the Coastguard Service.

INTRODUCTION

This book is the result of our acquiring habits which were encouraged in no small part by Moira Tangye, who, under the auspices of the WEA, set up the Boscastle History Group in 1997. As a project for this group we wrote a small booklet on Boscastle's history, which has been sold through local outlets ever since. Even though our family has been in Boscastle for many generations, we were amazed at how important this village and its inhabitants have been. Boscastle, nowadays, gives the superficial impression of a picturesque, tranquil spot, ideal for a summer break. Any clue to its past is disappearing beneath the tourist trappings that are growing at a faster rate than ever before.

Boscastle has been a manor since Norman times, taking its name from the first lords of the manor, the Breton family of Bottreaux. The manor was only sold in the 1950s and so retained a continuity of landlord, tenant and workforce for over 800 years. The harbour imported goods for a large part of North Cornwall and its overland trade stretched even as far as Saltash and Plymouth, and exported amongst other things a high number of emigrants to Upper Canada. The first successful Australian farmer came from here and it was a place visited by many, including the Prince of Wales, the King of Prussia, Sir Henry Irving, Thomas Hardy, Guy Gibson, Uffa Fox and the young Lady Tavistock and her parents.

It has been confirmed to us in the writing of this book that history is not an exact science and we hope you will forgive us our errors and omissions, for we are still learning and collecting information about the village. We have had invaluable help and contributions from many whose families live or once lived in Boscastle and we hope this publication fulfills their expectations. It is our hope that we have recorded some of the essence of Boscastle's past and that in reading *The Book of Boscastle* a better understanding of the present village may be gained.

Rod and Anne Knight
Boscastle

Chapter One

Celts, Churches and Crosses

The parishes of Forrabury and Minster lie within the Hundred of Lesnewth and together form the village of Boscastle and its surrounding area. They are divided by the River Jordan which flows northwards from Paradise. The two were amalgamated for ecclesiastical purposes in 1701 and for civil purposes in 1919.

Forrabury, at 508 acres in area, is one of the smallest parishes in Cornwall. Yet in its heyday it had both creek and harbour, quays, warehousing and quarries. It contains several elements of Cornish landscape history. An Iron-Age cliff castle stands on Willapark headland, an open field of 'stitches' lies on Forrabury Common, and below the Norman church is an ancient granite cross.

Willapark takes its name from the brythonic Celtic words 'whyllas' and 'parc' meaning 'lookout' and 'enclosure', or an enclosed lookout. The topographical words are as descriptive today as they were in Celtic times. There is a modern coastguard lookout on the site of an ancient univallate promontory fort 317 feet above sea level. It occupies an unrivalled coastal viewpoint looking towards Tintagel in the south-west and Cambeak and Strangles in the north-east.

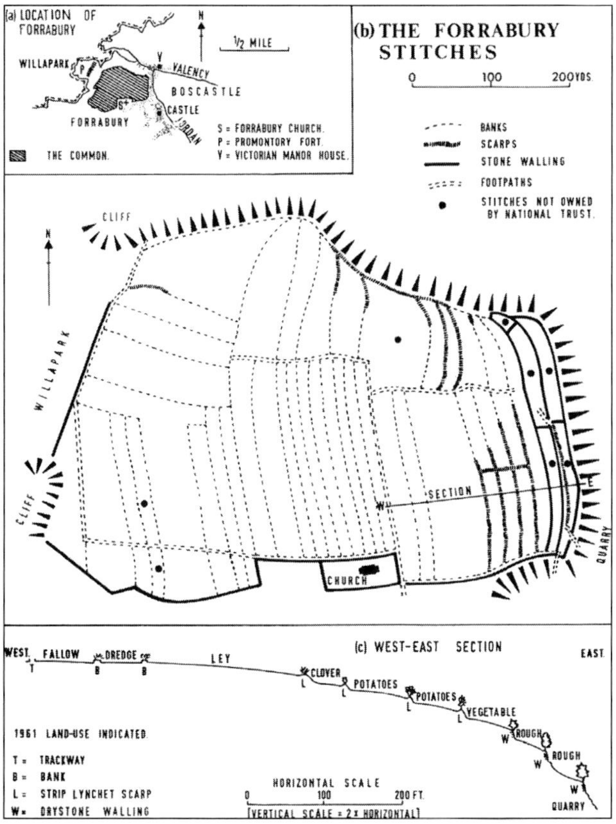

Plan of Forrabury stitches.
(P.D. Wood, Cornish Archaeology No. 2.)

The Iron-Age cliff castle on this headland consists of a single defensive rampart 110m long. It survives to a height of 1.8m and has a ditch 0.8m deep in front of it. The rampart is most prominent at its north-eastern end where it is at the foot of a steep slope. It is less distinct at its south-western end. The original entrance was probably where the modern footpath cuts through the bank. The whole area covers about three hectares. It forms part of Forrabury Common which covers, in total, 32 hectares.

On the common are the remains of an ancient field-farming system known as 'stitches'. They cover 20 hectares. The word 'stitch' is an old Cornish word for 'strips', believed by some to be the relics of an Iron-Age farming system. Roy Millward and Adrian Robinson (1971) put forward the theory that this Iron-Age open-field system was part of a Celtic in-field out-field method. A piece of land, the in-field, close to the settlement was cultivated continuously and fertilised in the winter with the dung of grazing animals. The out-field, a vast area around the hamlet, was used for pasture. Crops were grown here and there, for a year or two, on small patches of the out-field. If this is the truth of the origins of Forrabury Common, the field might be related to a Dark-Age Celtic settlement whose location may have been near the present church.

Certainly by the thirteenth century most hamlets would have been surrounded by arable fields divided into strips. The plan of one stitch owned by the Earl of Radnor appears in the *Lanhydrock Atlas* of 1694 and an heiress in the same family was the owner of a strip in 1839. The land was regarded, in a terrier of 1679, as common (Maclean, 1873), as opposed to the adjacent fields on the south which were individually owned. Local families in 2004 say that each householder in Forrabury had rights to the stitches. The individual occupiers grew what crops they wished from Lady Day (25 March) to Michaelmas (29 September). During the winter sheep or cattle were grazed. Some say that all householders had the right do this.

Despite the varying number of owners, the tithe map of 1839 shows 50 strips, most of which were eventually controlled by the manor. One of the owners of more than 20 strips became lord of the manor himself.

The manor agent and the stitch-holders made an agreement to exclude the cattle of non-stitch-holders and decided that their cattle could be impounded and held in the castle pound until a fine was paid.

In the 1940s the ratio of grazing animals was five sheep or two cattle per acre occupied by the tenant, and boys were employed to see that the animals did not stray from the common.

Originally there would have been about 60 stitches. The tithe map of 1839 shows 50 strips. In 2004 there are about 40. The original strips would have been one furlong by one chain (an acre), but over time some have been amalgamated and some cut down in size or sub-divided. They now vary in size from 1/2 to 1 1/2 acres. Most run from north to south but others are orientated east to west. Each is slightly curved to make ploughing easier (an aratric curve) and separated by a narrow ribbon of permanently uncultivated land. Where they have been ploughed on the slopes of the hill the soil has piled up forming small retaining banks or lynchets. On the steepest slopes they have been reinforced by stone walls. This is the only remaining example of a banked lynchet or terrace system in the British Isles.

A feature of the headland was the introduction of goats who were at one time confined by walls and a gate so they would not interfere with the nearby crops. These goats survived well into the twentieth century. Another curious feature was the construction of tunnels covered with slate tiles for the installation of Belgian hares, a valuable source of meat in winter. Writing in 1842, Cyrus Reading mentions Cornish choughs at Willapark. Sadly they are not here today but the peregrine falcon has returned to nest in the area.

On the southern edge of Forrabury Common is the parish church which is dedicated to St Symphorian. It is one of two churches that serve Boscastle – the other is at Minster. There was a church on the site in Norman times but little of it remains. A document of 1189 records the gift of Forrabury Church by William de Botreaux to Hartland Abbey. The first recorded rector is William de Stonhouse in 1308. In 1329 John Poddynge was excommunicated because he had 'instructus diabolico assaulted the Rector of Forebiri, giving him

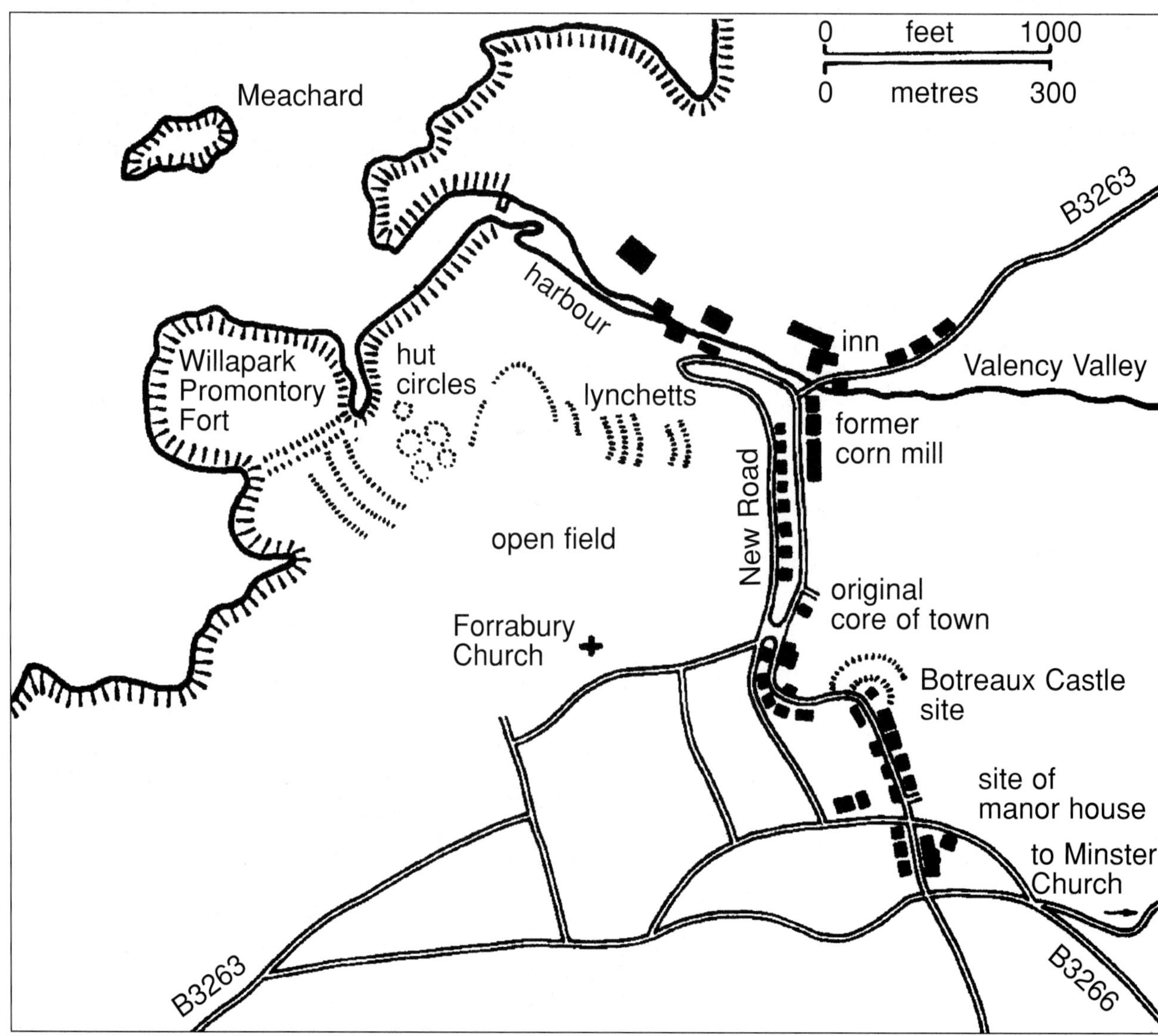

Plan showing the location of Forrabury stitches. (MILLWARD AND ROBINSON, 1971)

Boscastle from the air showing the stitches and Iron-Age cliff castle.

Harvesting the stitches at the foot of the Iron-Age cliff castle.

View of Boscastle from Trecarne Corner showing Forrabury Church, the stitches and Coastguard lookout.

Forrabury Church in 1937.

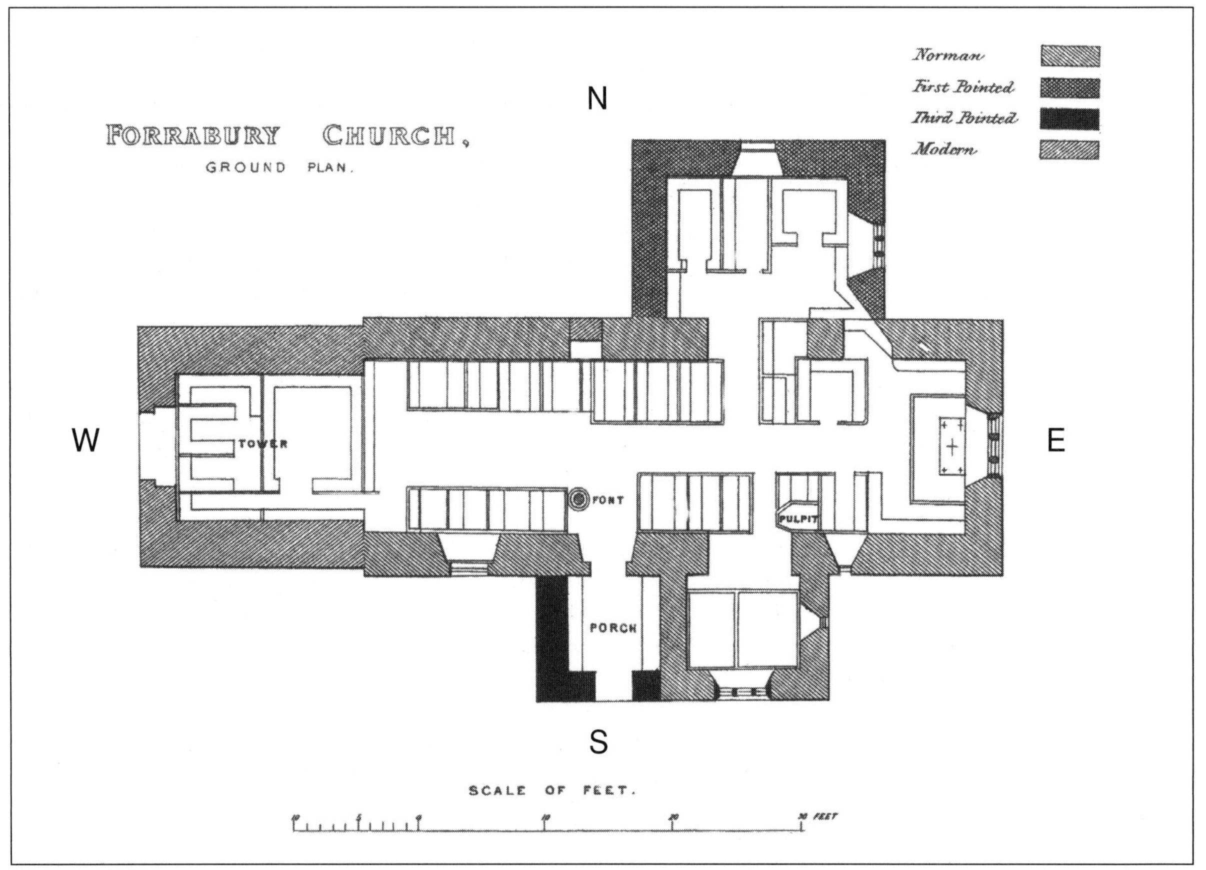

Floor plan of Forrabury Church in 1866, prior to the restoration the following year.

a public drubbing and slashing off an ear of his horse.' The oldest surviving part of the building is the porch which is dated 1520. In 1843 a terrific gale, the Jessie Logan gale, almost took the roof off and the extensive repairs cost £46.2s.11d.

In 1843 the Vestry minutes record that it was:

> *... unanimously resolved that the singers have been very neglectful and do not deserve the singing money, and until they better deserve it we propose leaving it in the hands of the churchwardens until the sense of the parishioners can be obtained!*

In 1867, in response to the need for extra seating, the south side of the church was taken down and rebuilt at a cost of £320.

Sir John Maclean visited the church in 1866, prior to the restoration. In his *Parochial and Family History of Forrabury and Minster* he described the church as it was at that time. It consisted of a chancel 11 feet by 13 feet 3 inches, nave 33 feet by 14 feet 3 inches, north chapel 14 feet 3 inches by 10 feet 7 inches, south chapel 11 feet by 7 feet 8 inches, and a south porch and western tower. He described the windows in the chancel as being modern and of a very bad type. The nave had a north door and one modern window. The north chapel had a triple lancet window in the east wall and a modern window at the north end. In the east wall was a trefoil-headed piscina (a stone basin for rinsing the chalice and carrying away water) and a niche for carrying the image of a saint. This was at the angle of the window-splay. A large hagioscope opened into the chancel, over which was another niche. The arches between the chancel and nave were of early-Norman work resting on plain abaci supported by responds. The south chapel was much smaller that the north. In the east wall was a lancet and at the south end a third-pointed three-light window. The chancel was separated from the nave by a carved oak screen of third-pointed work. The font, made from porphyry, was near the south door of the nave where it is at the time of writing.

In the nave were some carved oak bench-ends. They depicted the passion, two keys in saltire, cock and hen, swans swimming, an ape in a sitting position, and rabbits in a warren, one at the top of a burrow, another coming out and a third just disappearing. On the one which formed the end of the choir-stall was a bare-headed priest kneeling at a standard desk on which lies an open book. The pulpit was early-seventeenth century with panels ornamented with the arabesque carving of the period. Over the inner door of the porch was a bracket for an image.

The tower is of three heights, battlemented, with a circular-headed window on each side. It was built in 1750 on the base of an earlier tower. There is only one bell inscribed 'John Tink 1812'. He lived at Welltown Manor.

The interior of Forrabury Church showing some of the medieval woodwork retained during the restoration and incorporated in the altar, credence table and pulpit in the right-hand foreground.

During the renovations in 1867 the north chapel was converted into an aisle and a vestry was added to the south side. All the carved oak was removed and replaced with plain deal benches. The original cup-shaped font remains with its diagonal criss-cross carvings. Not all of the medieval woodwork has gone. Some has been incorporated in the altar, pulpit and credence table. The chancel floor, panelling, altar rails and screen were installed later in 1911. The altar in the side chapel is a memorial to the First World War. The altar here is a Jacobean table, above which is a beautiful embroidered collage of a dove made by Yvonne Ayling, wife of Revd Canon John Ayling and placed there in memory of $11^1/_2$ years spent happily in Boscastle (1991–2002).

Until 2001, the curtains behind this altar, which were of cream and gold damask, had been in place for 50 years and had been part of the postwar renovations. In April 2001 the heavy wooden frame on which the curtains were hung was removed. This revealed the organ-loft. Drapes of blue and gold brocade were hung on new gold rods and donated by Revd Canon John Ayling and his wife Yvonne as a 'thank you' for ten happy years at the church and to celebrate their ruby wedding anniversary. These were complimented by new altar drapes and a fabric hanging depicting a dove, worked in embroidery over applique. The following dedication was stitched into the back of the altar frontal:

> *Presented by John and Yvonne Ayling 22 September 2002 On the 40th Anniversary of John's Ordination as Deacon And in memory of Alec Shearwood (Priest) and Charles Gibson (Friend)*

Alec Shearwood served the parish from 1990 to 2000. He was a 'retired' priest who gave invaluable help during the interregnum after Revd David Nash retired, right up until a few months before his

Bernard Lowe's Angels. Revd Bernard Lowe is pictured with six choir boys. Left to right: *Buster Beadon, Cyril Russell, Claude Knight* (sitting cross-legged), *Bill Hilton, Percy Nicholls, ?.*

Wartime bride Gladys Rachel Bastick and groom William James (Jim) Kinsman RM outside the porch of Forrabury Church following their wedding on 20 October 1942.

death. Charles Gibson was a Cornishman, born in Launceston where his father was a well-known doctor. When he returned he came to live in Boscastle and was soon a well-known character himself. He was a devoted churchgoer whose readings in services will never be forgotten. Sadly, he too died of cancer. John and Yvonne Ayling wanted to recognise the contributions these two rather special men had made to Forrabury Church.

Much of the fabric work carried out in the church was made possible as a result of a memorial fund given in memory of Revd Neville Kirby. Neville and Maggie Kirby had lived in Bristol but were frequent visitors to Boscastle. Their aim was always to retire to the village. They purchased a cottage, St Hugh, and were about to settle in when Neville became critically ill. He died of a brain tumour, having spent most of his last months here.

The deeper-blue velvet curtains which surround the organ and those dividing the vestry from the nave also benefited from the fund, which paid for the material. It was made up by Yvonne Ayling and Pat Stanton-Nadin. The red hangings used at Whitsun and other days of celebration were made by Yvonne. They are red brocade lined with satin and feature a Celtic cross of knots worked in gold thread on each of the altar cloth, pulpit hanging, other sanctuary hangings, burse and veil. The purple hangings are of linen, lined with satin, and feature plain gold crosses. All these and the restoration of the green and white hangings were made possible by the Neville Kirby fund.

The church is dedicated to a little-known saint, Symphorian, who came from Autun in Burgundy. He was beheaded in AD282 for protesting against the worship of the goddess Cybele. He is commemorated on 22 August.

The town of Forrabury itself may have developed from an earlier Dark-Age Celtic settlement, as previously suggested. By 1650 it had fallen on hard times. England was in the grip of the Civil War (1642–60) and Charles I had been executed in 1649; Cornwall, divided in its loyalty to King or Parliament, had come out mainly for the King.

John Norden (1650) describes Forrabury as a:

> *Mayor towne, the meaneste and pooreste that can beare the name of towne, much lesse of an incorporation, for it consisteth but of 2 or 3 houses: It hath bene of more importance, as appeareth by the ruynes: But the fall of Tintagill and Botreaux hath bene the overthrow of this and many others upon this coast.*

The rectory house was described in a glebe terrier of 1679 as 'one dwelling house with two under rooms only, the walls of stone and covered with slatt.' Its exact position is not known but the glebe holdings were described in another terrier of glebe lands in the earlier times of Elizabeth I as being of about nine acres:

Bawndede on the southe wth ye Quenes heigh way: The weste with ye lands of John Tyncke: The north wth Farraburye down: Upon the este wth ye Quenes highe way: iij litell closses in all.
By me Roger Cowp Curatt

Since then there have been at least three other sites where rectories have stood: one was where Westerings is in 2004, to the south-west and on the opposite side of the road to the church; one was the Old Rectory built by Revd Kirkness in 1876 and almost opposite the church; and the new rectory was built in the 1970s. At the time of writing the road passes to the north of Westerings and the Old Rectory, but it appears at one time to have passed to the south. The buildings along here all have their backs to the present road. At one time the road from Tintagel came in from the west along Under Road passing in front of these houses and on towards the castle site. It is on this old road that Forrabury Cross used to stand, at the north-eastern end of Under Road where the football ground is in 2004. This field is known as Cross Park. The two neighbouring fields on its western boundary are called Middle Centry (Sanctuary) and Western Centry Fields.

In 2004 Forrabury Cross stands on a small piece of green just below the gates of the church. In the early spring it stands in a sea of daffodils and bluebells. It is set on a base of Tintagel greenstone and measures 5 feet 7 1/2 inches high. The head is 1 foot 6 inches wide by 8 inches thick. The shaft tapers to 13 inches at the top from 15 inches at the bottom. The head is round and decorated on both sides with a Greek-style cross. The side facing the church is very worn and there is some evidence that it was used as a gate-post, as there are three holes in it for gate hangers.

Arthur G. Langdon, in his book *Old Cornish Crosses*, says that there can be no doubt that like churchyard crosses such structures were erected for devotional purposes or for praying stations. He cites 'Dives et Pauper' a 'Worke emprynted by Wyken de Worde' in 1496 which asserts:

For thys reason ben crosses by ye waye than when folke passynge see ye crosses, they shoulde thynke on hym that deyed on ye cross, and worshippe him above al thynge.

In his will of 1447 D. Reginald Merthederwa, rector of Creed, in Cornwall, asked for new crosses to be put up in Cornwall at points where bodies were rested on the way to their burial, so that prayers could be said and the bearers could rest. Another theory put forward by Revd W. Haslam in the *Archaeological Journal* (*Vol. IV*, 1847) suggests that such crosses marked the way to the church. It is an old tradition that pilgrims followed such crosses to holy sites such as wells or chapels, and in doing so left alms there for the benefit of those who were not

The granite cross at the entrance to Forrabury Church. The holes made when it was used as a gate hanging can be clearly seen.

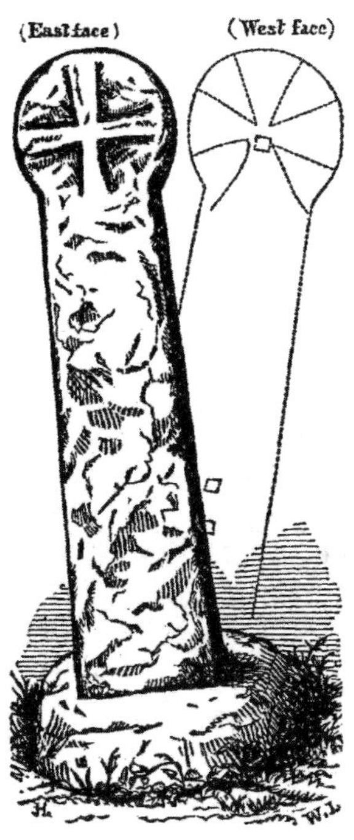

A sketch of the granite cross outside the churchyard at Forrabury showing the east and west faces. (MACLEAN)

A sketch of the base of Minster Cross showing the interlaced matwork, bosses and the interlaced cross. (MACLEAN)

so well off. Revd Burnard S. Lowe (1930) suggested that crosses were put up before churches and marked the place of an old preaching spot or an area of sanctuary for a limited period for those who had broken the law.

So there are many and varied suggested reasons for the existence of crosses, and in its position in 2004 Forrabury Cross could be said to be guarding the gate to the church, even if this was not the original intention.

However, the cross in the parish of Minster is nowhere near a church. Nor is it at a crossroads. Again we turn to Maclean for information. He states that the cross (only the shaft remains) is situated at the angle formed by the ancient roads from Tregear in St Kew, and Tintagel to Warbstow Beacon, all three sites having ancient caers or castles. The shaft was placed on this site in 1869 by Colonel S.G. Bake of Camelford, previously having been at Trekeek Farm since 1860 where it was used as a pivot for a horse-powered threshing-machine.

The shaft measures 7 feet 6 inches high excluding the tenon which is 11 inches. Above the tenon it measures 2 feet 4 inches wide tapering to 1 foot 6 inches at the top. It is 11 inches thick at the bottom. At the top a socket for the head remains. All four sides are carved and the front is inscribed. It is divided into three panels of differing sizes. The upper panel has a serpentine band and Stafford knots – did it at one time also have a dragon's head at the top? The centre panel is inscribed: 'CR VX IRC VR OC', and the lower panel contains a twist and ring pattern. The back of the shaft is divided into two sections, the upper part has figure-of-eight work with bosses sculpted in the centres. The lower panel contains two oval flattened rings forming the shape of an interlaced St Andrew's cross. Both sides of the shaft are carved. The right side is in better condition with a twisted-key pattern at the top and scroll work at the bottom. The left side is again in two panels, but the upper panel is too worn to distinguish what was on it. The lower panel contains a leaf and branch design.

Although Minster Cross at Waterpit Down does not guard the gateway to a church, it may mark the way to a holy site such as the well at Minster Church. The parish of Minster has another ancient stone, although this is not a cross. This type of stone, of a later period than the long stones, differs from them by being smaller and containing inscriptions. The majority are memorials erected to chieftains or other important persons. There are several of these inscribed stones in Cornwall which date from the fifth or sixth century. There is such an inscribed stone at Slaughter Bridge on the barton of Worthyvale. It has been said that the legendary King Arthur fought his last battle here against his nephew Mordred.

Leland (1535), in writing about the River Alan, notes 'some historyes cawl it Cablan. By this river Arture faught his last field yn token where of the people fynd there in plowynyg bones and harneys.' Carew (1602) writes that:

... upon the river Camel was the last dismal battle strooken between the noble King Arthur and his treacherous nephew Mordred wherein one took his death and the other his death's wound. For testimony whereof the folk thereabouts will show you a stone bearing Arthurs name, though now depraved to Artry.

Marianus Scotus (1028–86), a learned Scottish monk who was related to the Venerable Bede, in writing of a bloody battle here wrote the following lines:

Naturam Cambela Fontis
Mutatum stupet esse sui, transcendit inundans
Sanguineas torrens ripas, & ducit in aequor
Corpora caesorum, plures natare videres,
Et petere auxilium, quos undis vita reliquit.

The river Camel wonders that
His fountain's nature shows
So strange a change, the bloody stream
Upswelling overflows
His both side banks, and to the sea
The slaughtered bodies bears
Full many swim, and sue for aid
While wave their life outwears.

An illustration of the stone was drawn by Revd Iago of Bodmin in 1870. The inscription reads: *'LATINI IC IACIT FILIUS MAGARI'* (Latinus lies here son of Magari).

The dowager Lady Falmouth is said to have moved the stone from its original position, where it was being used as a footbridge, to its present site. There is nothing to link the stone with certainty to King Arthur, but many ancient chroniclers agree that a great battle was fought between the Britons and the Saxons at Gafulford, Gavelford, Camelford in the year 823. Henry, Earl of Huntingdon, says many thousands were slain on both sides. Perhaps the stone was erected as a monument to a chieftain who fell there in battle.

Unlike the parish church at Forrabury, which is set high up on the common above the sea, the parish church of Minster lies in the most beautiful and peaceful valley through which the River Valency flows, on the site of an ancient religious cell. No visible evidence of this remains, however, apart from fragments of pottery which are littered about the area near the parish church and the holy well.

There has been a religious foundation on this site since about AD500. A Welsh princess, named Madryn, gave healing there by prayer and water. She is said to be buried in the chancel of the church. Earth, air, fire and water were considered in prehistoric times to be the four constituent elements of the

Minster Church in 1909, described by the writer of this postcard as a pretty old church in a lovely valley.

The tower of Minster Church nestled into the richly wooded valley of Peter's Wood.

earth. Celtic man regarded them with reverence. Pure water was held in wonder and veneration. A spring was 'alive', so the origins of many of the later Christian acts and customs at springs and wells go back to these times. When saints arrived here they settled near a spring, for obvious reasons, and soon the water that the Celts revered for its 'spirit' was consecrated to Christian use. Gradually the reputation and power of the spring were transformed to the local saint who 'used' its powers for healing in the way that Madryn was said to have done at Minster.

Minster is mentioned in the Domesday Book of William the Conqueror. Here it is given its earlier name of Talkar and it is stated that:

> *Thurstan holds Talcar. Edwin held it before 1066 and paid tax for 1 furlong; ½ hide there, however land for 3 ploughs. 2 villagers and 6 smallholders have 1 plough. Pasture 20 acres. Value formerly and now 5 shillings.*

Following the Norman Conquest a priory was founded here by William, son of Nicholas Botterel who, for the good of his soul and the souls of his ancestors, granted the church of St Merthiane of La Minster and land called Kennegi and Trelay to God and the Benedictine monks of St Sergius and Bacchus of Anjou. He also granted these monks his manor at Polyphant and lands at Wolveston, Trefoward, Tredawell, Trevaga and Holewode. This charter was confirmed by Bishop Henry Marshall of Exeter, 1194–1206. The rector is still lord of the manor of Polyphant in 2004.

William de Botreaux, grandson of the William above, confirmed this grant but kept back wood for fuel for one plough land which he took from the prior's wood, with the prior's permission and under his inspection. William also allowed the monks to use his mill to grind their corn for the usual fee, unless they were prepared to wait their turn. If they did so they would not be charged. The object was to give the monks priority and not make them wait (*cursum suum expetare*). He also granted them common rights in his woods and pasture and all the necessary fuel they needed from his turbary (turf ground).

The first recorded prior of Talkarn was Friar Geoffrey de Swansseye in 1263. Priories such as the one at Minster, founded by Norman nobles, and generally being cells of abbeys in France, had uncertain tenancies. Whenever war broke out they were seized by the king or very heavily taxed. From 1241 to 1245 prior Philip of Tuardreyt (Tywardreath), of which the priory of Minster was part, paid £45 a year in taxation. This was a very large amount of money in those days.

During the Hundred Years War of 1337–1453 the priory was seized by the crown. In 1386 it was in a ruinous state. The priory went in and out of the hands of the king, the monks and the Botreaux family, until finally all alien priories were seized by the king in 1402. Soon afterwards it returned to the Botreaux family. The last recorded prior of Talkarn was John de Stratton of the order of St Benedict in 1385.

In 1340 the church of Talkarn (alias Minstre) was taxed by Pope Nicholas at £5. The ninth sheaf, fleece and lamb were taxed at the same rate and sold to John Leigh, Jordan Trebik, Henry Denche and Geoffrey Colman. The first rector of the church and parish of Talkarn was Reginald Welleslegh in 1407.

In 1878 the titheable land in the parish was estimated at 3,000 acres, comprising 2,025 acres arable, 20 acres meadow and pasture, 141 acres woodland and 40 acres of glebe or part of the clergy's living.

The rectory house at Minster may have been the old priory. It is described in a *Calendar of Cornish Glebe Terriers* on 21 April 1680 as a house on the east side of a court with three lower rooms, three chambers and a study. On the west side of the court were a hall, parlour, kitchen, chamber, dry house, stable, barn and outhouses. It was situated to the north of the church with the church forming the south side of a square. The north side opened into the valley forming the approach.

The monks' fish-pond was some 50 yards to the north below the orchard and measured 8 yards by 18 yards. In close proximity to it was Minster Holy Well. Around it were two fields of about 16 acres, the Eastern and Western Centurys, a copse of 7½ acres, three hills, the orchard and a town place of about five acres.

The house was allowed to fall into disrepair by Bishop Trelawney during the incumbency of Revd James Amey (1701/2), who was also rector of Forrabury and lived there rather than at Minster.

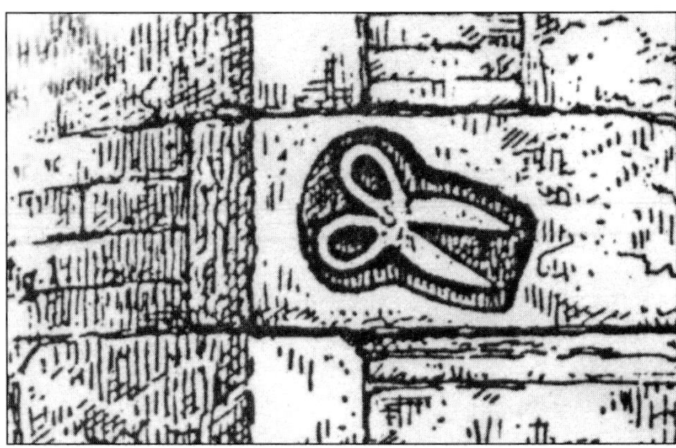

A sketch of a quoin, in the tower of Minster Church. Sculpted in low relief are what appear to be a pair of scissors.

It was taken down and completely demolished under a licence granted by Bishop Keppel on 1 October 1765. In 1914 Revd B.S. Lowe uncovered the remains of the walls but the First World War stopped further work.

The church is the mother church of Boscastle. The name Madryn has been changed and the church is dedicated to St Matheriana, Mertheriana or Merthiana the Virgin. William of Worcester, writing in 1478, recorded:

> *Sancta Matheriana the Virgin lies in the parish of Minster... She did a miracle on a certain man in lethargy and a certain girl on the feast of St James in the past year, and the feast takes place about the ninth of April.*

The original priory church was Norman, erected by William de Botreaux in 1150. The building was restored and enlarged in 1507 when the south aisle, replacement porch and upper part of the tower were built. This was during the incumbency of John Trelawney who was rector from 1507 to 1536. His arms (ar. (a chev. Sa.) between three oak leaves vert.) were removed from the east window of the south aisle to the tower window in the nineteenth century. At that time the church was in poor repair yet again. It was agreed at a Vestry meeting in 1868 to 'restore' it after raising sufficient money. However, one Sunday night in 1869, after the service, the roof fell in. Miss Hellyar voluntarily offered to restore the nave, aisle and tower at her own expense and the rector agreed to restore the chancel. The chancel is the oldest part of the building and the one-light window in the north wall seems to be where the door from the old priory came into the church.

Plans and estimates were submitted by Mr J.P. St Aubyn in 1869 and the work was done the following year under his supervision. The fine old carved wagon or barrel-vault roof, with its carved images of angels, was sold. A large part of it was bought by Mr Gayer of Trethevy and some by Mr Scott of the Wellington Hotel. The church reopened on 4 January 1871. By then the box pews, carved bench-ends and the singers' gallery were either burnt, sold or given away, as were the three-decker pulpit, the manor pews and the south aisle chapel. Sir John Maclean recorded that formerly this church had a very fine carved oak chancel screen which was said to have been removed on the orders of a rural dean at the beginning of the 1800s. It was usual to separate the chancel from the nave by a screen, often very intricately carved and filled with richly painted panels. Over this would be a loft or a beam on which stood statues of the Virgin Mary and St John either side of a crucifix. The entrance to this rood-loft can still be seen, although it is now filled in. On special occasions a number of candles would be lit – hence the name candlebeam.

The restored church consisted of a chancel, 14 feet by 16 feet, one bay raised three steps above the nave, a sanctuary 11 feet by 12 feet and south chancel aisle or chapel the same length as the chancel and 12 feet 6 inches wide. The nave was 50 feet by 17 feet and made up of four bays divided from the south aisle by granite monolith columns. The south aisle was the same length as the nave and 12 feet 9 inches wide. A western tower 13 feet 8 inches by 10 feet has an unusual hipped or saddleback roof and one of the quoins has a pair of scissors sculpted in a sunken panel in low relief. The porch was completely rebuilt. The Norman font is of porphyry and is criss-crossed with diagonal lines representing net or basket weave. It is lead-lined and the bowl and stem are original but the base and step are more modern. The altar, dating from 1883, is made of old oak from the late Dr Wade's stables, and the cost was met by Revd E.A. Hammick, rector 1877–85. The east end of the south aisle was separated from the chancel by a solid screen erected in 1705. At its north-eastern end was a monument to Sir John Cotton. This was removed and put in its present position in 1885. The reredos was added in 1890. The credence table is made of two old oak bench-ends from Forrabury Church which had been restored in 1867.

A 'positive' or pipe-organ replaced the old harmonium and was provided at a cost of £121 in 1908. Since then this has again been replaced by an electonic organ. Many of the monuments in the aisle used to cover the numerous vaults beneath its floor and the gangway of the nave. In 1869 these vaults were found to be water-logged and were filled in, as part of the restoration.

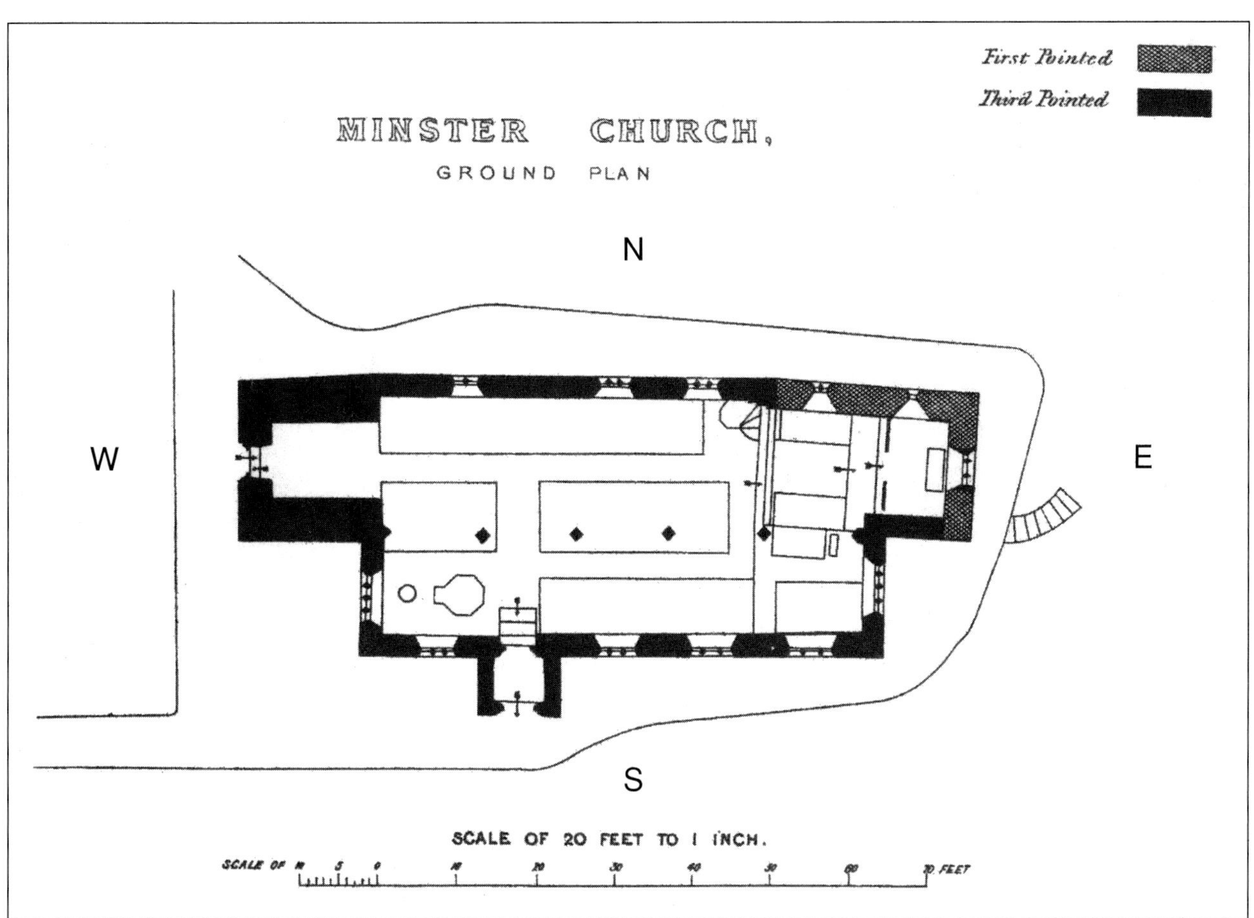

Ground plan of Minster Church. The eastern end of the much older priory building is not quite aligned with the main body of the church.

The unusual hipped roof of the tower of Minster Church.

The interior of Minster Church showing the oil-lamps used prior to the 1960s.

The history of the tower is difficult to ascertain. An inventory taken in 1550 mentions three bells. A former lofty tower was said to have been struck by lightning and this may account for Revd J. Wallis stating in 1847 that Minster had no tower. Legend has it that when the lofty tower was being built the stone was mysteriously removed again at night. No one saw who did it, although they could be heard hard at work each night.

Sedding, in his *Norman Architecture in Cornwall*, suggests that the tower was 'reared in the thirteenth century but remodelled by the builders of the aisle... Some of the old belfry jamb-stones are now doing duty in the lych-gate.'

There is one bell now inscribed 'Com praise the lord, 1728.' It came from Bodmin and went by the name of the 'tinking bell'. Of note is the fact that Forrabury Church has a bell inscribed 'John Tink 1812'.

A couple of bench-ends were saved following the renovation and now form part of the altar in Forrabury Church, a tribute to the quality of the carving destroyed.

Very few alterations have been made since the restoration carried out by St Aubyn. The old rood-beam had gone by 1843 and a new one with the crucifix was put in place in 1911 by Revd A. Cornish. The crucifix was carved in Oberammargau.

In the 1960s the church was electrified and the old oil-lamps were sold. Some can still be seen in the Wellington Hotel.

The parish of Minster includes a large part of Boscastle, stretching from the sea to Camelford Station. It includes the site of the old Norman castle, the old manor-house and the old market house. Until recent times it also housed the majority of the villagers of Boscastle. This is reflected in the registers of marriages and baptisms.

Chapter Two

Castles, Knights and Lords of the Manor

We have looked at the possibility that Forrabury was founded on a Dark-Age Celtic settlement and the evidence of an Iron-Age cliff castle on Willapark. The Celts spoke the brythonic Celtic language and are remembered for their distinctive roundhouses. The Celtic Iron Age lasted roughly from 500BC to AD1, the time of the Roman invasion of England. Cornwall was already trading with the Romans who were buying tin, wheat and hides. Whilst the rest of England came under full Roman rule Cornwall remained autonomous and could more accurately be described as Romano-British. There are few Roman sites in Cornwall and the closest Roman city was Exeter (Isca Dumnoniorum). The nearest evidence of Roman influence to Boscastle is the milestone at Trethevy. It is a squared granite stone 1.3m high and is inscribed: *'C DOMIN GALLO ET VOLVIS'* (To the Emperor Caesar our Lords Gallus and Volusianus).

When the Romans left Britain there remained a legacy that was very important to the Cornish – Christianity. There followed, between the arrival of the English in 449 and the coming of the Normans in 1066, the period known as the Dark Ages. The English were not Christian but still worshipped gods such as Wodin and Thor, but they did not reach Cornwall until after they had been converted to Christianity, and so the Celtic Cornish Christians can fairly say that they have had the same religion for 1,500 years.

The Dark Ages were a time of few records but left us with our inscribed stones, like the one at Slaughterbridge, our stone crosses at Minster and Forrabury, and many of our Cornish saints or holy people like Madryn. During this period there was continual fighting between the Celts and the English and, although the Cornish were subdued by the English, they were never fully conquered and still retained their language and Celtic Christian religion. Even so, Anglo-Saxons were known to have been in the area of north-east Cornwall. King Centwine won a battle in North Devon and occupied north-east Cornwall. Some of the place names here have Anglo-Saxon origins, such as Widemouth (Oe Wid),

Boscastle harbour in the early 1920s with the Iron-Age cliff castle and Coastguard lookout at the top left. Two cargo vessels are moored in the shelter of the pier.

Canworthy (Oe Worthig), Crackington Haven (Oe Haefen) and Otterham (Oe Hamm).

Centwine also fought a battle at Slaughterbridge in 722. King Egbert regained north-east Cornwall in AD815 and there followed the battle of Gafalforda. Egbert of Wessex was the first king of a united England in 829. Further evidence of the Anglo-Saxons in the area can be seen at Lanteglos-by-Camelford, where there is a stone inscribed with an early form of English. Nearly 700 years after this period Richard Carew (1602) recorded that the Cornish people still showed a strong dislike for the English.

Against this background of continual battles with the Anglo-Saxon English, the Cornish also had to contend with the Vikings. Evidence of their presence can be seen in the island which is visible to the north-east of Boscastle – Lundy is old Norse for Puffin Island. At the time when Alfred the Great was King of Wessex, puffins were threatening to overrun his kingdom. Cornwall, in addition, had to contend with raiding pirates from Ireland.

This then is the scene into which the Normans arrived – the people who had the biggest influence on modern Boscastle. They are also the people who gave the village its name. Following the Norman Conquest of Britain in 1066, William, Duke of Normandy, was crowned King of England on Christmas Day of that year. He settled much of the lands of the English nobility on his own followers. Later in 1086 he instigated a survey of the land to find out exactly what he had and who held it. This information was collated and became the 'Book of Winchester', perhaps better known as the Domesday Book. The Domesday Book records, as we have seen, the local settlement of Talkar (later to become Talkarn), alias Minster.

The survey was used not only for a tax assessment, it also assessed the land and its use so that 'every man should know his right and not usurp another.' It showed waste and underused land. North Cornwall must have seemed bleak and sparsely populated. Yet in the middle of a 30 mile stretch of inhospitable coastline was a sheltered inlet from the sea, a highway for commerce into this inaccessible land.

According to the Domesday list for Cornwall, William the Conqueror's half-brother Robert Count of Mortain held 'Talcar' and Thurstan held it for the Earl Mortain. William de Botreaux was given lands here and built a castle in order to stamp Norman authority on the area. This castle, Botreaux Castle, gave its name to the village. The Botreaux family came from Brittany in France. The people of Brittany spoke the same brythonic Celtic language as the people of Cornwall and they would have been able to converse with each other. The family descended from King Rollo, the first king of Normandy, and was related to Alan Fergant (the Red) Earl of Brittany, who was created Earl of Richmond in England by William the Conqueror for his services at the battle of Hastings. The name Fergant, possibly Ferphant, a phant being a toad, as in Polyphant (Pool of the Toads), may account for the three toads which appear on the Fergant and Boterell coats of arms.

Alan Fergant was the fourth son of Eudes Count de Panthievre and was a man of great wealth and prowess. His brother Etienne was Count of Panthievre and married Havise Countess of Guinchamp. Their son Geoffrey Botherel, Count of Lamballe, settled in England. He is recorded in Wiltshire in 1107–33, in Nettleshead, Surrey in 1139, and in Hatfield Regis in 1139. He married Vigolenta and their son William Boterele is recorded variously in Wiltshire in 1107–47 and then mainly in Cornwall from 1130. Thus began a dynasty of Boterells, or family Botreaux, which lasted until 1462 when the last Botreaux lord of the manor of Botreaux Castle was killed at the second Battle of St Albans.

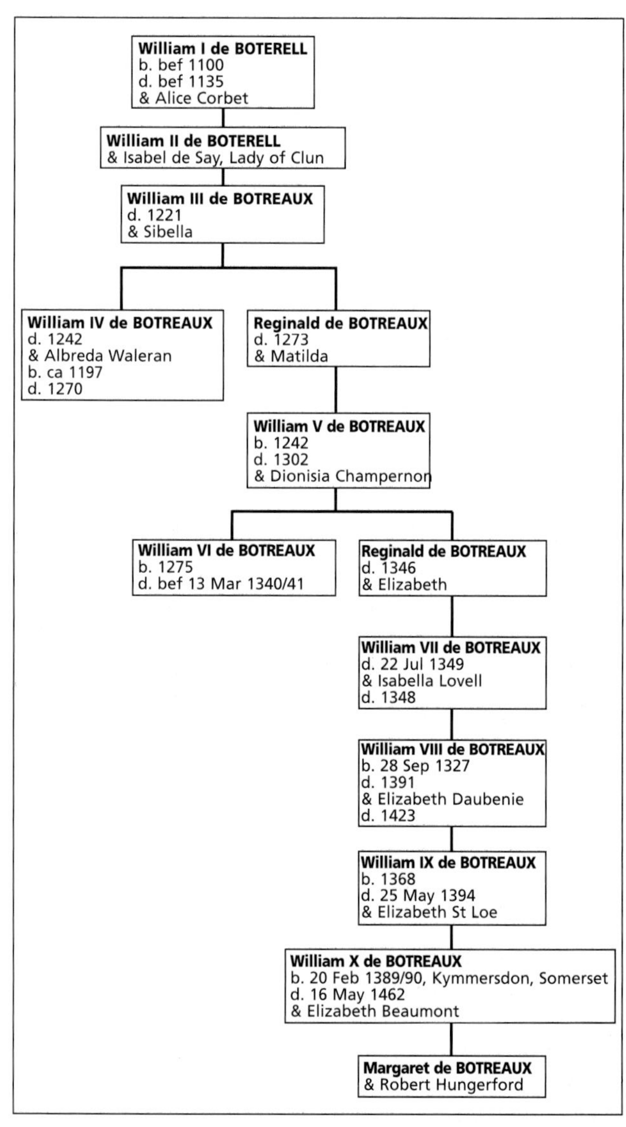

Pedigree of the Botreaux family showing the lords of the manor. The names in bold type show the progression of the title.

The following spellings of the name occur in medieval records: (de Merio suo de) Castello Boterel (Assize Rolls, 1284); Castel Botereaus (ibid 1287); Botereles castel (ibid 1302 and 1370); Chastelboterel (Calendar of Charter Rolls, 1312); Castelboterel (Court Rolls, 1334); Botterellescastel (Seizin, 1338); Botrescastell (Patent Rolls, 1383 and Closed Rolls, 1392); Boterelles Castell (Episcopal Registers, 1400); Butters Castell (Calendar of Wills, Court of Canterbury, 1536). In about 1550 Leland gave it as Botreaux Castelle vulgo Boscastel.

The family name may be derived from a place in Normandy now called Les Bottereaux (Ekwall), or from a small place shown on a map of Brittany of 1513. It shows, in the extreme south-east close to the Brittany–Normandy border, Tibidi Botorel. Another possible solution is that the name originally came from Cornwall. Brittany was the first British colonial settlement in history. It was overrun by a mass migration of the Celtic Cornish who were fleeing from the Kerns (Irish). The Amoricans in Brittany were displaced by the Cornish and the Cornish language was established there. The words 'bod', 'bos' and 'bo' mean 'dwelling'; 'Terril' is a Cornish Celtic personal name – hence Botorel, or 'Terril's dwelling'.

The Botreaux family were highly connected. William Boterell I married Alice Corbet, the daughter of Sir Roger Corbet and the sister of Sybell who was a concubine of Henry I. This marriage may have resulted in the Botreaux family acquiring the manor of Worthyvale, which had fallen to the crown by forfeiture. The Botreaux family owned several manors and much land, particularly between Boscastle and Launceston, which was the ancient capital of Cornwall and the centre for justice and commerce. The Botreaux family were involved not only in national Government and with royalty, but served as sheriffs of Cornwall, knights of the shire, keeper of the keys to the king's castles and guardians of the priories.

In 1166 William Botreaux II paid scutage (money paid in lieu of personal service to the king) for 12 knights' fees in Cornwall because he had not accompanied the King on an expedition to Galway the previous year. He again paid scutage for 12 knights' fees in Cornwall for the King's Scottish and Welsh expeditions. Perhaps he found himself tied up with more pressing matters. He was Sheriff of Cornwall from 1205–09 and died in 1220, when his son William III came into possession of his father's lands.

William IV took part, with other barons, in a rebellion against King Henry III in 1232, and some of his lands were seized. He died in 1243 and his lands passed to his brother Reginald. Reginald also took part against the King and had his lands seized. Prior to 1258 he was a witness to the Charter of St Leonards Hospital for lepers at Launceston near the current site of Polson Bridge. He died in 1272.

William V was summoned on several occasions to perform military service – in 1277 against Llewellyn Prince of Wales and again in 1282. In 1299 he served the King overseas, and in 1300 against the Scots amongst others. He married Dionysia, daughter of Sir William Champernown. He died in 1302 having received a knighthood and been made Sir William Botreaux.

On 4 February 1302 William Boterell had to contribute towards the King's levy on the occasion of his eldest daughter's marriage. A contemporary record states that:

The King instructs the Sheriff of Cornwall and Robert Gifford to let Willelmus de Boterall pay 25/- for each small manor for the aid of marrying his eldest daughter instead of 40/- as in the past.

On the reverse it is noted 'William de Boterall holds in Lesnewth seven small manors.' (Henderson ms RIC.)

He was succeeded by his son William VI who already held a prominent position. He had been assessed in 1297 as holding lands or rents of the value of £20 or more and was therefore summoned to perform military service overseas with horses and arms. In 1301 and 1306 he fought against the Scots. He was knight for the shire in 1305 and again in 1322. He was Sheriff of Cornwall from 1320–23, and in 1325 he was appointed governor of Tintagel Castle. In 1331 he was made steward and keeper of all the castles, manors and parks in Cornwall. He died in 1340.

William VI was succeeded by his brother Reginald. In 1324 he had been one of the joint guardians of the alien priories in Cornwall, of which Minster was one. He was appointed Sheriff of Cornwall and Governor of St Michael's Mount in 1338. In that year on 5 May an inquiry was made into the possessions of the Black Prince at Dunheved (Launceston). This showed William de Boterell holding 12 manors in and around 'Boterellescastel'. It also showed, as evidence that the English and the Cornish were considered races apart, 'John The Englishman' as holding one fee in Wadenast.

William's obligation to the Black Prince was to provide, in time of great war, at his own expense for 40 days, one man for each manor held by him. These men were to be sufficiently armed for defence of the castle at Launceston.

On his death, his son William VII succeeded him. He had married his wife Isabella Lovell without licence. As a result all her lands were forfeited to the crown and were granted to Thomas de Ferrars and Theobald de Monteny on 1 September 1337. William did not get back these lands until ten years later in 1347. He died in 1349, a few days after his wife, leaving his 12-year-old son as heir.

William VIII was born in 1337. In this year the population of Minster was 75 and the town of Botro

Castle had a population of 181. After achieving majority he inherited his father's lands in 1359. He had married Elizabeth, daughter of Sir Ralph D'Aubigny. He was summoned to Parliament on 24 February 1368 as a baron. On 23 February 1369 he was paid £26.6s. to cover expenses for himself, his men at arms and archers in the war. A month later he received further payment as a reward for ten men at arms travelling abroad with the King. He travelled to Portugal in 1381 and 1382 to aid Ferdinand against John, King of Spain. He died in 1391 and was succeeded by his son William IX who died three years later, leaving his five-year-old son William X as his heir.

William X was born at Walton Manor in Kymmersdon, Somerset, on 20 February 1389 or 1390. He married twice and had two daughters. Only Margaret survived him. He obtained a licence in 1413 to travel with his men and servants to Rome and Jerusalem. Two years later, as William Lord Botreaux, he set out again in service of the King.

William's name came up in early chancery proceedings in 1433. On 1 January the previous year John Brykles, a merchant from London, alleged that Thomas Treffrye had taken possession of 15 tuns of wine. The wine had been forcibly taken from a Breton ship bound for London. The master of the ship *Mawdelyn (Magdalene)* was a Dutchman, Laurence Boy. He and his crew took the wine to Fowey on Treffrye's instructions, where Treffrye delivered eight pipes of wine, in person, to Lord Botreaux who had carried it away. The rest he sold to confederates, victuallers, receivers and maintainers.

Lord Botreaux died on 15 May 1462 at the second battle of St Albans. He owned Botreaux Castle and 15 other manors in Cornwall. He left no son. Through his daughter Margaret, the widow of Sir Robert Hungerford, the Botreaux baronies passed to the Hungerford family.

Some of the surnames recorded that same year (1462) in the parishes of Forrabury and Minster relate to families still in the area in 2004 and include Gayor, Jollow, Veale, Mugford, Hambly, Knight, Wickett, Harper, Tubb, Callaway, Garde, Worthyvale, Kinsman, Garland, Philpe, Duke, Wakem, Blake, Slogatt, Stevens, Hoskin, Edwards, Gibbon, Hardy, Turner, Cowling, Juell, Kittowe, Bath, Mill, Symons and Bone.

An indication of the Botreaux importance in Cornwall is shown by the fact that many of them were buried at St Thomas Priory in the county capital of Launceston. The family gave the advowsons of the churches of Egloskerry, Tremaine and St Gregory of Hill to the priory, in perpetuity, on condition that, when William or any of his heirs was buried there, an armed man would ride before the body. That armed man would then be given food and accommodation at the priory for himself and his horse for life. Evidence was given in 1328 before justices that this had happened. William de Botreaux had been buried at the priory and John Chamberleyn had ridden before his body. He was succeeded by Reginald who on his death was accompanied by Roger LeKey to his burial. Reginald's son was also buried at the priory, accompanied by William Wynnolove. Reginald's heir William was accompanied by John Skewys. Skewys gave evidence that Chamberleyn, LeKeys and Wynnolove had all benefitted from the Botreaux legacy and was claiming his own entitlements which were being denied to him.

The castle built by the Botreaux family stood on a steep prominence in the Jordan Valley. The castle was of a motte-and-bailey type. Mottes were bases for mobile bands of cavalry, with archers, which were the Norman military units. They were usually conical mounds of earth, with a flat top, surrounded by a ditch. William de Botreaux built the earth motte of Botreaux Castle, part of which is still visible at the time of writing. It is accessed by a path beside what is now the war memorial in Fore Street and opposite a pair of early cottages called Smugglers and Tinkers.

The earth mound was topped with stout stone walls enclosing the building or tower inside. This was used as a watch-tower, for the storage of weapons, as a firing post and a refuge. Attached to the motte would be a banked and palisaded enclosure, the bailey. This was used for horses and for food preparation and storage.

We have been unable to find any contemporary records of the castle, the earliest being William of Worcester, writing in 1461, who alludes to the castle as '*Castrum vocatum Botreaux Castel distat per duo militaria ultra Tintagel Castel.*' (Davies Gilberts *History of Cornwall Vol. IV,* 228.) Carew, writing in 1602, stated that:

The diversified rooms of a prison in the castle for both sexes, better preserved by the inhabitants memory than by their own endurance, show the same, heretofore, to have existed some large jurisdiction.

John Norden, writing in 1650, recorded that 'It was first builded by a baron of that name (Botreaux), and continued long a Baronye and ended or discontinued by Henry Earl of Huntingdon.' Norden also included a drawing of Tintagel Castle, which had a similar floor plan to Botreaux Castle.

In 1980 P. Sheppard noted, in *Historic Towns of Cornwall,* that some stonework was recovered from the mound in 1812 and that both the inner and outer walls were then easily distinguishable. In 1906 in his *Victoria County History of Cornwall,* J.B. Cornish stated that no sign of any building remains, and this confirms what is recorded by Lysons in 1814 – that only a mound remains. This would lead us to believe that before 1812 stonework was removed, but as yet we have uncovered no major building work for which the stones may have been used. The remains

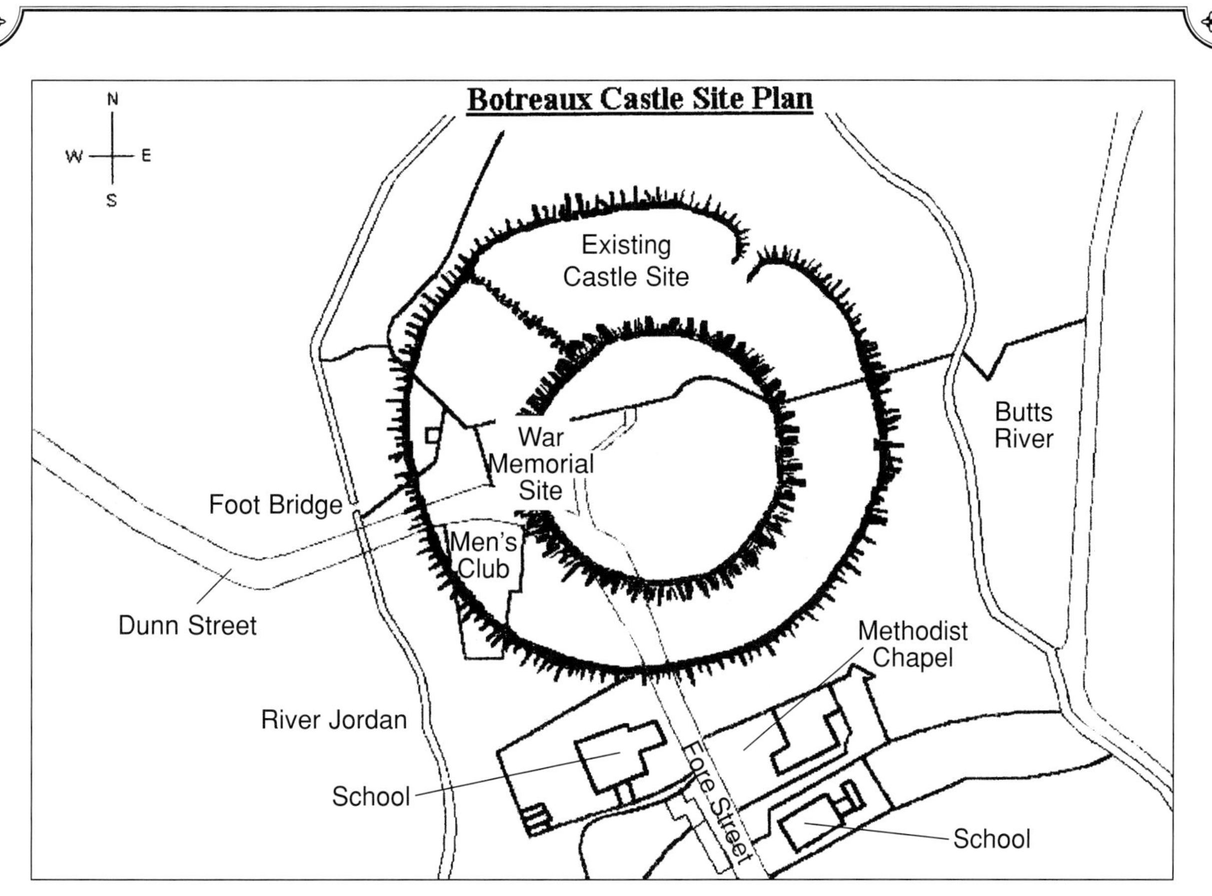

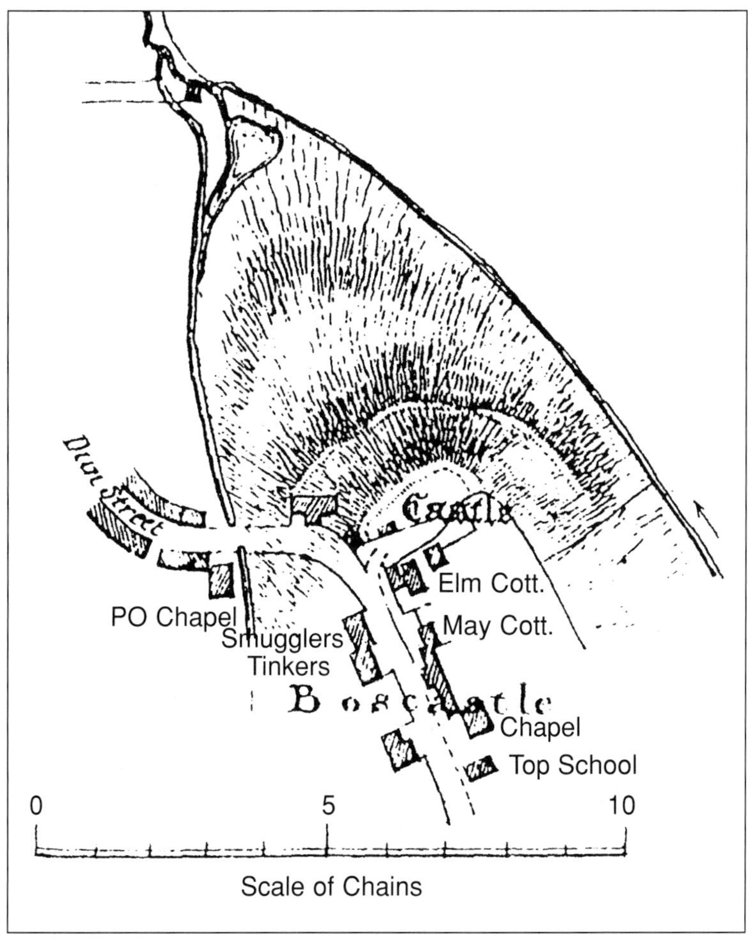

Above: *Plan showing the site of lower Fore Street and Dunn Street in 2004, with an overlay showing the extent of the original castle.*

Left: *Plan of the site of Botreaux Castle, produced in 1847.*

Fore Street, 1905. The entrance to the castle site is via the path leading off to the right-hand side of the street opposite the last house.

of the manor-house were demolished in 1818 and sold at auction by George Harman, committed of the estate on Miss Ann Amy. Did the castle stonework go the same way? The castle remains were examined and surveyed by McLaughlan in 1852. He noted that:

> *... about half the entrenched mound at the end of the promontory still remains, from which it seems probable that there was an outwork extending down the slope towards the mill.*

In 1873 Maclean stated:

> *It* [the castle] *is situate on the sharp spur of a hill at the junction of two valleys. On the lower, or northern side, the sites of the outer and of the inner walls are very distinguishable. They were of a circular form and are marked by mounds of rubbish, from which, we are informed, ashlar stones have from time to time been removed for building purposes. The defence on this side must have been strong but what protection existed on the other sides is not easy now to discern, the site being now occupied by cottages and gardens.*
>
> *We apprehend, however, that the castle could never have offered much resistance to an enemy, being commanded by higher ground on three of its sides.*

Most recently, the OS reported that:

> *The castle presumably stood on a level site now occupied by a cottage and garden (at SX 0994 9081). It*

Smugglers and Tinkers Cottages. The war memorial is just visible on the right-hand side at the entrance to the castle site.

Smuggler and Tinkers, Fore Street. These are some of the earliest houses in the village and are built on the edge of the old castle site.

was probably isolated from the high grounds to the south by a ditch across the spur but all trace of this is now effaced by dwellings and gardens in Fore Street. The surviving earthworks on the north are somewhat enigmatic. The steep natural slopes of the spur have been scarped approximately 10 metres below the top to form a crescentic terrace up to 6 metres wide. An inturned terrace cuts into this terrace.

A projected image of the castle ground plan overlaying the current street layout can be seen on page 27.

When the Men's Club was demolished and replaced with the new sports and recreation centre in 2000, an archaeological assessment of the site was carried out by the Exeter Archaeological Unit (Report No. 00.06). Tim Grant, a full-time archaeologist, was assisted by Olaf Bayer, who was completing his MA. They had two days to carry out their examination before building work began. In their conclusions they stated that no evidence was found on the eastern part of the site of a castle defensive ditch, and that any such ditch was probably either set tight against the mound on the line of Dunn Street/Fore Street, or further west. They also stated that a surviving depression that runs roughly parallel with the southern boundary of the site may represent the line of an excavated ditch extending the natural stream gully, and that the central division of the site may represent the original western edge of the bailey. The gentle curve of the northern end of this central boundary closely resembles the surviving inturned entrance on the north-eastern side of the bailey area.

Pottery finds on the site covered a large time-span but the earlier finds for the period 1200–1470 include one sherd of coarseware and 39 sherds of North Devon coarseware.

On 16 October 2000, in the later stages of the building of the sports and recreation centre, one of the workmen found what he thought might be a cannon ball made of metal about $3^1/_2$ inches across and weighing 5lb 4oz. It was identified by John Gould of the Cornwall Archaeological Unit as coming from a 6lb field cannon used from Tudor times until the mid-1800s. It was probably from a Civil War cache. Following the find, June Metcalfe confirmed that she had found a similar cannon ball in the garden of Orchard House when she lived there.

After the First World War the Gard family built the village war memorial in Dunn Street on part of the site of the old castle. They had to dig deep to find bedrock to lay the foundations and in doing so found some large pieces of dressed granite, which were in all likelihood from the castle building. These have been incorporated into the steps to the war memorial.

The Botreaux family were responsible for other buildings in the village, one of which survived, albeit in ruins until the late 1800s. St James' Chapel stood on the site of the present village hall at the top of Boscastle, in Gunpool Lane. It was the personal chapel of the Botreaux family and Botreaux Castle. Being built before the reformation, like both Forrabury and Minster, it was originally a Roman Catholic chapel. Dedicated to St James the Apostle, it was built because monks took over Minster Church.

Boscastle village hall concert, 1960. Among those pictured are: *Bill Hockin, Sandra Knight, Norma Piper, Julie Olde, Mary Gard, Pamela Mugford, Mary Higgins, Barbara Sandercock, Nicky Nicholls, Peter Kinsman, Wendy Brewer, Elizabeth Bowering, Marion Piper, Jacqueline Symons, Pamela Mugford, Joyce Hancock, Kenny Piper, Bill Perry, Iris Olde, Vi Biddick, Mrs H. Hicks, Effie Brewer, Clifton Sandercock, Tacker Wickett.*

It had the advantage of being near its congregation in Boscastle. In medieval times any church dedicated to St James would probably have had a hostel for pilgrims nearby and possibly a basic hospital. Boscastle was a stopping-off place for pilgrims on their way to the shrine of St James of Compostella in Spain. Some sailed from South Wales to land in North Devon. Here they joined others who had travelled across land. There is a line of St James' churches, showing their route through Kilkhampton, Jacobstow and Boscastle. The pilgrims would then travel on to Falmouth or Fowey to take ships to Spain.

The chapel was situated just south of the castle and adjoining the Market House. It consisted of chancel, nave and western tower. The tower was 17ft square and the chapel was 60ft by 22ft. A sketch was made of it in ruins in 1846 by Mrs Gibbons, the wife of Revd G.B. Gibbons and daughter of Sir William Trelawney. The date of its foundation is not known but records show that in the William Decimerius returns to Edward the Third it returned an amount of ninepence halfpenny.

Licences to celebrate Divine Offices were granted in September 1400 and April 1421, when it was described as the Chapel of St James the Apostle of Botreaux Castle within the parish of Minster. It was therefore not merely a chantry or gild chapel, but was used for congregational purposes. By 1744 it was in ruins and described in the Bishop of Exeter's survey as 'the remains of what they tell me was formerly a chapel.' In 1800 its fortunes changed and it was re-roofed, and the tower held a bell inscribed '*Sante Johannis ora pro nobis*'. The bell was rung by a Mrs Mathews to notify the times of the services in the parish churches of Forrabury and Minster. It was also tolled for funerals. One day it was rung too enthusiastically for a wedding and cracked! It was removed and kept at the Boscastle Inn (Kiddlywink) in Fore Street until it was stolen.

A sketch by Mrs Gibbons made in 1846 of the ruins of the tower of St James' Chapel.

Parts of the old building were cannibalised and reused in the village hall. Some of the granite stones were built into the Wellington Hotel. The stone arch over the old village water-supply in Gunpool may also be from the chapel. Several granite stones were used as kerbing in Fore Street. We do not know the date when it was finally demolished, but Sir John Maclean, writing in his survey of 1873, describes it as being situated 'until lately'.

With the chapel were two other properties, a dwelling-house, orchard and gardens on the site of the National School (Top School) in Fore Street and a strip of land running from the chapel, behind Orchard House, to what is New Road in 2004. This was the burial-ground to the chapel. Some burials were carried out within the chapel, signs of which have been unearthed when building work has been undertaken on the site. During the building of the St James' Mission rooms in 1899 a vault was discovered under the grassy mound which was at the roadside, where the small steps lead to the back door of the hall. Jim Pickard is reputed to have descended into the vault and, on reporting what he found to the rector, was told to cover it up again.

When the chapel was finally pulled down there was much anger in the village. A spate of vitriolic correspondence, some from churchwarden Langford, was published in the local newspaper. The lord of the manor and Revd Kirkness were accused of engineering its demolition! It was Revd William John Kirkness who carried out major restoration on Forrabury Church but oversaw the demise of St James' Chapel. He had become rector of Forrabury in 1843 and died on 15 June 1877, aged 68.

Rector Henry Mitchinson Coverly Price MA reversed some of the earlier thinking. He launched an appeal to raise funds to build St James' Mission Chapel on the old site. He was rector of Forrabury from 1895 to 1906 when he died as the result of a carriage accident.

During the reign of George III two Acts of Parliament were passed which promoted the building of additional churches in populous parishes. Further Acts followed in the reign of Queen Victoria to try to make the previous Acts more effectual. On 28 September 1901 a Trust was set up under the Church Buildings Act, conveying the land to the Trust. The opening date of St James' Mission Chapel had been a year earlier, in September 1900. Subscriptions to the Buildings and Fittings Fund had raised the total of £408.19s.8d. needed. Individual subscriptions came from many people including the lord of the manor, Drs Arthur and Charles Wade,

Forrabury & Minster,
BOSCASTLE.

Church Services.

July, August, September, 1909.

FORRABURY. 8 a.m. Holy Communion every Sunday.
1st, 3rd, and 5th Sundays, 6 p.m. Evensong and Sermon.
2nd and 4th, Mattins, Sermon, Holy Communion.
1st Sunday, Children's Service, 2.45 p.m.

MINSTER. 1st, 3rd, 5th Sundays, Mattins, Sermon, Holy Communion.
2nd and 4th Sundays, Evensong and Sermon, 6 p.m.
On the First Sunday in each Month there is a Choral Eucharist at 11.30 a.m.

Special Preachers at both Services. July 11th, Rev. ROWLAND CARDWELL, Rector of Lezant.
„ 18th, Rev. CANON SAMPSON, Diocesan Missioner.
„ 24th, Rev. MINOR CANON CHILDS-CLARKE, S. Paul's Cathedral.
August 1st, Rev. MINOR CANON MORGAN-PAYLOR, Manchester Cathedral (Evensong only.)

DAILY SERVICES. Holy Communion 8 a.m. Tuesdays and Thursdays.
Mattins, Mondays, Saturdays 8 a.m., Tuesdays, Thursdays 8.30, Wednesdays, Fridays 11.0
Evensong Daily 7 p.m., (unless otherwise announced.)

{As both Churches and the Mission Room have recently been entirely renovated, Members of the Congregation are earnestly invited to contribute liberally, as heavy Expenses have been incurred.}

ESPECIAL NEEDS include—
At MINSTER CHURCH £10 Debt on the New Organ; £5 Debt on re-painting the Church; £5 required for painting exterior, &c. £30 for enlargement of the Churchyard.

At FORRABURY CHURCH, £11 is required to defray cost of renovation, and the Organ requires cleaning and re-building as soon as funds permit.

"Let us proportion our alms to our ability, lest we provoke God to proportion His Blessings to our alms."

ARTHUR CORNISH, Rector.
J. J. L. MITCHELL, A. V. HARRIS, Churchwardens of Forrabury.
July 1st, 1909. A. G. FENN, H. HOSKIN, Churchwardens of Minster.

A poster from 1909 with details of services in the Mission Rooms for July, August and September.

Forrabury & Minster,
BOSCASTLE.

Lent, 1903.

"Therefore also now saith the LORD, turn ye even to ME, with all your heart, and with fasting, and with weeping, and with mourning, and rend your HEART, and NOT your GARMENTS, and turn unto the LORD your GOD." *Joel ii. 12, 13.*

Lenten Services.

SUNDAYS.

HOLY COMMUNION (Forrabury) at 8 a.m., and (Minster) March 1st, 15th, and 29th, at noon.
MATTINS & SERMON, or LITANY (Minster) at 11 a.m. EVENSONG & SERMON at 6-30 p.m.

WEEKDAYS (Forrabury).

HOLY COMMUNION, Feb. 25th (Ash Wednesday); March 5th (Intercession for Home Missions), 12th, 19th, 25th (Annunciation B.V.M.), and April 2nd, 8 a.m.
MATTINS, Wednesday and Friday at 11 a.m.; other days at 8 a.m.
EVENSONG, Wednesday and Friday (with Sermon), at 7 p.m.; other days 6 p.m.

On Thursday Afternoons (3 p.m.)
The REV. ARTHUR G. CHAPMAN, B.A., will deliver a
COURSE OF LECTURES
(Which will be illustrated by special Lantern Slides) in
S. JAMES' MISSION ROOM,

SYLLABUS:
Feb. 26—Early Church History—The Apostolic Age.
March 5— „ „ The Age of Persecution.
„ 12— „ „ The Age of Controversy.
„ 19— „ „ The Age of Evangelization in N. Europe.
„ 26—Origin and History of the Prayer Book (pt. i.)
April 2— „ „ „ „ (pt. ii.)

On Friday Evenings (7 p.m.)
A SERIES OF SERMONS will be preached by the
REV. J. E. CAREY (*Rector of Otterham*), in
FORRABURY CHURCH,

As follows. SUBJECTS:
Feb. 27—"The Cross as the Source of Hope."
Mar. 6—"The awakened Soul."
„ 13—"Forgiveness of sin."
„ 20—"The life of obedience."
„ 27—"Perfect through suffering."
April 3—"Rest for your souls."

FORRABURY RECTORY,
Quinquagesima, 1903.

HENRY M. C. PRICE, M.A.,
Rector.

Poster for Lent in 1903 giving notice of a course of lectures and lantern slides in the Mission Rooms.

S. James' Mission Chapel,
BOSCASTLE.

LIST OF SUBSCRIBERS.

	£	s.	d.
H. P. Leschallas, Esq. (Lord of the Manor) ..	25	0	0
Arthur Wade, Esq., J.P.	20	0	0
W. T. Martyn, Esq., B.A.	20	0	0
Colonel and Mrs. Hawker	10	0	0
Miss Power	10	0	0
The Rector	10	0	0
In Memoriam, G. A. P.	5	5	0
Mrs. Wade	5	0	0
Miss Wade	5	0	0
Miss Pay	3	3	0
A Friend (J.P.)	3	11	0
E. W. L. Maeer, Esq.	2	2	0
Mrs. White	2	2	0
Mrs. Douglas	1	1	0
Mrs. Ghrimes..	1	1	0
Mrs. Harrison...	1	1	0
Mrs. Wildy	1	1	0
Mr. Adams	1	0	0
Mrs. Gibbons	1	0	0
Miss Langford	1	0	0
Mrs. Lewis	1	0	0
Rev. F. G. Mattinson	1	0	0
Mrs. Tonge	1	0	0
Mr. and Mrs. R. B. Carr		10	0
Mr. Desborough		10	0
Miss E. A. Jackson		10	0
Mrs. Johnson..		10	0
Mrs. Maeer		10	0
Miss Napier		10	0
Rev. R. J. Roe		10	0
Mr. and Mrs. Daintree		5	0
Sale of Work 1898	7	14	0
„ 1899	43	1	1
„ 1900	16	12	0
Easter Cards under 10s.	4	13	6
Choir Concert and Dance	12	8	6
Church Box	6	10	10
	226	1	11

List of subscribers to the St James' Mission Chapel, now called the Mission Rooms.

S. JAMES' MISSION ROOM,
BOSCASTLE.

BUILDING AND FITTINGS FUND.

(1)

Subscriptions to the Building and Fittings Fund.

Receipts.				£	s.	d.
Mr. Leschallas				25	0	0
The late Dr. Arthur Wade				25	0	0
Mr. W. T. Martyn				20	0	0
Miss Power				15	0	0
The Rector				15	0	0
Col. & Mrs. Hawker				10	0	0
An old Friend (J. P.)				5	13	0
"In Memoriam" G. A. P.				5	5	0
Mrs. A. W. C. Price				5	0	0
Mrs. Wade				5	0	0
Miss Wade				5	0	0
Mrs. White				4	4	0
Miss Pay				4	3	0
Mr. Maeer				2	2	0
Mrs. Tonge (Didsbury)				2	0	0
Mrs. Douglas				1	1	0
Mrs. Ghrimes				1	1	0
Mrs. Harrison				1	1	0
Mrs. Wildy				1	1	0
Mr. Adams				1	0	0
Rev. Stephen Wade				1	1	0
Mrs. Gibbons				1	0	0
Miss E. A. Jackson				1	0	0
Miss Langford				1	0	0
Mrs. Lewis				1	0	0
Mr. J. H. Martyn				1	0	0
Rev. F. C. Mattinson				1	0	0
"A Cornish Churchwoman				1	0	0
Mr. & Mrs. R. B. Carr					10	0
Mr. Desborough					10	0
Mrs. Johnson					10	0
Mr. Kirkness					10	0
Mrs. Maeer					10	0
Miss Napier					10	0
Rev. R. J. Roe					10	0
Hon. Mr. Waldegrave					10	0
Mr. & Mrs. Daintree					5	0
Mrs. Hertzel					5	0
Miss Mabel Hine					5	0
Anonymous					2	6
Miss Mary Stacy					2	6
Easter Cards under 10s.				4	13	6
Collected by—						
Mrs. Taylor	1	2	0			
Miss Pay	1	0	0			
Miss Katie Symons ...		17	8			
Miss Mourant		4	0			
				3	3	8
Church Box				11	11	10
Church Building Society Grant ...				20	0	0
Sale of Work (1898)				7	14	0
„ and Garden Party (1899) ...				48	1	1
„ „ „ (1900) ...				15	8	9
„ „ „ (1901) ...				10	11	6
„ „ „ (1902) ...				1	8	0
„ „ „ portion (1903)				18	3	3
Choir Concert and Dance (1900) ...				12	8	6
Rummage Sale (1900)				6	17	0
„ (1901)				5	12	0
„ (1902)				6	15	11
Concert, Miss Edwards (1901)				1	0	0
„ New Year's Day (1901) ...				2	18	0
Entertainment (Whit Wed'y, 1903) moiety				3	13	0
Sundry Donations				2	11	7
Committee of Girls' Club					5	10
Loans				45	0	0
Bank Interest					3	9
Balance from Special Fittings Fund ..				19	6	6
Total Receipts ...				£408	19	8

Payments.	£	s.	d.
To the Contractors (Messrs. Brown and Russell	295	10	0
Architect (Mr. O. Peter)	20	0	0
The Solicitors, Ecclesiastical Commiss'n'rs	10	17	10
Mr. Brown, Platform, Tables, &c. ...	10	2	0
Messrs. Hayman	30	0	0
Diocesan Secretary, Licence	1	4	0
Sundry Expenses of Secretary	1	15	0
Insurance, two years		10	6
Fixing Stove		7	1
Loans Repaid	20	0	0
At Bank or in hand	18	18	3
	£408	19	8

(2)

Special for Furnishing, &c., the Mission Room, Dedication Day, Sept. 13, 1900.

Receipts.				£	s.	d.
Donations—						
H. P. Leschallas, Esq. ...	10	10	0			
Rev. R. J. Roe	5	0	0			
F. A. G.	2	0	0			
Dr. Chas. Wade	1	1	0			
Mrs. White	1	0	0			
Wm. Rowe, Esq.		10	6			
Mrs. and the Misses Foxmale		10	0			
				20	11	6
Offertory at Dedication Service ...				7	11	0
Concert by Rev. S. Wade				13	13	6
Profit on Tea				2	6	7
Entertainment				3	3	9½
Sale of Work				3	16	0
				£51	2	4½

Disbursements.	£	s.	d.
Chairs and Freight	17	5	8
Wippell and Sons, Kneelers, Carpet, Desks, Rails, &c.	13	12	0
Sundries, Blinds, &c.		12	11½
Eccles. Insurance, &c.		5	3
Balance to General Account	19	6	6
	£51	2	4½

(3)

Loan Account.

Received.	£	s.	d.
Rev. H. M. C. Price	25	0	0
W. T. Martyn, Esq.	10	0	0
The late A. Wade, Esq.	10	0	0
Total amount borrowed ...	45	0	0

Paid.	£	s.	d.
Loans repaid	20	0	0
At Bank or in hand	18	13	3
Balance required	6	6	9
	£45	0	0

Details of the initial subscriptions to the St James' Mission Rooms.

Ladies of the Women's Institute in 1951. Left to right, back row: *Nella Mitchell, Pam Pridham, Violet Mugford, Annie Beard, Christine Olde, Muriel Knight, Zelma Allen, Miss Carr, Elsie Williams, Jess Perry, Mrs Kellow, May Tippett, Mrs Nash;* middle row: *Miss Sleep, Annie Pridham, Miss Edwards, Miss Turner, Miss Robinson, Mrs W. Pridham, Mrs K. Higgins, Mrs Serena Brown, Anne Billing, Miss Gay, Elsie Tippet, Mrs N. Ferret, Mrs C. Ferrett, Bertha Smith;* front row: *Miss M. Beadon, Betty Honey, Connie Olde, Gwen Parnell, Molly Nicholls, Rita Symons, Effie Brewer, Kath Snowden, Jane Lobb, Mary Hilton, Vi Honey, Dora Cann, Miss Calloway.*

The crowning of the carnival queen in 1953 in the Mission Rooms. Marion Piper hands the crown to Doreen Fernley who is seen crowning Betty Bartlett. Seated are Ann Cory and Joyce Biscombe.

The school Nativity play in the Mission Rooms in 1978.

Colonel and Mrs Hawker and 'A Cornish Churchwoman'. The village raised money through sales of work, garden parties, concerts, dances and rummage sales, much in the same way as in the early-twenty-first century. Apart from £11.11s.0d. from the Church Donations Box and a £20 Church Building Society grant, all the money was raised by private subscription, making it entirely appropriate that the building is now used by the whole village as a village amenity.

The original fittings included kneelers, rails and an altar at the eastern end of the hall, where the stage stands in 2004. Rector Price clearly intended having weekday services there, although there is no evidence to suggest that any actually took place. Lectures were certainly held. During Lent 1903 six weekly lectures were delivered by Revd Arthur G. Chapman which he illustrated with special lantern slides. By this time the building was being referred to as St James' Mission Room.

Thanks to the efforts of Revd John Ayling the building and the adjacent land is now used as a parish or village hall. It is run as a charity and governed by a Lease and Trust Deed made on 1 September 1993 between the Church authorities and Forrabury and Minster Parish Council. It is still a requirement of the deed that Forrabury and Minster Parochial Church Council may use it free of charge on 23 separate occasions each year, and that it must only be used on Sundays in accordance with the rights and doctrines of the Church of England, but otherwise it is for use as a village hall for the inhabitants of the parishes of Forrabury and Minster. The charity is administered by a Committee of Management who are the trustees of the charity and governed by the Charities Act 1960.

Over the years the hall has been used for many and varied purposes. Having started as a place for religious worship and study, it has been used by the Parochial Church Council, the Mothers' Union, British Legion and Women's Institute. In 1952 the WI planted a beautiful pink cherry that stood at the east end of the hall for the Queen's coronation.

Boscastle school has made use of the rooms for school parties and plays. Many of us have seen our children's school Nativity play there just before Christmas. Other education has taken place there. It is used by the Workers' Education Authority for their classes and by a pre-school playgroup and youth club, as well as the Institute of Cornish Studies. Much fun has been had, as well as the odd argument at whist and beetle drives, jumble sales and craft fairs. During the Second World War the Ginner Mawer School of Greek Deportment and Dance were evacuated to Boscastle. They used the hall for lessons as well as public performances. In more modern times we have had a wonderful succession of productions from the 'Cave of Harmony'.

Since the opening of the new Boscastle Sports Hall less sporting activities have been carried out in the hall, although it is still equipped for bowls and table-tennis. It is fully equipped with stage and stage lighting, facilities for lectures and talks and a full range of tables, seating, crocks and crockery for the large parties and wedding receptions that regularly take place there. A site initially used in Norman times for worship by the villagers is still in use in the twenty-first century as a village amenity.

On the death of William, Lord Botreaux, Knight, on 15 May 1462, the manor passed to his daughter Margaret who had married Sir Robert Hungerford. She was over 40 years of age when she inherited and carried 19 manors in Cornwall into the Hungerford family. The family of Margaret's husband Robert sold the manor of Botreaux to John Hender in 1575.

The family of Hender is of great antiquity in this area. Their name possibly derives from the manor of Hender in Trigg. David Hender levied a fine on John de Cornwaille, in Talkarn, in 1343 (Pede's *Finium*, 17th year of the reign of Edward III). John Hender was the son of William Hender of Botreaux Castle. Some of the families living in Forrabury and Minster in that year had names that are still familiar in the area in 2004, and include Tyncke, Dawe, Hocken, Stephens, Martin, Roucke (Rooke), Veyle (Veale), Garland, Pethycke (Pethick), Yolton and Bridgman.

John Hender was responsible for building the Elizabethan manor-house situated at the top of the village. It lay on the west side of Fore Street. A few remains were still standing in the 1870s. When John Hender died his daughter Elizabeth inherited the manor. She was the wife of William Cotton and through her the Cottons became lords of the manor.

The family of Cotton derives its name from the manor of Cotton in the county of Chester. William was the eldest son of William Cotton senr, who was educated at Queen's College, Cambridge and, whilst Prebendary of St Paul's, London and Archdeacon of Lewes, was elected to the See of Exeter. The Bishop died on 26 August 1621 and is buried in Exeter Cathedral. His son William had followed him into the Church. On 6 October 1606 he was collated to the office of Precentor in the Cathedral of Exeter and on 10 March 1613 he was admitted to the rectory of Silverton in Devon. Six years later, on 17 March 1619, he became Archdeacon of Totnes, a post he held for only a short time because on 15 February 1621 he became Bishop at Silverton. He is described as 'a person of meek and humble temper, of grand and sober conversation and of exemplary piety, charity and learning.' (Walker's *Sufferings of the Clergy*, p.24.) In his will, dated 26 April 1652, he left money to the parishes of Forrabury and Minster, amongst other things for the benefit of the poor.

On William's death in 1656 he was succeeded by his son Edward. Edward was educated at Christ Church, Oxford and was also admitted to Holy

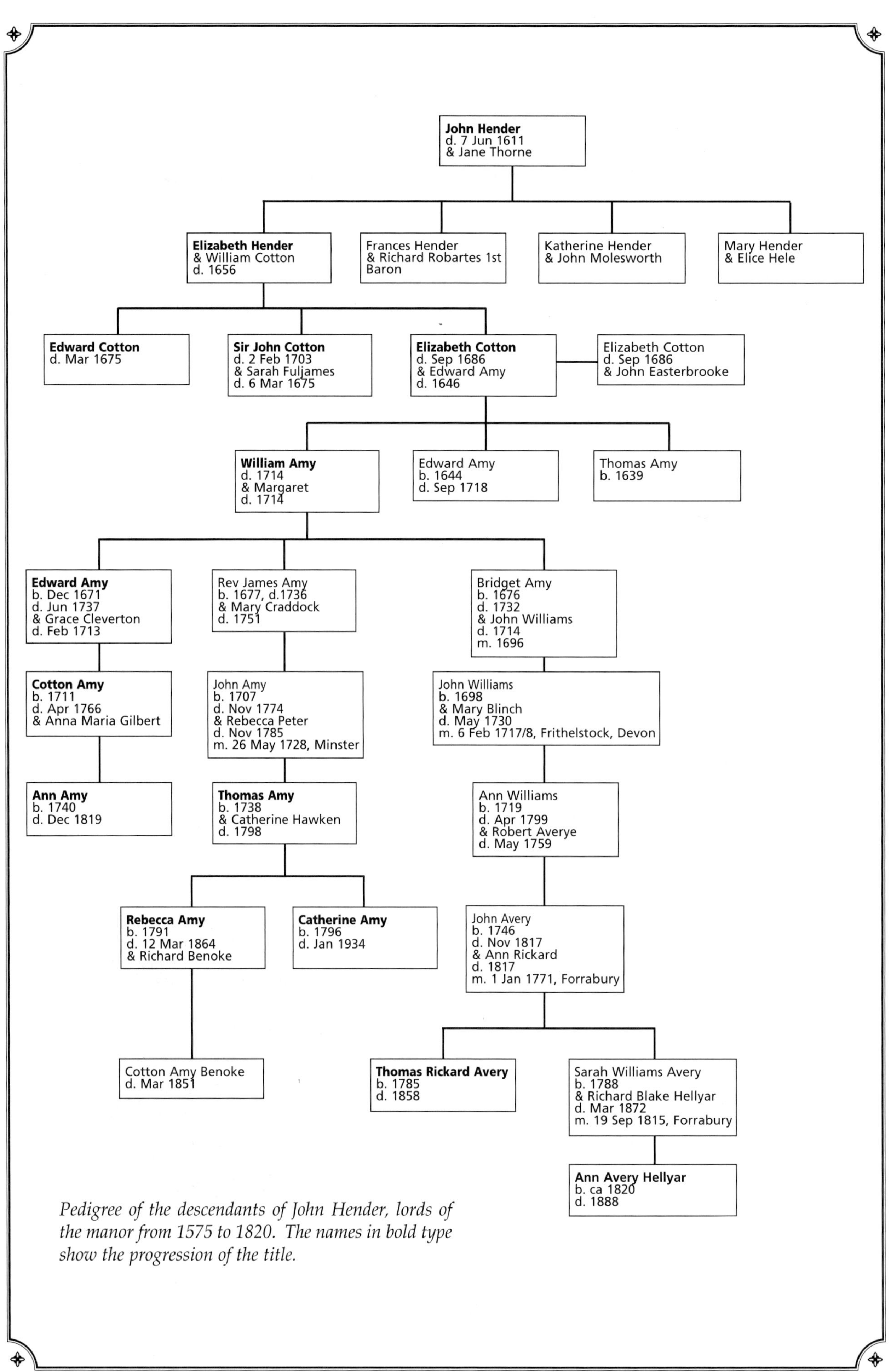

Pedigree of the descendants of John Hender, lords of the manor from 1575 to 1820. The names in bold type show the progression of the title.

Orders in June 1660. During the Civil War he had, like his father, remained steadfast in his loyalty to the King, voluntarily contributing to the Royal Army. He was present at the surrender of Exeter to Sir Thomas Fairfax, Commander-in-Chief of the Parliamentarian army. Fairfax with Oliver Cromwell formed the New Model Army which defeated Charles I at the Battle of Naseby on 14 June 1645. Because of this Edward, like his father, was deprived of his ecclesiastical positions, had his goods plundered and was turned out of his parsonage. Edward died on 16 December 1675. In his will he left many charitable bequests and gifts to the poor. He was buried in Exeter Cathedral beneath a monument that describes him as charitable and pious. Yet the Cathedral Registers (Bodleian Library 35,227) describe him, albeit after his death, as a person of disreputable character and one who shockingly profaned the Sacrament of Holy Baptism.

Cotton coat of arms.

Edward's brother John Cotton succeeded to the manor of Botreaux Castle. He was knighted by James II on 9 July 1685 for his loyalty to the King. He died in 1703 and the manor passed to his sister Elizabeth's grandson, Edward Amy. One of Edward's brothers, James, was rector of Forrabury and Minster. The manor continued in the family of Edward Amy until 1819 on the death of his last direct descendant, Ann. Ann Amy was a 'lunatic' and died without marrying at the age of 79. The manor passed to Edward's second cousin, Thomas Amy. He had two daughters – Rebecca Ann who married Richard Benoke, and Catherine. From the marriage of their great-aunt Bridget Amy descended Mr Thomas Rickard Avery and he, a distant family member, purchased the manor, leaving it in 1858 to his niece Ann Avery Helyar.

A long 300 years after John Hender had bought the manor in 1575 it ceased to be in the hands of his descendants. On the death of Miss Ann Avery Hellyar in 1885 it was put up for sale by her executors and was bought by Mr Henry Pigé-Leschallas. He was a successful Victorian businessman of Huguenot origin. He and his wife had six children and they lived at Highams, a large house at Sunningdale in Surrey. Born a Pigé, he had lengthened his surname on inheriting the estate of his cousin John Leschallas in 1874. The hyphen and therefore the Pigé faded from the surname in the next generation. He bought the manor of Boscastle and, at the age of 60 in 1893, he bought the estate of Glenfinart, close to the village of Ardentinny on the shores of Loch Long in Argyllshire, as a second home for use in the summer and as a shooting estate.

Crest, shield and motto of Henry Pige-Leschallas.

He immediately embellished the house, which had belonged to the Douglas clan, and on the wall above the portico displayed the Leschallas crest, shield and motto 'de tout mon coeur'. The crest consists of a vine support post, the old L'echalas, up which a fruitful vine climbs. The shield has two overlapping hearts. The family emblem can also be

The silver vase with plaque inscribed 'Presented to Captain J.H.P. Leschallas on the occasion of his marriage by the tenants of Boscastle and Otterham Manor Estates 22 June 1904.'

seen in Boscastle on the southern-most villa on New Road, one of the many building projects undertaken in the village. Henry Pigé-Leschallas died at the age of 71 in October 1903, not long after his eldest son returned from the Boer War. Just before his death he had purchased the Otterham Manor estate for £5,000.

His son, John H.P. Leschallas, married Kathleen Badham at Westminster nine months later. They were both aged 29. On his father's death John inherited Highams, Glenfinart and the manors of Boscastle and Otterham. They decided that his widowed mother would remain at Highams and they made their home at Glenfinart from their marriage in 1904 until 1926. The village of Boscastle celebrated the wedding by presenting the couple with a silver Warwick vase similar to that given to the bridegroom's sister on her marriage two years earlier. The vase was inscribed 'Presented to Captain J.H.P. Leschallas on the occasion of his marriage by the tenants of Boscastle and Otterham Manor Estates 22 June 1904.' It was modelled on a famous ancient Roman pottery vase excavated near Tivoli in 1771. Known as the Warwick vase, the original was displayed at Warwick Castle until being removed to the Burrell Museum, Glasgow.

Left: *Alice, wife of Henry Pigé-Leschallas.*

Below: *Henry Pigé-Leschallas, who became lord of the manor in 1885.*

A family group in 1912 of Captain John H.P. Leschallas, who became lord of the manor in 1903, with his wife and three children Ian, Sheila and Richard.

On the day of the wedding, 22 June 1904, all the tenantry of the manor sat down to a dinner provided by Captain Leschallas. The catering was carried out by Mr H.W. Ince of the Wellington Hotel. After the dinner a tea was provided for all the children and young people of Boscastle. The arrangements for the tea were carried out by Mesdammes Couch, F. Pearn, J.A. Pearn, Sharrock, Sanders, Northcote, Brown, Nicholls, Wivell, Honey and Dingle, and the Misses Sharrock, Faull, Northcote, Garland and Wivell. The room was decorated with flags, art muslin and evergreens. After the tea all the children were presented with an orange and a packet of sweets. They adjourned to a field, kindly lent by Dr Charlie Wade, for sports, which were organised by H.W. Ince, J. Cowling, E.W. Couch and W. Nicholls. They were entertained by Boscastle Band which was conducted by Mr W. Prout.

The Leschallas family had taken over the running of the manor in difficult times. Henry Pigé-Leschallas was a businessman, first and foremost. His purchase of the manor would have been an investment. However, the country was involved in the Boer War in South Africa from 1899 to 1902 and 12 years later was thrown into the First World War.

When Britain declared war on Germany on 4 August 1914, the 40-year-old major, who had already served in South Africa with the Queen's Boys, had already written to a senior officer in the Argyll and Sutherland Highlanders volunteering his services to the regiment. In a letter dated 4 August he was offered the position of captain. Two weeks later he was in Devonport.

John Leschallas served with the British Expeditionary Force on the Western Front and records in his letters home being under fire in the trenches. Despite the war, work went on at home with the construction of the villas, Bottreaux House and Lundy View, the New Bridge in Quaytown and the opening of the Public Hall which took place in November 1909. The building which was opened by Capt J.H.P. Leschallas had acetylene lighting and was said to cost about £8 per annum to maintain. Due ceremony was given to the opening with the band being present and Mr Ernest Couch's young ladies' choir who 'rendered a tableaux and song'.

The Leschallas family acquired additional property which went into the manor estate following the death of Colonel Hawker, who had taken out mortgages with Leschallas on several of his properties. The family were also responsible for overseeing the installation of a water and sewerage system in the village, to which he made a substantial contribution. Both J.H.P. Leschallas and his son presided over the Court Leet held at the Wellington Hotel where the manor provided a dinner and discussed the matters of the day. Officers of the manor, such as the pig ringer and town crier, were appointed. Most villagers kept a pig for meat. If the pig escaped from its pen the pig ringer was responsible for rounding it up, putting a ring in its nose and returning it to the owner on payment of a fine. The cost of bringing Boscastle into the twentieth century, together with the vast improvements being made to Glenfinart in Scotland, appear to have put the then Major Leschallas' outgoings considerably in excess of his income. In order to make ends meet various parts of the Glenfinart estate, together with some of the Ardentinny properties, were sold. Maintaining Highams proved a heavy burden and the manor of Boscastle was sold to George Bellamy in 1918, followed by the sale of Glenfinart House and its estate in 1926.

The Bellamy family kept the manor only from the end of the First World War to the end of the Second World War when they sold it to Thomas Percy Fulford, a corn merchant from Launceston. He bought almost the entire village and many of the surrounding farms for £95,000. It was a speculative venture and he immediately put it up for auction to be sold as a whole or 144 lots in 1946. Fortunately, he decided to cancel the auction and offered each tenant the opportunity to buy their property and land for 'a reasonable sum'. Many cottages were sold for around £200 each. Other tenants chose not to buy properties, many of which were in a poor state of repair, still with outside toilets and only having very basic amenities.

After nearly 900 years Boscastle ceased to be a manor and became open to the influences of the outside world. Houses, which had been the homes of people who worked and supported the community, became second homes and holiday businesses until the early-twenty-first century, when Boscastle's own families can no longer afford to live in the homes that had been theirs for over 800 years.

Chapter Three

Piers, Palaces and Pilchards

The Harbour

In 2004 Boscastle harbour presents a romantic and peaceful appearance to the summer visitor. However, its past was somewhat different. This small harbour was the only sheltered anchorage on the rugged and dangerous 30 miles of coast between Appledore and Padstow. It has been in continuous use since the Celts first fished here and has had her own ships since the earliest surviving port registers of the 1560s. The Cornish fishing industry is no less ancient than mining.

Despite the twisting entrance channel past the rocky island of Meachard and the protection of Penally Point, there can be a heavy swell into the harbour. If there is a strong westerly wind over a period of time then a heavy slow ground sea comes in, making it dangerous to lie alongside or in shallow water. Early on, therefore, it was found necessary to add some additional protection in the form of a breakwater or quay. There is no recorded date of when the first quay was erected, although it is often attributed to Sir Richard Grenville in 1584. Records show, however, that a quay had been built at least twice before this and had cost local inhabitants over £200. Records from 1536 make no mention of any quay or pier, although one is recorded early in the reign of Queen Elizabeth I. In 1547 the Charities Act Commissioners recommended that a portion of the local stipendary priest's wages be alloted 'towards the maintenance of the said keye whyche shall be a gracious and merciful deede of charitie.'

In 1549 the Church of St Thomas at Launceston made a contribution towards repairs to the quay. The community of Boscastle, in the first instance, raised the money for their own pier. It was public property. However, the harbour, including the pier and quays, was an integral part of the manor and always changed hands with it. The lord of the manor acted as Trustee of the Exchequer for all harbour dues and tolls. He had the responsibility of using these monies to keep the harbour workings in a good state of repair.

Boscastle harbour in 1930 – the Blowhole in action.

Boscastle harbour from the air in 1929. The tortuous entrance is almost hidden from the seaward side.

Rough seas. Even behind the shelter of the two quays the harbour at Boscastle can be a dangerous place to be.

When Grenville came upon the scene the quay was in such a bad state of repair that it was causing severe financial problems for the local people. Between 4 April and 6 August 1584 they had spent nearly £50 on repairs and it had been estimated that another £50 would need to be spent. Sir Richard Grenville, who was High Sheriff of Cornwall, asked the townsmen to furnish him with a memorandum of works, and this they did:

The Charge of the Keye of Botreaux Castell sett down by the Townesmen thereof The Peire and Key of Botreaux Castell hath bene of late tyme twise builded, ye wth hath cost the poore Inhabiters and their well willers above 200li, & the same lately decaied, to the great hinderaunce & vtter vndoinge of a multitude wth thereby are daily relieved and susteyned. But the same key is nowe begonne and sett in a newe place by the good ayde and directions of the right worshippll Sr Richard Greynvile, Knight, and is thought of the skilfull workemen and others, by Goddes grace, most like for ever to contynewe.

The charge wherof beganne the 4th daie of Aprill 1584 and hathe contynewed nowe 4 monethes vntill the 6 daie of Auguste, being 2 partes fynished. We haue dailie 20 men to worke, of the wth fower men's worke every daie hath bene geven by the neighbors wthout any charges ever sence the worke beganne, wth men, if we had hyred, wolde have stoode us, as the rest, 6d the daie for eche man.

4 of the skilful workemen, wch are Keymakers apointed by Sr Richard Greynevile, hath for wagys 8d a daie, and their meat and drink 5d a. daie, for a man. So thir wages, for 4 monthes paste, amounteth to – xijli xijs

It. We pay for every of their boarde 2s. 8d. a week, that is for 4 men 4 monthes paste – viijli. xd. viijd.

It. We have 4 other workmen for drawinge of stones and bearing the barrowe and other woork, to whome we pay 7d. a daie, and they finde themselve's, so their wagys for 4 monthes past – xili. iiijd.

It. We have 8 other laborers which are only barrowe men, and those haue for wagys 6d a daie and find themselfes, their wages. for 4 monthes past. is – ixli. xijd.

It The Mr. of this woorke contynewed 6 wekes, he had. 12d. a daye & meate & drink during his. tyme, wch I – iijli.

It The tymber wch is now occupied about the Key standes the Inhabitantes in the some of – iijli. vjs. viijd.

It. The work wch is to be done will stand the same inhabitantes as muche as that that is past, by reason that the stuffe is not nowe to be gotten but wth great charges being sette furre of, and that wch is made was of the old Keye stones Wch was very neere at hande, and wth much more ease to be had

This hetherto is the true copie of the note that the inhabitants of Botreaux Castell gave me, at my desire, whereby I might computate the charge of there woorke according to the quantitie thereof by the Perches, wch is in grose as followethe

The Piers is in length on the backe side, being somewhat compas – 160 foote
The length in the myddeste of the woorke is – 104 foote
The length on the insyde is – 91 foote
The bredthe of the worke at the grounde is – 30 foote
The worke that is alredie made is in heighte – 20 foote
The bredthe thereof at that heighthe is – 24 foote

An ideal spot to sit in the sun. Holidaymakers enjoying the view in the 1960s.

For want of leisure at this tyme I am not able to reduce this cube or piere into perches and to adde the summes of the charges as before together, and to deuyde the same according to the nomber of the perches, wherebye it might be sene what charge euery perche of woorke amountethe vnto, wth Mr. Arthur Gregory or Mr. Hylle will easelye do at Mr. Secretarie's direction, whereby his honor shall be better judge how the woerke at Douer may be made. The substance and sufficiency of the worke, the laying of the stones, and hole manner of ye workemanshippe hathe bene shewed vuto Capitane Hoorde and consydered of by him to the ends he sholde advertize therof, as to directe for the making of ony peace of like worke at Colstone, if Mr. Secretarye so think meete.

(Taken from State Papers, Greynevile)

Grenville's dimensions and description fit the existing pier that stands on the southern and western side of the harbour in 2004. Seven years after completing the work Grenville lost his life in the *Revenge*.

The pier is built in the traditional way with large upright stones, dry built without mortar to withstand the action of the sea.

In 1740 Mr Cotton Amy restored Grenville's pier and built the harbour wall at great expense, and was allowed in partial payment to levy an additional due on all ships entering the port. These dues were still being paid in the 1870s and amounted to £150 a year. They were vested in Miss Ann Avery Hellyar.

The harbour of Boscastle came within the limits of the port of Padstow which extended from Hartland Point in the east, to Peranzabuloe in the west. (Parliamentary Survey 28, Charles II, AD1675).

In 1805 an application was made to put a bill before Parliament to improve the harbour by cutting a canal or basin from a point between Pelly Beak and Valency Bridge into the harbour. It is possible that the Blowhole is the result of an exploratory cut.

The outer breakwater was built on the north side of the harbour in about 1820. This pier lasted for more than a century but was damaged by a mine which exploded in the outer harbour on 6 August 1941, and within a year the sea had demolished it.

In 1861 Walter White, librarian to the Royal Society, visited Boscastle and wrote:

You will be astonished at the harbour. A narrow tortuous inlet which appears scarcely big enough for a jolly boat is made available for vessels of considerable tonnage... We have heard a good deal of late about the remarkable harbour in the Crimea but Boscastle is a miracle compared to Balaclava.

In 1891, what was described as a 'large bathing pond' was cut opposite the outer pier on the instructions of the lord of the manor. Just below the steps leading down to the bathing pool is a rock pool used for the storage of shellfish. A grill was hinged over the top, and the hinges were set in lead.

Looking into Boscastle past the two piers. The one in the foreground was damaged by a sea mine in 1941. The other was rebuilt in 1584 by Sir Richard Grenville.

The Boscastle Manor estate continued as a family property until it was sold soon after the Second World War. It was bought as a speculative venture by Mr Tom Fulford, a prominent miller and agricultural merchant in North Devon. He sold off much of the estate but, realising its historical importance, gave the harbour and Willapark headland to the National Trust in 1955.

They took the decision to rebuild the outer quay which had been demolished by the sea. In 1962 the Trust's building gang from Cotehele carried out the work. A light railway was built along the north side of the harbour to deliver the huge blocks of masonry which came from the piers of Laira Bridge near Plymouth. The masons had to lash themselves to the breakwater with safety ropes. They worked between the tides in some of the winter's worst weather.

The National Trust has also undertaken work on the slipways and in the upper part of the harbour. They were responsible, in partnership with the

District Council, for the building of the large car park on a greenfield site opposite the Cobweb Inn and for its extension on to fields which had been given to the village in memory of the men who lost their lives in the two world wars. These fields had been used traditionally for the villagers' fêtes and fairs, for the annual school sports, for band concerts and maypole dancing. The weekly summer Flora Dance also ended there. The demise of these activities followed the development of the fields.

Fishing

The harbour's first commercial use was for fishing. In Cornwall there were four principal types of fishing – seining, drifting, long-lining and crabbing.

The earliest reference to fishing in Boscastle was found in the records of St Thomas Church at Launceston, in which is it penned:

> *In 1438 there was an unseemly quarrel and blood was shed in the churchyard so that after solemn inquiry the yard was closed as being polluted although a pestilence was raging at the time. The offender was a fisherman from Boscastle and he was punished.*

In his *Survey of Cornwall* (1602) Richard Carew recorded: 'I feel I shall breed you nauseum while I play the fishmonger, and yet so large a commodity may not pass away in silence.' He goes on to describe the great variety and plentifulness of a large number of different species available. He talks of trout, salmon, winkles, limpets, cockles, mussels, shrimps, crabs, lobsters, oysters (you may still find piles of oyster shells below the site of Botreaux Castle to this day), rays, thornbacks, sole, flukes, dabs, plaice, brit, sprats, barne, smelts, whiting, scad, chad, sharks, cuttlefish, eels, conger, basse, mullet and porpoise.

By the reign of Elizabeth I, seining or inshore fishing for pilchards had become an important part of the industry in Cornwall. The number of fishing boats belonging to the port of Boscastle were recorded as four in 1608, four in 1626, two in 1634, and three in 1687. Fish cellars were called 'palaces'. The pilchards arrived at harvest time. A watch would be kept for the shoals on the cliff tops by men called huers. The fish would appear like a reddish-brown slick just below the surface. When the shoal was sighted the huer would shout a warning. Boats would be manoeuvred into position and a net pulled around in a large circle, enclosing the pilchards and pulling them ashore. The fish were taken as quickly as possible to the palaces where they were layered in square piles or 'bulks', with salt to extract the moisture. This had to be done speedily and throughout the night if necessary.

Men, women and children all worked together. After the pilchards had remained 'in bulk' for several weeks they were put in barrels or hogshead casks, which were placed above a sloping wooden trough set close to the back wall of the building. A circular wooden cover was placed over the fish and pressed with stone weights to extract the oil. If they were to be sent to hot countries they would also be smoked. The Italian buyers were some of the main consumers.

In June 1811 there was offered for sale in Boscastle:

> *... all those capital fish cellars, capable of containing for curing from 1000 to 2000 hogheads of pilchards together with a large salt house and appurtenances adjoining... a large quantity of fish salt, also the sein called or known by the appellation of the Boscastle sein with the boats tackle and material.*

The cellars, seine and materials were said to have been scarcely used and as good as any in the county. 'Large and spacious' cellars belonging to the Boscastle seine, measuring 111 feet long by 62 feet wide, were again on the market in May 1820. They were said to be conveniently situated and could be converted to workmen's accommodation, workshops or warehousing.

In 1856 the Boscastle fishermen were fishing by placing a net across the harbour entrance when the tide began to ebb, trapping the fish in the harbour.

Cornish fishermen owned their own boats and took a share of the profits when there were any. They were proud men but when the catch was poor or prices were low they would find times hard. On 19 February 1906 *The Launceston Weekly News* reported in the Boscastle news section that the fishermen had recently had some good catches of whiting. On the previous Monday they had brought in 300 very large whiting which were sold at 12 shillings per 100.

As well as net fishing there were boats used to catch lobsters and crabs. These were caught using dome-shaped pots made of withies which were specially grown in Valency Valley by the fishermen, many of whom were also farmers (a common feature among those living by the sea).

In that same year two Boscastle fishing boats put to sea with a total of five men on board. In one were William Nicholls and Joseph Bath, owner of the first boat registered in Padstow with the number 13. In the other boat were Thomas Honey, Henry Honey and Richard Bath. They sailed at 7a.m. to line fish. A heavy gale got up from the south-south-east and the boat carrying the three men managed to get back to harbour. William Nicholls and Joseph Bath first attempted to row and then to sail back, but their sails were blown away and the boat drifted out to sea. Fortunately, Mr Holbry, the Chief Coastguard Officer, saw the boat in difficulties whilst on watch in the lookout on Willapark. He telephoned the Port Isaac lifeboat station. The lifeboat, under coxswain Hain, came into the harbour for instruction. Meanwhile, William Nicholls and Joseph Bath had been picked up by a passing ketch which took them eventually to the port of Pembroke. The men of the Port Isaac lifeboat returned home by land in the height of the gale and their boat was returned on the following Friday.

The fishermen had left Boscastle on Thursday and arrived back safely the following Tuesday, after travelling home by train to Camelford Station. Mr J. Taylor of Trevalga gave them a lift home from the station in his trap, and they were received by a cheering group of villagers who were waiting for them. Mr Nicholls appeared none the worse for the adventure, but Mr Bath was suffering from cramp in his back which had caused him to give up rowing. Neither man had been to bed since the previous Wednesday night. The men described how they had been rescued by the ketch *President Garfield* of Bude. Its managing owner was J.W.

The rescued and the rescuer. This picture by Richard Webber shows Frederick Martin and the walnut-cased clock and barometer presented to him for rescuing William Nicholls and Joseph Bath.

Banbury and it ran from Cardiff to Bude with flour for W.W. Petherick. Its captain and part owner was Frederick Martin. He had tried to tow their boat to safety but as the gale increased in force had had to cut it adrift. The *President Garfield* had been heading down the channel but had turned and tried to make for Bude. Finding it impossible to get into Bude it then headed for Hartland Point and, finding no shelter there, to Ilfracombe. Eventually the decision was made to run at an angle across the channel and make for the Welsh coast. They came ashore and William Nicholls telegraphed his wife to say they were safe. They stayed on board the ketch until Monday but were unable to put to sea for Bude. The Shipwreck Mariners Society was contacted at Milford Haven and, having provided the men with a substantial meal, set them on the 6p.m. train for home.

The men complained that they had been unable to predict the gale as the barometer fixed outside the Wellington Hotel for the last 25 years had been removed and, since the death of Mr William Sloggat-Hawker who had been Lloyds Agent, no warning telegrams were received.

Following the rescue a few friends opened a subscription to an award fund. Subscriptions were limited to two shillings each and enough was collected to buy a 'handsome polished walnut clock with a thermometer and barometer.' Inscribed on its silver plate was the inscription:

Presented to Captain Frederick Martin of Bude by Boscastle friends in recognition of services in rescuing two Boscastle fishermen whose lives were in extreme peril in a gale February 22 1906.

The presentation took place at a public meeting. The recipient Captain Frederick Martin had been brought to Boscastle and the presentation was made by Mr D.F. Ward and supported by manor agent Mr R. Couch, who expressed sympathy at the loss of the *President Garfield* in March when she struck Barrel Rock under Summerleaze cliffs and ran ashore in Bude, breaking her tiller and damaging her rudder. She was later completely thrown on to rocks and became a total wreck.

Even in the harbour vessels were not always safe and their safety was often threatened by the heavy swells which are a feature of this coast. A system was devised to help prevent damage to the ships known as 'vearing and hauling'. The manor provided substantial ropes made of coir to resist rotting. Oak posts on the quayside and on the opposite side of the harbour allowed vessels to be secured and if a ground sea was expected the call would go out for helpers to man the ropes. When the surge came into the harbour the vessel would be driven ahead, putting strain on the ropes astern which were secured to the ropes on the other side of the harbour. Men took in the slack using a turn made around the post. As the vessel moved astern with the retreating surge the ropes were paid out to check the vessel's movement. This would go on as long as needed, sometimes all night. To prevent undue wear to the posts a boy was detailed to apply tallow where and when it was needed.

Quaytown

The working area around Boscastle harbour is known as Quaytown. A great deal of research into this area has been done by Michael Webber, a local man who spent much of his life in the village. He had the fore-thought to not only study records of the area but also talk to the villagers and record their memories. He donated much of his work to the Boscastle Archive

Boscastle harbour in 1870 by artist William Gibbons. This picture shows Highwater Cottage and Bourne Stream on the left, and Penally Terrace on the hillside on the right. In the foreground is Palace Stables which was finally demolished to build the Youth Hostel and the Harbour Light.

and it is from this that a great deal of the following details come.

Michael's grandfather, Richard Webber, was a local businessman, but he was also a keen and very productive photographer who recorded a great deal of village life at the beginning of the twentieth century. We have the paintings and drawings done by many artists who visited the area before photography was available. One of these early paintings was done by Plymouth artist William Gibbons. He depicts the harbour in 1850 looking towards Pelly Point. On the left-hand side are Highwater Cottage, once the Sundial Inn, and Bourne Stream, previously called Amy Cottage after Miss Amy who lived there. She was a relation of the Hellyar family. On the right, set into the hillside, is Penally Terrace which is described on the 1842 tithe map as 'cellars'. As previously mentioned, the name 'Palace' refers to a fish cellar. In the open yard the pilchards were stacked before being processed. The buildings often had sleeping quarters on the first floor above the cellar and there would have been fireplaces to enable the workers to cook their food, as well as for heating. The fish processors – men, women and children – were itinerant workers and would follow the shoal along the coast, moving from port to port. They were paid by the seine owners and were experts at their job.

On the south side of the building, which overlooks the harbour and is arranged around a courtyard, is accommodation in the form of houses, said by some to have been built for the captains of Boscastle ships. At the time of Gibbons' painting they were lived in by the families of Mary Ann James (the National School mistress), Richard Bartlett (a labourer), William Rowe (a farm labourer) and Sarah Giddy and her son Thomas, who was also a labourer. By the time the manor was sold Penally Terrace had five houses at the front and three more at the rear.

Below Penally Terrace, Gibbons painted the picturesque group of buildings called Palace Stables. These buildings included the Coastguard boathouse at the north-western end. In 1912 a storm broke down the doors of this building and the boat was washed out and wrecked. The Coastguard received regular supplies of provisions by sea in the vessel *Margaret*. About this time this system of supply ceased and the building became used for housing the hobbling boat. The next building in the centre section of the group were the fish cellars and a smoke house. At the rear was living accommodation where Florence Nightingale Richards was born. After moving to Tintagel she became the keeper of the keys of Tintagel Castle.

Palace Stables evolved over time and stabling for ponies that hauled coal from the colliers in the harbour and pigs' houses were added to the eastern end of the building. In 1957 the stables were converted by builder Percy Jones working with Jim Pickard, mason, and William Nicholls, carpenter, for Norman Webber, and became the Pixie House, known in 2004 as the Harbour Light. Norman had bought it from T.P. Fulford, the last lord of the manor, for £75. They installed the gothic granite arched windows which had been salvaged from Trevalga Rectory and were so convincing that they persuaded a local council official that the building was of Tudor origin! It is one of the most photographed buildings in Cornwall and is owned in 2004 by Norman's daughter Trixie.

The buildings behind the Harbour Light were virtually demolished and a 24-bed Youth Hostel built in 1961/2. The building work was carried out by contractor Edward Dennis of Camelford. On Saturday 21 July 1962 the hostel was officially opened by HRH Princess Chula Chakrabongse of Thailand. Guests invited to the opening ceremony included members of the YHA and Mr James Scott-Hopkins, MP. Local dignitaries included Mrs J. Symons, who was chairman of the Boscastle Parish Council, Mrs

Taken in the 1950s by press photographer George W.F. Ellis, this picture shows tank traps still in position on the slipways on either side of the river.

Boscastle Youth Hostel, which was opened in 1962.

The Pixie House Shop in 1969 with its granite arched windows which came from Trevalga Rectory.

J.B. Whitehouse JP, Revd Dr R.G.L. Beazley, vicar of Boscastle, and Pat Day who became the first warden.

Other buildings in the Quaytown area in 1885 were as follows. On the right looking inland is the tall building called Fox's Cellars (known in 2004 as Harbour Terrace). It had three large openings facing the harbour for the reception of goods brought in by trading vessels. The building at its rear has the tapered louvred chimney of a fish smoke house. It was used later as a store for china clay from Stannon Clay Works, and Mrs Winnie Gent could remember this building being used as a salt store. Harbour Terrace was converted into residential use in 1875. Its walls were altered to incorporate sash windows with brick surrounds. The manor housed fishermen and farm workers there.

The large group of buildings on the opposite bank of the river, where the Witches Museum is now, were also fish cellars but used in later years as rope lockers and boat stores, and to store the horse-drawn vehicles owned by the Wellington Hotel. After the horses had been unharnessed and taken to their stables opposite the Wellington Hotel, men would get hold of the shafts and run down beside the river with a trap or wagonette. On the building was a cement strip which faced the river and read 'Wellington Hotel Stables'. The building once housed Vivian's Manure Store.

Michael Webber recalls that, as a lad, he was told that the building was a treasure house of maritime relics. Figureheads, sea-chests, old naval uniforms and swords were all there. Of course he and other young lads couldn't wait to get in and the removal of roofing slates at the rear allowed them to enter this Aladdin's Cave. They lowered themselves down on ropes but needless to say were disappointed to find no treasure. The place was filled with old boats, including the *Banshee* owned by George Bellamy and the 12ft *Venus* belonging to Bill Hocken.

Between this building and what is now Harbour Light was a small stone building. It stood in an open area between the bridge and Cellars Hill. It was the tally house for the clerk who kept a record of the loaded carts coming up from the harbour. Later, the building was used for rendering down seal blubber for dressing horse harnesses. This was sold in jars for this purpose and also in ointments. The building on the south side contains a gift shop and living accommodation in 2004. At the western end of the buildings was a line of square holes. These were used in the pilchard-pressing business to allow the excess oil and water to drain away.

On the quayside there was also a cottage known as Honeymoon Cottage. It was used by the manor to house newly-wed couples. It can't have been too pleasant a place to live as at one time it stood right next to one of two limekilns which operated in the harbour area. The other still stands at the rear of the buildings next to what is now the National Trust shop. A limekiln has stood in Boscastle for more than 200 years.

In 1792 a sale was held at the King's Arms in Bodmin. The property being offered included the Sundial Inn with stabling and a cellar together with a limekiln, warehouse and rights to the wharfage alongside the harbour. The property was in the possession of James Gard and Samuel Panter. Limekilns are among the most widely spread of industrial remains. During the nineteenth century nearly every river or creek in Cornwall possessed at least one and Boscastle had two. The harbour provided a safe place for the stone to be unloaded. Limestone is scarce in Cornwall and so it was nearly all bought in. It is burnt to produce quicklime which could be used as a fertiliser and in lime mortar and limewash, or whitewash for painting houses.

When limestone is heated to just over 900°C carbon dioxide is given off and lime is left:

$$\text{Heat} + CaCO_3 = CaO + CO_2$$

i.e., 900°C + Limestone = Quicklime + Carbon Dioxide.

To light a limekiln from cold the lime burner would put a combustible layer of something like faggots or scrap timber at the bottom, followed by layers of culm (a type of anthracite) and limestone. He would keep adding layers of culm and limestone until the kiln was full, or 'the pot was charged'. About five times the weight of limestone was added to one part of culm. The kiln was then lit and, when burning fiercely, the fire doors would be closed. Once alight, the kiln could be used on a continuous or running basis by drawing off the burnt lime at the bottom and topping up with more culm and limestone. Lime was exported through the harbour as well as being used locally and carried overland. It provided employment for local men like Henry Hockin, who came to Boscastle with his wife Elizabeth and family in the 1870s to dray lime with his horse and cart for the Hawkers. Beside the limekiln by the wall in front of the National Trust shop was a saw-pit, part of the carpentry business carried out in several buildings nearby, including what is, at the time of writing, the Harbour Café. This has had various uses in its past including a carpenter's shop, the town hall in the early 1900s, when the upper floor was removed, and the Apollo Cinema. It became the Harbour Café when the Piper family bought it in the 1950s. At one time it carried the legend 'Vivian's Manure Store' on the roof. In what is the present kitchen was a gas engine used to power a saw which cut much of the timber used for the repair of manor properties.

The building called Seagulls was once a manganese mill. It is on the south side of the river beside the bridge which was built in August 1887 by Henry Pigé-Leschallas, then the lord of the manor. Manganese was produced in quantity in this area. It

The lower bridge built in 1887. On the right-hand side is the unconverted building which became the Pixie Shop and, beside it, the set of gates leading to Penally Terrace.

is a black mineral used in the production of glass. The manganese mill was advertised by Mr Avery, the then lord of the manor, on 28 January 1850, for long-term let. It was described as 'recently occupied by Messrs Williams & Co of Scorrier' as a manganese mill, having a large stream of water and suited to the flour, brewing or paper-manufacture trades. The water was supplied from the River Jordan via a subterranean leat from the upper bridge area near the Wellington Hotel. The leat fed the water-wheel which was situated behind the building in a wide trough or sump. When Norman Webber was laying a floor in the building many years later he discovered a millstone and the remains of manganese ore. Another millstone was found in the road outside during the laying of the sewer in 1947. Shipments of manganese ore from Boscastle amounted to 200 tons in 1820, 1,000 tons in 1830, and 180 tons in 1840 (*Royal Cornwall Gazette,* 25 July 1851).

Small deposits of manganese were found in Valency Valley and small exploratory adits were dug into the south side of the valley, but not enough ore was found to make them viable. Other minerals were mined in the area. Near the cliff edge at Welltown was the Great Welltown Lead and Silver Mine of 1837. The fenced shaft can still be seen beside the coastal footpath. The shaft connects to the cave below and during stormy weather a fine mist of spray issues from the mouth of the shaft. At the bottom of the shaft was a strong wooden door to prevent the sea from surging into the workings.

In the *Mining Journal* of 1845 there is mention of mineral lodes being visible in the cliffs at Boscastle. Exploratory adits driven from the foot of the cliffs found silver lead leaders 12 to 18 inches wide. On one of these, at what is believed to be Wheal Neptune, a winze was sunk 12 fathoms below the drift.

One mile out of Boscastle just south of Tredorne farmhouse was Wheal Boscastle. It had a 16 inch steam pumping engine and in 1845, when the lode was cut in the 20-fathom level, it was said to be four feet wide and composed of beautiful yellow ore and a strong gossan.

In the 1840s prospecting trials were being carried out at Wheal Beeny. In this sett, which extended along the cliff top for nearly a mile, an adit from the sea intersected three east–west lodes and two cross courses. On one of the lodes a level was driven to 28 fathoms with values ranging from 30 to 40 ounces of silver to the ton and 50 per cent for lead.

Along the south of the River Valency, opposite the National Trust shop, is the old carpenter's shop. This was built by Mr Prout, who was bandmaster of the Boscastle Band and at one time the Bath City Band. Amongst the many woodworking jobs carried out, wheels for carts and wagons were made or repaired and, when ready for their metal rims, were wheeled across the river over a narrow wooden bridge to the old forge situated in what is the National Trust shop

Harbour Cottage, 1920. Set into the hillside behind is the old shippen.

The Old Forge being converted for the National Trust.

The Pearn family of carpenters.

in 2004. The granite base for this little bridge can still be seen on the bank of the former saw-pit. The metal rims made at the forge were fitted on to the wheels and then returned across the river to the carpenter's shop for fitting to the relevant vehicle.

The Pearn family took over the carpenter's shop from Mr Prout. There had been five generations of Pearn carpenters in the village from the early 1700s. Mr Pearn was estate foreman to the Bellamy family, and he and his two sons carried on the trade until they were bought out by Arthur Olde, who continued the business which included making coffins when the need arose. On retiring Arthur converted it into the Carpenter's Kitchen tearooms.

Next door was the old Rocket House, built in 1898 at a cost of £143.3s.0d. by the Board of Trade for storing the Life-Saving Rocket Apparatus. It was later replaced with a newer brick building on the opposite side of the river, used at the time of writing by the National Trust as a storehouse.

Shipbuilding

Most of the ships which were needed at Boscastle in the nineteenth century were two masted with a square rig and were known as brigs. They had long bowsprits and rounded tubby hulls designed for carrying capacity rather than speed. This type of vessel continued for many years, being only slowly replaced by schooners which had a larger mast towards the stern. They were rigged with fore and aft sails, enabling the vessels to head into wind and tack more efficiently. Towards the middle of the nineteenth century the schooners were re-rigged as ketches – the masts were moved. The foremast was larger and the rear or mizen-mast was about two-thirds the size. Many of these vessels sailed with just two men and a boy and they still had no engines.

Quaytown was at its height in the mid-nineteenth century, when Thomas Rickard Avery was lord of the manor and lived at what is Valency House in 2004. He was a shipowner and a dealer in tea, general groceries, iron, coal, timber, beer, porter, hemp and

The wreck of the Thomasine and Mary, *1926. She was built in Boscastle by Thomas Rickard Avery.*

Moored alongside the quay, this vessel is being unloaded into the horse-drawn cart below.

tallow. He was also a quarry owner and owned East Delabole Slate Quarry, of which California Quarry, south of Willapark headland, and Buckator Quarry at Beeny were a part.

T.R. Avery also owned a shipbuilding yard at Boscastle situated next to Highwater Cottage, or the Sundial Inn (1792). The yard had been cut into the rock face and extends about 50 yards towards the harbour. This area was used to build such ships as the ketch the *Thomasine and Mary,* one of half a dozen ships to be built at Boscastle. Sadly, she was wrecked in 1926 in Walton Bay, Portishead, carrying barley for Hayle.

In the river bed below the yard, set close to the harbour wall, are at least five square holes cut to take wooden posts. The holes are 12 feet apart and the wooden posts set in them supported the temporary slipway for launching the newly built vessels. One old Boscastle resident, Luxon Pickard, used to relate that the launchings were arranged to coincide with Boscastle fair day. This ensured the presence of plenty of strong farmers who, suitably rewarded with free beer, made the launching easier. Ropes and pulleys would be needed to launch the vessel sideways down the 'ways'. The ways would extend down towards the river bed so that the maximum depth of water was available, and launching would take place at high tide.

By the middle of the nineteenth century Boscastle had grown in importance as a trading port. As many as 300 ships of up to 100 tons called in a year. They were mainly bringing in coal, wines and spirits, and taking out slate and lime. In 1870, 4,000 tons of coal were shipped into the harbour and it was reported that 13 vessels were in the harbour at one time. The last trading vessels to come in with such a cargo were the *Lively* and the *Francis Beddoe.* They were 90-ton cargo boats from Appledore which brought in coal, manure and iron.

William Francis Burnard of Bridge House recalled in 1962 how well he remembered the *Lively,* the *Beddoe* and another small steamship called *Sir Francis Drake.* They all brought in general cargoes, mostly coals, and when the weather conditions were favourable they came in on one tide and went out on the next. There was plenty of manpower available at the time – men, he said, who worked with heart and will. There were two merchants who had large stores for coals and other goods and when the ships came to discharge their cargoes, although the merchants had their own horses and wagons, there were a number of farmers who sent their carts and horses to help. Much harness was broken at the time through heavy haulage and had to be speedily repaired at Burnard's saddlery and harness-making establishment. There was one outstanding farmer, he recalls, a very nice man but not always even-tempered when he and his horses were busy. His horses were strong and powerful. On one particular occasion when the

The Francis Beddoe *and the* Lively *in harbour together in 1910.*

The steamship Beaver *and the* Lewisman *being unloaded by horse and cart.*

horses were backing to tip up the cart in the store they were not responding quickly enough to his demands and he let forth a volume of language described by Mr Burnard as 'not attributable to the purest English'.

The captains of the *Beddoe* and the *Lively* were well known in the village. They took part in the Whit-Wednesday Sports which consisted of horse-racing, cycle racing and flat racing, as well as many other sports. The day ended with a tug-of-war competition in which the two captains took an active part.

The steamship Beaver *alongside the quay.*

When the *Francis Beddoe* came in with her last cargo the usual gang were not there to unload her. Pentecost Symons had died on 9 September 1916 and they were attending his funeral. The members of the Symons family who lived at the Old Post House in Fore Street owned several horse-drawn conveyances and wagons for their business. The replacement men detailed to unload the vessel refused to work unless supplied with a good amount of beer. Daniel Ward, the consignee, gave them a jar of ginger-beer champagne which didn't satisfy them, and they made their feelings known. Mr Ward said it would be the last time he would employ the *Francis Beddoe* to bring in his coal and so it proved. He switched his trade to the new railway freight business.

Many of the buildings in the harbour area, including some which have now been converted for housing, were used for storage of goods and for carrying on the trades associated with the port. In addition to the fish cellars and limekilns there were warehouses, smithies, stables, rope lockers, oil stores, candle makers, carpenters, spirit and liquor stores, brew houses, inns and pubs. The port also handled timber, hardwares, salt, bricks, pottery, potters' clay, iron, drainage tiles and corn.

At low tide local farmers would be employed with their carts to go along the river bed to the harbour where the ketches lay against the quay or moored from the pier and posts. A section of the vessel's bulwarks could be removed and a wooden chute fitted into the gap so that coal tipped onto it would slide down into the carts below. Old photographs show these carts at work transporting the cargoes to the warehouses. Each vessel held 80 to 100 tons and each cart could carry about one ton, so it was a very labour-intensive job involving a great deal of traffic to and fro. A ketch had a crew of three – master, mate and boy. Some ketches made two trips a week between Lydney in Wales and Boscastle. As the tide came in the operation had to be changed to the quayside. This was a more complicated operation involving a series of pulleys and ropes. The vessel's main gaff, which carried the huge mainsail, was tucked away with the main boom and sail beneath a tarpaulin cover and swung away to one side, so as to not obstruct the hatchway. In place of the main gaff a discharging boom was rigged with an iron pulley wheel at the outer end. A rope from the winch or to a horse led up through the gaff pulley down into the hold. The wicker basket known as a caundle and holding about $2^{1}/_{2}$ cwts would be filled by a local labourer who was in the hold. When the caundle was full it was hoisted up level with a horizontal plank fixed from the side of the vessel to a position over the hold. A man caught the caundle and ran along the plank, swinging it over the quayside into the waiting cart. A horse was often used to help hoist the baskets. Whilst one was being unloaded into a wagon or cart another was being filled in the hold. The man who ran the plank was invariably barefoot, as were all the sailors during times of hardship. Shoes or boots were only worn ashore or on Sundays and children went barefoot.

In the harbour bed, when the sand has been washed away and the tide is very low, the twin tracks made by the carts can be seen worn into the bedrock.

In the days of sail, before the advent of engines, to enable vessels to enter port there was a special

Right: *Leaving harbour. This photograph was taken by Richard Webber and shows a vessel leaving the harbour.*

Below: *The hobbling boat leaves the harbour to assist another ship. The two along the quayside are already being unloaded. This picture was taken by Richard Webber before the outbreak of the First World War.*

Entering harbour. A Richard Webber photograph of the hobbling boat towing a vessel into harbour.

The Dewdrop *was a 200-ton Brigantine owned by Thomas Rickard Avery.*

A sailing vessel rounding Penally Head in 1915.

system in place. From the Bristol Channel the ship would head for the prominent headland of Tintagel, and as they closed with Tintagel headland their next landfall was a flagpole on Penally Point. Off here they would wait for the rising tide before attempting to enter the harbour. As soon as there was enough water in the harbour a ball would be hoisted on the flagpole. Once the vessel entered the narrow seas between Meachard and Willapark the local hobblers would be on hand to tow the vessel into the harbour. The hobbling boat was a vital part of negotiating the tortuous entrance to the harbour. A ship wanting to make port had to drop anchor in the waters between Willapark Head and Penally Point and await the hobbling boat which would come out and tow her in. Mr James Pickard, who lived at 4 Harbour Terrace, was a member of the crew of the hobbling boat called *Nancy.* He and Dan Kinsman were the last two hobblers to be paid off and were part of a crew of six men. Their boat was about 30 feet in length and propelled by oars. One such hobbling boat was made by carpenter Fred Pearn, who cut a fishing boat in half and lengthened her so that it could accommodate the six-man crew. These boats had no pilot, only the oarsmen.

Leaving the harbour could be a more complicated affair. The hobbling boat would take a line from the sailing vessel out beyond the harbour mouth, pass it through an anchor ring and back to shore. Harbour labourers then hauled on the warp, dragging the vessel out to the open sea.

Ships left Boscastle carrying cargoes of slate, bark, wool, barley, oats, wheat, malt, china clay, china

The sailing smack William McCann *is left aground in June 1986. The ebbing tide caught the crew by surprise.*

Dan Kinsman, one of the last men to crew the hobbling boat, is pictured with his wife. Her sister Queenie Thomas and three daughters sit in front.

stone, manganese and copper ore, even emigrants to the far-flung colonies, particularly Upper Canada. The 200-ton brigantine *Dewdrop,* under the ownership of T.R. Avery, sailed between Boscastle, Padstow and Quebec, St Johns, New Brunswick, New York and Mirimanchi from 1833 to 1852. She carried a crew of 11. Her masters included Edwin Key, Ralph Brown, T. Rickard and J. Burke. The fares charged in the 1830s were between £3 and £6, although steerage passengers were expected to provide their own food and cooking arrangements.

Another ship which plied the route between Padstow and Quebec between 1840 and 1850 was the 513-ton barque *Clio.* Her owners were the Avery family. A crew list from 1842 shows three Boscastle crewmen on board – John Browne aged 25, a seaman, with Thomas Garland aged 18 and William Nicholls aged 16, both apprentices. They joined the ship in March 1842 and when it returned to Padstow in July against the names of Garland and Nicholls appear the words '23 May, at Quebec. Ran away'. They found the harsh life on board with little reward not to their liking and both ran off to join the Royal Navy.

The future of the harbour, and with it the fortunes of Boscastle, changed with the coming of the railway. In 1886 a new road in and out of the village was built, which linked Boscastle to the London South Western Railway station in the furthest corner of Minster parish at Melorne (Camelford Station). It opened in 1893. The coming of the railway saw a quick demise in the coastal shipping trade, aided and abetted by the threat from German submarines during the First World War. A once industrious and important port which served much of North Cornwall and West Devon was left to await its fate.

Local boatmen found this barge adrift off Pentargon in February 1977 and manoeuvred it into the harbour to safety.

Chapter Four

Inns and Pubs

Water, Winks & the Duke of Wellington

In the early days the cottages of the village entirely lacked sanitary arrangements. There was no piped water or system for the disposal of sewage. Hot-water systems were naturally unknown with the result that the inhabitants had little opportunity for washing either their clothes or their bodies. Laundry had to be carried to the water-supply and after being washed was hung out to dry on the surrounding furze brakes. This system of drying carried on well into the late-nineteenth century, as can be seen from some of the postcards of the time.

It reflects well on the character of Cornish people that they retained a reputation for cleanliness and decency, even under such conditions.

Until the development in the late-twentieth century for vehicular access to the back of the properties in the area of Fore Street, there was evidence of an old water-supply that fed down to the castle site. A stone conduit ran from the Butts River across Butts Lane into the triangular field between the lane and the river. A level cutting through this field carried the old watercourse to the castle and was later adapted to supply the cottages in Fore Street. It ran to the rear of Myrtle House, where the water exited from a spout into a drain and then to the rear of the play area of the National School (Top School). It then ran past the back of the cottages on the lower side of the chapel to Elm Cottage. Another such leat ran across Paradise Road behind the houses in High Street to the forge behind the Napoleon Inn, and across what is now the 'New' Road into Gunpool trough.

Apart from the water supplied by the rivers Valency, Jordan and Butts, the village had several springs, including one in the orchard between the school and New Road. This supplied the 'Villas' along the New Road. A waste and foul-water drain led from these villas to a septic tank in the garden of Ambrose Pearn's cottage which stood next to the old bridge by the Wellington Hotel. This cottage was demolished to widen the road when a new bridge was built in 1960, after the disastrous floods of 1958/59 damaged the original one. There was a cast-iron water tap between Glenfinart and Meachard Villas in New Road until it was demolished one day when Dr Hillier's car ran into it.

Another spring ran from the old turkey house at the foot of Forrabury Hill, under the New Road and the Slip Road to an outlet opposite the Scotts' front door. It was known as Granny's Dribble. One local gentleman on his way home from the Wellington Hotel stopped nearby to relieve a call of nature. Having been there a long time it was remarked on. Apparently he thought that as he could hear water running he should remain there.

Collecting water at Gunpool shute in 1916.

At the water shute in Gunpool is Mrs Warne of Vulcan Cottage, Fore Street.

Other cast-iron taps were to be found at the old cottages in Paradise, at the junction of Paradise and High Street opposite Minster Cottage, outside Kiddlywink in Fore Street and opposite Trevalver Cottage on Old Road, just below Granny's Dribble. They all served the main areas of habitation.

A supply of fresh drinking-water was therefore not easy to come by, and throughout the entire 1800s waterborne diseases such as cholera and typhoid were prevelant. It was often safer to drink beer, cider or whey.

Boscastle merchant, Thomas Pope Rosevear, wrote in his journal in November 1831:

The first week of this month the awful plague of colera broke out at Sunderland... imported from Hamburg thro' the want of sufficient precaution on the part of the authorities and officers of Customs at that place. The first subject was a man named Rottenburgh, a shoemaker, aged 35 seized 30 Oct died 31 at Sunderland. To the 9th 22 persons had fallen by it.

Two public-health Acts were passed in 1848 and 1875 respectively. The first Act was advisory but the second compelled action to provide clean, safe water and for the safe disposal of waste.

In 1893 several cases of typhoid were reported locally. In January 1895 the lord of the manor, Mr Henry Pigé-Leschallas, stated his willingness to contribute substantially to any scheme of drainage which might be undertaken by the rural sanitary authority. The initial building of Boscastle's water-supply was completed in April 1895. When the loan taken out to enable this work was repaid in 1935, new mains were laid. The notebook kept by William 'Nixie' Nicholls shows what a major undertaking it was.

The Boscastle Water Works Committee, which was set up in 1910, had already vastly increased the water capacity in 1912 by building a second reservoir capable of holding 12,000 gallons and was linked to the old reservoir which held 3,500 gallons. The supply was drawn from shallow springs below Polrunny Farm and a spring in the valley below Tubbs Ground. The springs below Polrunny were fed into two small reservoirs at Parade which were built under the supervision of Mr William Gard.

As demand increased attempts were made to supplement the supply by pumping more water from a borehole at New Bridge, which gave approximately 700 gallons an hour. During the early 1960s surplus water from a spring owned by the two Misses Olde was piped into the larger reservoir, giving a further 250–300 gallons an hour.

The village was supplied from the Parade or New Bridge reservoirs and the area from Paradise to the Coastguard Houses at Cambeak, and the properties along the Tintagel Road were fed from the Tubbs Ground Reservoir.

In 1966 a new reservoir was built at the top of Gibbs Lane by Sidney Jewell of Wadebridge. Michael Webber worked on it as a shutter carpenter. This reservoir is part of the North Cornwall mains system which took over from the old Parade and Tubbs Ground Reservoirs of the Boscastle Water Works which were inadequate because during summertime droughts demand for water always exceeded supply, particularly at the upper end of the village. It also had a lot of iron dissolved in it which was acidic and in turn dissolved the old lead water pipes.

In 1988 the village water-supply along with that of the whole of North Cornwall became contaminated by aluminium sulphate when a delivery lorry accidentally tipped a delivery into the wrong tank at the Lowermoor Treatment Works. People all over the area reported health problems ranging from aches and pains, memory and concentration loss, to nail and hair loss.

William 'Nixie' Nicholls was works foreman during the laying of the water mains in 1935.

Gibbs Lane Reservoir under construction in 1966.

In the years since then the reservoir and the mains have been cleaned and relined, public enquiries have come and gone, local residents received letters from the water board, the local authority, the government's Department of Health and a variety of study groups, and yet the long-term effects of this poisoning incident have not been established. Local consumers were, however, compensated by South West Water. In the case of the author this amounted to £8.20 for a family of three.

Better to stick to the beer, cider and whey you might suggest. Before the advent of piped water this is what many people chose to do, even though beer and cider were taxed. From the sixteenth century onwards legislation had favoured the victualler over the drinking-house owner. It encouraged the provision of respectable accommodation as well as refreshments. In 1825 the reduction in the duty on English-made spirits was said to have increased the cases of drunkeness throughout the country. The increase in spirit drinking was one of the chief causes of the Golburn Act of 1830. The tax on beer and cider was removed. Their retail sale was opened to any ratepayer on payment of two guineas and surety of

£20 to the excise officer for a licence. This had to be displayed to the public. With this new Act the authorities lost the ability to control the pattern of the licensed trade. The results were immediate. Within 12 months 24,432 new retailers of beer and cider had set up businesses in Cornwall alone, and a rash of new 'alehouses' appeared in Boscastle. Some were known as kiddlywinks, or simply winks. The name is still used in 2004 in the house opposite the village hall in Fore Street. At one time there were 20 such premises in and around Boscastle.

The Act established that licensed premises could remain open between five in the morning and ten at night, but not on Sundays between ten and one or three and five.

Dunn Street, Fore Street and High Street were the main areas where people lived. They contained the shops and services needed for day-to-day living. Quaytown mainly contained the buildings that served the harbour and Bridge was used for warehousing and services for both.

In the village High Street in the mid-1800s there was a butcher's and slaughterhouse at Hilldene with a malt-house behind, a general store at what is St Christophers at the time of writing, an apothecary and dressmakers next door, a cobbler between Hilldene and the Napoleon, and a carpenter's shop and forge at the rear of the Napoleon Inn. There was a Bible Christian Siloam Chapel at the junction of Mount Pleasant and High Street and later a police house next to Fernleigh. In Paradise Road was a general grocery, known in 2004 as Dolphins, and across the road at what is the entrance to Summer Winds there was a butcher's shop which was converted in the late 1950s to a greengrocer's shop. Further along the road at Paradise Farm was a grain store and another butcher's.

Until the arrival of the railways in 1886 most goods were brought in by sea. They were stored in the buildings at Quaytown and Bridge before being loaded on to mules, ponies, ox carts or wagons for distribution. The main road in and out of Boscastle for all traffic, foot, horse or oxen-drawn wagons, was up and down Old Hill, Dunn Street, Fore Street, High Street and on up to High Gates. This route became known even into the twentieth century as Oxen Road because of the numbers of oxen that were used for heavy haulage.

The horses and oxen used for carrying such goods were mostly specially bred and were of necessity very hardy. For example, the carriage of sand, lime and manure for the fields was in wooden dung pots. These were barrel shaped and hung one each side of the animal's back. One elderly resident said that she hoped never to see the return of the horse-carried goods, for the animals were so heavily laden that they often had to be beaten to get them to climb the hill. In November 1867 a correspondent with the *West Briton* wrote:

> *While I am writing this a string of sand-loaded carts are passing up a steep road before my window. This incline is certainly near a mile in length; it has been well and skilfully made by Boscastleites, but it needs three horses to drag about a cubic yard and a half of sea sand up the hill. So highly valued is this sand that it is frequently drawn from the sea shore up apparently impossible inclines and over such rough roads that none but the active little Cornish cart horses could surmount. And in places where the cliffs are so steep that only pathways exist, they carry the sand from the shore to the top of the cliffs in bags on the backs of donkeys, from whence it is carted on to the land. About from five to ten loads of sand per acre and mixed with heaps of turf gathered from under the hedges, collections of weeds and some farmyard manure and this forms a good dressing. The sand it appears is more valued in the interior of the county than by the farmers in the immediate vicinity of the sea shore.*

The very steepness of the hill meant that animals had to be changed frequently. One such changing post was the Brig Inn which was equipped to stable, feed, water and change the horses, and whilst this was happening refreshment could be taken. The building contains many of the original features of the style of building adopted by the manor workforce – slate roof, slate stone walls rendered at the front of the property, massive stone chimneys and small-paned irregular windows. Methods of construction made use of the stone freely available locally – Delabole slate or slate from nearby cliff quarries. The manor-house at Welltown is a good intact example of a small Elizabethan yeoman's house with many features common to houses of the period. The farmhouse at Redivallen dates from the same period. Local residents remember that before it became one of the growing number of holiday lets the Brig Inn sign was a wooden ship mounted on a pole set into a flagstone at the front of the building. Although this stone is no longer in its original position it can still be identified in the front garden by the hole cut into it. In the

The Brig Inn, High Street, which ceased trading in the late 1800s.

1950s the house still contained some of the inn seating. The rear of the building was used as stabling, as was the cottage below called Hillside.

The first recorded mention of the Brig Inn is from 1824, when the *Royal Cornwall Gazette* recorded the death of the wife of Abraham Matcott, landlord. Abraham Matcott had married Anne Dennis on 26 August 1785. Before becoming an innkeeper he had been a shipowner. In 1817 he purchased the sloop *John* from Samuel Billing of Padstow. With a captain, Thomas Rawson, in command the ship traded coal and general goods between Wales and the local ports. On 21 January 1820, sailing from Llanelly for Swansea, *John* foundered in Roselly Bay, with all hands.

The Brig Inn seems to have been a fairly law-abiding establishment, although the *West Briton* newspaper carried a report on 16 January 1857 of a riot that took place at the time of the landlord William Marshall, and also in 1860 the landlord Thomas Prout was fined for breaking one of the conditions of the Golburn Act. He was fined five shillings for keeping illegal Sunday hours.

The inn ceased trading in the late 1800s and became the home of the Downing family. Mr Downing had a small business carrying goods by horse and trap, and continued to make use of the stables. The haulage business could be quite hazardous and old Mr Downing had a lucky escape when backing his cart too close to the edge of the quay. The cart and pony fell over the edge into the harbour. Luckily he was able to right the cart and the pony suffered no injuries and was fit enough to pull it up the slipway to safety, and Mr Downing was able to carry on and later become a film star.

The film which starred Billy Hale and Gordon Harker was called *Phantom Light* and was filmed, in part, at Homeleigh, the name then given to the Brig Inn. It featured the house in its former guise as an inn with Mr Downing as an elderly pipe-smoking customer sitting outside. The plot was that, unbeknown to the drinkers or to Mr Downing, a shipwreck was taking place. On a signal from the director to indicate a maroon going off Mr Downing was to jump up from his seat and rush into the pub, announcing to one and all that a ship was in trouble.

Mr Downing looked exactly as the film crew had hoped. Unfortunately, every time they started filming and before the director gave him the signal, he would get to his feet and dash indoors. After a few minutes he would return to take up his position. It took the company some time to discover that he was concerned that his fire in the black range would go out. To let it do so meant no heat, hot water or means of cooking. Like any sensible person this was more important to him than being a film star!

Further down the hill is the Napoleon Inn. Records here start later in 1856 in the time of landlord William Bone, whose name gave rise to Boney's Bar in the front of the building. This was not quite such a law-abiding place. In 1859 William Bone was fined for keeping a disorderly house and for allowing gambling. In December 1886 the *West Briton* newspaper carried a report of a disturbance at and outside the Napoleon. Twelve months later landlord Peter Cotton was fined for being drunk and incapable and for threatening the police.

John Lane took over as landlord of the Napoleon in 1913. He had been born near Launceston and worked as a waiter in the Theatre Royal Hotel, Plymouth during his early years. There he met many famous people including the actor Sir Henry Irving who gave John a gold watch and chain for waiting on him at some function. John then moved to the Falcon Hotel at Bude before coming to the Boscastle Hotel (now the Wellington) during the early 1900s. His wife Elizabeth was from Boscastle, being the youngest daughter of John Smeeth who was a customs man in the village. Elizabeth was born in 1860. John built the bars similar to how they are at the time of writing and was a canny businessman.

Landlord John Noah Lane and his wife Elizabeth in 1914.

Outside the Napoleon Inn in 1917. Pictured are: *Tom Hockin, Tom Sharrock, Jack Scott, Jim Pickard and landlord John Noah Lane.*

Outside the Napoleon Inn during 1930 are the landlord John Noah Lane, his wife Elizabeth and their children.

The public bar of the Napoleon Inn. Landlord Herbert John 'Bert' May is behind the bar. Seated at the bar is Charlie Jose and standing is Walter Knight. The identity of other man is unknown.

North Cornwall Hunt outside the Napoleon Inn for the Stirrup Cup in 1960. Landlord John Doubleday is pictured with Jimmy West. Percy West and Richard England were joint masters.

The Alvis Car Club meet at the Napoleon Inn in the 1960s.

When the North Cornwall Hunt met at the inn one ploy was to pay the master to delay the start of the hunt, thus keeping the followers in his bars and increasing his trade for as long as possible.

John and Elizabeth retired from the Napoleon in 1946 when their son-in-law Herbert John (Bert) May came out of the Army and took over from them. They did not move very far, however – just across the road to the top flat in St Christophers where they could keep a watchful eye on the business.

In the 1960s John and Ba Doubleday took over and continued the old traditions, including those with the North Cornwall Hunt. John had an abiding interest in Alvis cars, being an owner of a Grey Lady, and encouraged the Alvis Car Club to hold meetings there. The Mills family of Corentin took in foreign students during the holidays, many whom were Muslims from the Middle East, and Ba Doubleday was always on hand to serve them milk as they did not drink alcohol.

Further down the hill again, where the public toilets are in 2004, was the Mumpers Inn. A mumper was an itinerant beggar. This establishment catered for the wandering population of the country. After a good booze up, if they had a penny left in their pocket, they could buy a night's accommodation and sleep on the floor on a straw-filled palliasse. Those who drank all their money away had to content themselves with rope lines stretched across the room, over which the visitors suspended themselves. This type of accommodation gave rise to the expression 'sleeping on a clothes line'. Life was never easy for these itinerants. On 15 March 1841 an inquest was held in Boscastle on the body of an old man aged 86. He had been found lying in the road with his thigh broken and was taken into the village and the surgeon was called. He lived a life of travelling around the country selling matches and was known as Scotch Willie. Before he died he was able to give his age and to describe how he had fallen during the night and had lain there unable to move all night. He was unable to give his true name and so was buried at Minster Church on 15 March 1841 as a 'person unknown'. It is supposed that he was to all intents and purposes a beggar. Ten months earlier six vagrants had been committed from Boscastle by Revd S. Chilcott for one month at the treadmill. Some of them had matches organs, white mice (to give the impression they could support themselves) which were of no avail as they were considered to have been begging.

Returning to Fore Street we come to the Boscastle Inn opposite the Old Post House where the Lynhay and Kiddlywink are in 2004. In 1930 Revd Wilfred J.C. Armstrong described this building as:

> *An old house part of which abuts into the street. It will be well worth the visitor's while to ask to be allowed to see over it. The story goes that this was one of the depots to which the smugglers brought their goods. This also was one of the old 'pubs', it was in fact, the main house and was called the Old Boscastle Inn, it had too its own skittle alley. The visitor will be shown the little room on the left with its door well provided with numerous bolts and bars.*
>
> *This door was originally a side door exiting straight into the street, it was said to be so made that the smugglers might gain entrance without disturbing the inmates. Another door, now blocked, leads into a room beyond; beyond which again is a curious low doorway, with a pointed head, that might remind one of Ali Baba and the forty thieves.*

On the right of the entrance hall is what was a public bar. Wooden battens nailed vertically made the partition, behind which the beer and wine were stored. This is the inn which held the old bell from St James' Chapel after it became cracked.

Behind the building was a brew house which, together with the inn itself, dates back to the 1700s. A report in the *Sherborne Mercury* dated 24 October 1803 names the landlord as John Witherell, who was followed by the Panter family. In the time of John Panter on 5 July 1858 the seemingly small building

The Boscastle Inn, Fore Street in the 1870s. On the left-hand side of the road is Mr Parsons' shoemaker's shop. Richard Holt is standing in the doorway. (BY KIND PERMISSION OF THE CORNISH STUDIES LIBRARY)

accommodated a seated party of 50 people for dinner. The Boscastle Inn ceased to trade at the turn of the century and for a brief period at the beginning of the twentieth century was used as a men's club and billiard room. The money for this was donated by Mr Juswant Rikh, a minor Indian potentate from Jaipur who lived in the village at Pengar with his wife and children.

Carrying on down the hill past the castle site we come to Dunn Street. Here there were two pubs – the Commercial Inn and the Dolphin. Of the two the earliest records are of the Commercial Inn. The *West Briton* carried a report on a survey of the house on 22 September 1826 when the innkeeper was Charles Jenkyn. The old church council meetings were held in this building. At the time of writing it is a private house and has been renamed Moonlight.

Dunn Street in 1935. The building on the right with the bow windows was the Dolphin Inn and later became Keals butcher's shop.

The Dolphin was on the opposite side of the street and is called St Hugh in 2004. An alarming report about the Dolphin appeared in the *Royal Cornwall Gazette* on 7 July 1865, titled 'A frightful leap and a wonderful escape.' Apparently Thomas Cox had gone to bed in one of the upper rooms. Between one and two o'clock on the Sunday morning he jumped out of the window. The height from the ground was reported as 40 feet and his fall was broken by the slate roof of the outhouse below. Although cut and bruised, Thomas Cox survived. According to the report he was under the influence of drink and enjoyed the immunity which generally attaches to drunken men. The building which houses the Dolphin is distinguished by two curved bay windows looking on to the street, which are said to have been removed from a ship, possibly the schooner *Dolphin* which traded through the harbour. The pediment above the top floor, which is quite unusual for Boscastle, carried the name of the inn.

If we continue down the Old Hill to the Bridge area of the village the first inn we come to is the Wellington Hotel. This was previously known as the Joiners Arms. In 1830 the landlady was Mrs Phillipa Panter. Her husband John had died in 1814 when aged 38. They had married on 24 June 1802

The Wellington Hotel. In the foreground on the left is the Wellington Mill tearooms and on the right the hotel stables.

and had at least four children – Ann, Mary, Thomazin and John, who was born in 1808. By 1838 John Panter was landlord of the Bos Castle Hotel, as it was then known. John's wife Ann was born in Minster in 1813. The story gets a little confusing when looking at the fortunes of the Panter family as Moses Panter was landlord of the Boscastle Inn in the first half of the 1800s and succeeded by his son John in the middle of the century, quite a bit later than John Panter of the Bos Castle Hotel.

Stagecoaches first appeared in Cornwall at the beginning of the nineteenth century, the first route being by mail coach from Exeter to Falmouth through Launceston and Bodmin. The 'stages' became well-known and welcoming inns developed along the routes. The Bos Castle Hotel was one such stage and is one of the oldest coaching inns on the north coast. The continued use of stagecoaches was essential to the hotel's trade right into the 1920s. An advertisement in the *Plymouth, Devonport and Stonehouse Herald* dated 29 July 1849 read:

The Albion Omnibus, with first rate horses and driver, leaves Saltash every Wednesday at 10 o'clock precisely, passes Callington and reaches Fivelanes at twenty past three, where it remains for one hour and finally reaches Boscastle with Mail Coach regularity at seven o'clock. Fares whole distance, 4s.6d inside, 3s.4d outside.

The Bude to Boscastle coach was owned by the Brendon family from Bude and the horses were changed at the Wainhouse Inn.

Two men of local families still living in the village in 2004 who were involved with the stagecoaches were Dan Hockin and John Symons. The Hockin family have a long connection with Boscastle. The Cornwall Muster Roll for 1569 shows both John and Thomas Hockin living in Minster. Daniel Hockin was one of six brothers and three sisters who lived with their parents at Penally

The Bude to Boscastle coach in 1900. Holding the leading horse is Dan Hockin.

The Wellington Hotel coffee room in 1910.

Barman Scott with customers Bill Barkwill and Alfie Blight at the Wellington bar in 1958.

Cottage in the 1850s. Their father, Henry Hockin, was a merchant wagoner who worked for the Hawker family of Penally House, so he was no stranger to horses. John Symons' family was also familiar with the carriage trade. He lived at the Old Post House in Fore Street where he had several horse-drawn vehicles and wagons.

It is claimed that the Bos Castle Hotel was renamed Scott's Wellington in 1852 on the death of the Duke of Wellington, who died that year, but the Scott family did not open the hotel until the 1860s. It was, however, extended in 1853 and advertised in the *Royal Cornwall Gazette* on 29 April to be let as a 'new hotel at Boscastle bridge, ready in a month'. On 14 October 1853 H. & A. Bone announced the fitting up of the hotel in the same newspaper. It was probably at this time that it was named the Wellington Hotel.

According to the *West Briton* it was again being advertised to let in 1856 when it came into the hands of William and Ann Scott. They carried out further extension work before opening, when, it is believed, the tower was added and it became the Wellington Family Hotel. They continued in business there until Ann died in 1889. William moved to Paradise House at the top of the village and he died there in 1898.

The Wellington Hotel had its own electricity for a while, generated by water-wheels fed by the leat from Valency Valley. As late as 1920 the Wellington was dependent on horse-drawn coaches for its guests. It had its own stables across the road and kept the vehicles beside the river in buildings near

Scott's Wellington Hotel. This photograph was taken in the 1870s.

The Wellington Hotel. On the right are the New Road Villas (built 1887). Note that the tower has not yet been built on Valley View.

what is the Witches House in 2004. A number of prominent people have visited the hotel, including Edward VII, who came with a royal party in the 1870s. Sir Henry Irving, the first actor to be knighted, was another distinguished guest. He was said to be very interested in a lady of the village who was reported to have magical powers. It is a fact that he gave her a quarterly allowance, paid through the wife of a local doctor.

Thomas Hardy stayed there in 1913 after the death of his first wife and whilst working on the refurbishment of St Juliot Church. The King of Prussia was a royal guest in April 1895 when he and a party of three coaches were given luncheon. They later visited the quay.

During the Second World War the hotel was run by Dorothy Stock who took it over from a Mr Wilmott. Dorothy and her husband had returned to this country in 1938 from Kenya, where they had had coffee plantations. With the threat of war looming they wished to be in the old country. Dorothy's daughter Peggy lived with her and her son John was a RAF bomber pilot. John brought fellow pilot Guy Gibson, later of dam-buster fame, home with him on leave from Scampton. After losing John, who was shot down into the North Sea, Dorothy took the local air station, RAF Davidstow Moor, under her wing. She allowed the officers to use part of the hotel as a

Flying Officer John Stock, RAF, son of Dorothy Stock, proprietor of the Wellington Hotel, 1940.

home from home. They in turn adopted her, calling her Mummy Stock and sometimes, because of her strict nature, Mother Stock! Members of 547 squadron in particular became frequent visitors, if not for the beer, then more for the association with the young girls of the Ginner Mawer School of Deportment and Greek Dance. They had been evacuated to the village from London in the early days of the war. The attractions of the young airmen of 547 squadron and the young female dancers was a strong one and many couples married after the war.

Officers and aircrew were constant visitors during 1943 until they moved to Thorney Island and Aldergrove on 25 October 1943 – but not before Dorothy had given a dinner at the Wellington for the squadron.

Many other squadrons visited and were glad of the comforts afforded by the hotel. One other that was particularly grateful was 524 squadron, formed at Davidstow on 7 April 1944. Equipped with Wellingtons, its duties were to include night patrols over the Channel close to the French coast, searching for the dreaded German E-boats which had been the scourge of channel shipping throughout the war.

With the D-Day landings imminent, Coastal Command's task was to protect naval shipping crossing the Channel with troops from the threat of German U-boats and E-boats. 524 squadron's forte was searching out and attacking the fast and elusive E-boat. Despite poor weather, radio and radar jamming and many other unplanned events, the crews were always assured of a welcome at the Wellington. When the squadron moved to Docking, Norfolk at the end of June 1944 the squadron presented Dorothy with a silver salver inscribed with all the officers' names and the following inscription: 'To MRS M. STOCK, Flight Commander.'

During this time the Wellington was visited by other well-known people including the young Henrietta Tiarks (now Lady Tavistock) with her mother and father, Wing Commander Tiarks. The pianist Mary Starling, who later married John Williams and lived in the village, also visited, as did 16 members of the Polish Air Force Theatre in October 1943 and Uffa Fox, the yachtsman and designer who had worked on the development of the airborne lifeboat, in August 1944.

Like other inns and hotels in the village the Wellington was not without its incidents. On 9 November 1895 the *Launceston Weekly News* carried a report entitled 'Shocking Occurrence at Boscastle'. On the previous Tuesday Dr William Chalmers of Lyme Regis, who had been staying at the hotel, committed suicide by jumping over the cliff at Penally Terrace. Several people including Mr Ralph Fuge and Mr Mitchell tried to get near him but he deliberately jumped over headlong, pitching on the rocks, then falling into the sea. An inquest was held at the manor-house by Mr Hambly, with Mr R. Couch as foreman of the jury. Mr Rundle Brendon, proprietor of the Wellington Hotel, said the deceased had come there about two months previous and had occasionally been in a low, despondent state. Other witnesses including Mrs Fry of Manor House and Dr Charles Wade, and both Mr Fuge and Mr Mitchell gave an account of how they had tried to grab Dr Chalmers and had thrown a rope over him but to no avail. Dr Wade said he had been treating the deceased for gout and was aware that he was depressed over a cheque or money matters, but not to the extent of suicide. The jury returned a verdict of suicide during temporary insanity.

Captain Limney of the ketch *Lively* and a member of his crew had a novel method of causing a stir in the lower part of Boscastle whenever his vessel visited the harbour. After the day's work of unloading was done one of the crew would have an iron collar fastened around his neck and would be led by a chain on all fours up to the Wellington Hotel. This man would perform various tricks for beer and cause quite a bit of fun.

On the top floor of the Wellington Old Mill the temperature was always higher than elsewhere and the sailors and local men would, after the pubs had shut, retire to this building with a large cloam jar of ale. One man decided to investigate the workings of the mill machinery and in the process got into one of the wooden chutes. His friends heard his cries for help and discovered him wallowing in a huge bin full of flour. As he was so drunk they sent him home, and his wife never recovered from the shock of opening the door and seeing a pale apparition bearing a resemblance to her husband.

Close to the Wellington Hotel across the bridge in Valency Row, Back Street was an inn described by Grus Redding (1842) as 'the Robin, homely but clean and neat as everywhere in Cornwall, right hospitable to the stranger.' Further along Valency Row towards the harbour was the Ship with its brewhouse next door. The landlord in 1820 was William Stacey. The Mably family took over from William Stacey and continued to trade there for 30 years. During this time the landlord, Henry Mably, was fined for keeping late hours (1859) and for allowing card playing (1860). William Brenton had been summoned by him for assault. It appears that Brenton had, with five others, arrived in Boscastle and been employed as a shipwright. They had lodged at the Ship but later moved to another nearby inn. Mably had gone to call on them and had been assaulted. The evidence was found to be contradictory and the bench dismissed the case. Henry Mably also appeared before them, summoned by William Prior for allowing cards to be played. The bench fined him five shillings and all expenses for both cases.

On 17 September 1877 the *West Briton* reported that Mr Forward, landlord of the Ship, had been

Eating pasties outside the Ship Inn.

William Cory Scott and his wife Mary with their children William Charles, Annie Mary Maud, John and Frederick William, 1897.

Manor House, 1930. This picture was taken from Manor House Garden which later became part of the tourist car park.

charged with adulterating the beer with salt to promote thirst and occulos indicus to increase its potency. The chairman of the bench declared it to be a well-kept and regulated house. He ordered a mitigated fine of £1.

At the turn of the century this inn was in the hands of the Scott family. William Cory Scott had been born in 1864. He was the son of John and Caroline Scott of Pelly Cellars and was known as Cory Scott. He married Mary Sandercock at St Juliot Church on 16 July 1887. They lived at Dunfarley Cottage before moving to the Ship Inn when he was a livery servant. They had four children: William Charles, who became a policeman; Annie Mary Maud, who died of tuberculosis aged 21; John Elson who was known as Jack and became the driver of a two-horse coach employed by the Wellington Hotel; and Frederick William Cory who took over the Manor House. The Ship closed after the landlady's sons were called up for service in the First World War. She was not permitted to hold the licences as a widow on her own.

Four pewter measures from the Ship Inn have remained in the family. There are three pot-bellied tankards and one thimble-shaped measure. They have been stamped several times each by Weights and Measures. They were given lately to Justin Scott on his eighteenth birthday with the legend which states they were used in the Ship Inn by his great-, great-grandparents, (William) Cory and Mary Scott.

After it closed the Ship Inn became Atlantic House and was the home of Mr and Mrs Jim Bath. He had a horse and cart and worked as a rubbish collector. It later became the home of the Rogers family who supplied milk and cream from their dairy. Thomas Henry Rogers was known as Harry. He and his wife Sarah later moved to Home Farm with their daughter Elsie Maud and son Archibald. When Archie married Doreen Cann she also went to live at Home Farm where she took in occasional bed-and-breakfast guests. Harry and his family moved to Trehane House in Fore Street. John Brown (known as Ginger) was the next inhabitant of the Ship Inn with his wife Serena and son Stuart.

The Scotts remained in business in Boscastle. Fred had started his working life as a footman at Pencarrow House, the home of the Molesworth St Aubyn family. He later worked at the Grenville Hotel under the manageress Mrs Reynolds, who had employed him previously in Penzance. He was called up in 1916 and saw service with the 1st Herts Regiment, the 2/5th East Surrey Regiment and the 25th Battalion the King's Liverpool Regiment. In 1920 he went with an expeditionary force to Egypt and the Holy Land. After the war he worked at the Falcon Hotel for George Brendon and married Helen, who was known as Nellie, in 1918. In 1922 they moved to Boscastle and took over the Manor House in 1927, which they turned into an hotel. They

Melorne Hotel, Camelford Station, after it was destroyed by fire in 1917.

continued in business there until 1965, bringing up their children Frank and Arthur who were born in 1921 and were twins. Both were awarded the Burma Star in later life and Mary, Barbara, Freda and Priscilla completed the family.

As well as running the hotel and bringing up a large family they sold teas on the hotel lawn opposite the house, where there was also a tennis-court which was rented to players and used by the family.

Amongst their guests at Manor House were the potter Bernard Leach and his daughters Jessamine and Eleanor. The girls were part of the Ginner Mawer School which was run by Mrs Dyer, who lived at Corentin and gave dance instruction, and Mrs Paragini who lived at Bourne Stream and was responsible for drama classes.

There were several other inns or pubs that at one time served Boscastle, including the Sundial on the quay which we have already mentioned as being offered for sale in 1792, when the landlords were James Gard and Samuel Panter. There were several whose locations are no longer known. They include the Jessie Logan, named after a vessel that traded between Calcutta and Liverpool and was wrecked off Boscastle. Ann Richards was the landlady in 1847. The Waggoners Arms is another whose location is unknown. In the 1840s the landlord was John Chapman.

Named after its landlord Richard Garland, another inn was said to be known by its sign, 'The Garland'. It was sadly to feature in newspaper reports of 1821 which told of a tragic occurence. On leaving the inn several men had become rumbustuous. After Nicholas James Gard had left the group and gone into the home he shared with his parents, Henry Hoskin had entered the house and taunted him. Neighbours then witnessed Hoskin staggering from the house with a single knife wound which was to cause his death. His attacker was arrested and charged with murder and, after being found guilty, was sentenced to death. During the time he was held in gaol his father, also called Nicholas Gard, collapsed and died, not living long enough to see his son hanged. Twelve months after this incident the landlord of the Garland was declared bankrupt.

Another premises which had a sad ending was the Melorne Hotel by Camelford Station. In 1856 the landlord was W. Hawker. This hotel was destroyed by a fire which completely gutted the building in January 1917. The fire was recounted by Mr Hugh Godber, a signalman at the nearby railway station. It is said that nothing was known of the fire until next morning when the hotel owners were found huddled in a nearby barn for shelter. The hoteliers, Mr and Mrs Thomas, and their three sons left for South Africa shortly after and, although rebuilt, the Melorne never again functioned as an hotel.

One other inn on the outskirts of the village was the First and Last, known as Hillsborough Farm at the time of writing, which is part of Home Farm and under the ownership of the National Trust. It was also known by the more earthy name of Cock in Breeches. Its landlord in 1842 was Thomas Moore. He and his wife Eliza had 12 children. Perhaps this was the origin of the saying 'don't have any more Mrs Moore!'

Of the 16 inns and pubs we have mentioned that flourished in the 1800s we have only two left in 2004

The Cobweb Inn. The car park to the right of the building has not yet been built and the storehouses still stand on the site.

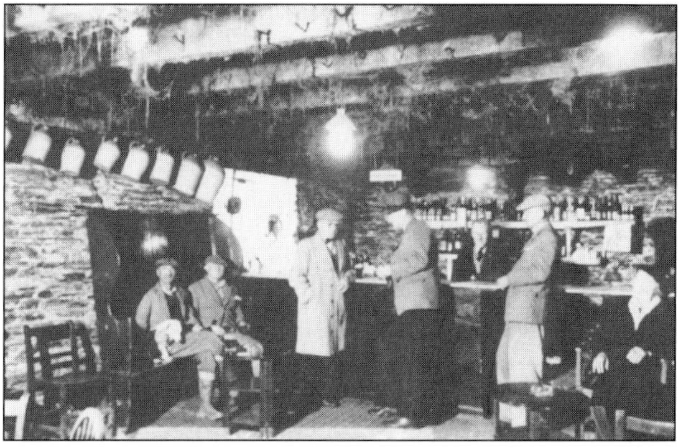

The Cobweb Inn, complete with the few remaining cobwebs hanging from the beams.

– the Napoleon Inn at the top of the village and the Wellington Hotel at the bottom. Boscastle's third pub today is the Cobweb Inn and it is quite a newcomer to the scene. Until 1947 the Cobweb was used as a storehouse by Rosevear & Sloggatt, then Hawkers, then Bowerings, then Bowering & Olde, and finally Charlie Bowering. It was known as Launceston Cellar. It served as an off-licence from the 1700s and bottled its own beer, wine and spirits, and was a bonded warehouse where the beer, wines and spirits were stored in barrels under the charge of Customs. After being unloaded from ships it was tested for alcoholic strength and Customs' approval, before being sold on to inns and pubs or through its off-licence sales.

In its foundations the Cobweb has large square black stones with a smooth appearance, similar to those on the walls of the footpaths which lead from the Old Road to the New Road Villas. These stones are like those from Harveys Foundry in Hayle and of the Copperhouse Foundry nearby. They are the waste 'slag' from iron castings. The molten slag was poured into moulds and allowed to harden into building blocks.

The store's second floor was used as a practice room by Boscastle Band and as somewhere to store their instruments. In the 1960s it was an art gallery for a brief spell. Contributors to the Boscastle Gallery were Margaret Blakeborough, Christopher Cork, Arthur Dongray, Bridget Holden, Frank Middleditch and Carole Vincent. The gallery was opened in 1966. The third floor was used to store agricultural manure and the top floor, which could be accessed from Private Path, initially held corn but later held all sorts of ironware including crocks, boilers, saucepans, frying-pans, kettles, cast drainpipes, bolts, chains, corrugated-iron sheeting, ploughshares and iron rods for use by the blacksmith in shoeing the oxen and horses. Nearby were coal stores of considerable size at the foot of Penally Hill. This building was reduced in size to provide car parking when the Cobweb became a public house.

In 1906 W.S. Hawker formed a partnership with Harry Bowering who had arrived from London in 1904 with Lillian, his wife of three years. Unfortunately for Harry Bowering, W.S. Hawker committed suicide the following summer and his widow emigrated to Australia. Hawker had owned the buildings concerned – office, stores and the cellar. The business owned two sheds at Camelford Station, the horses, wagons and stock, and traded in grain, coals, seed, tea, beer, wines, spirits, manure and sundries. After Hawker's death Harry Bowering continued in business as an agricultural and coal merchant and a baker and confectioner. Bowerings (Boscastle) Ltd now had two shareholders – Harry Bowering himself and Harold Rush. Amongst the employees were W. Force, J.C. Warren, A. Ferrett, C. Hiscock, L. Parnell and F. Pearn.

When Harry died his son Charles took over the business. He held business shares with Harold Rush's widow. They had differing ideas about how the business should continue and so agreed that Charlie should take the bakery side and Mrs Rush the coal and agricultural interests at Camelford Station. Work in the bakery started early. Jim Kinsman started work there when he left school in 1936. He worked a six-day week for ten shillings and started work at 4a.m.

After the Ship Inn closed at the end of the First World War its licence was transferred to Launceston Cellar. It allowed the purchase of drink on six days a week but was not trading as a public house. Mr Statton worked in the wine and spirit store. He and his wife lived at Penally Court. Mrs Statton acted as a midwife in the village, assisting the doctors with confinements. She brought many Boscastle children into the world and laid them out when they died. The first licencee was Percy Jones, later to be the husband of Doreen Jones who taught at the primary school. He gave up the licence trade to become a council surveyor.

In 1947 Mr Cecil Beadon took over and turned the ground floor into a bar. The pub got its name from the cobwebs that hung from the ceiling in a thick, black mat. They had been encouraged by the merchants who believed they kept the flies away from the kegs. Over the years they have gradually disintegrated, until today, in line with modern hygiene standards, there are none to be seen.

Cecil Beadon lived at Riverside on the opposite side of the road beside the main bridge. This house was converted in 1984 to an hotel and restaurant but in Beadon's day it was one of two homes. The other was called Brooklets and was lived in by Mr William (Bill) Ferrett and his wife Violet, who was the daughter of Henry Rogers, a local omnibus coachman.

Chapter Five

Pirates, Smugglers and Wreckers

The area of lower Boscastle to the east of Quaytown is known as Bridge. It gets its name from the road bridge which carries traffic across the Valency River. The Valency rises just four miles away near Otterham Station. When the Bridge Garage was being converted in 1923, inspection pits were dug before the floor was levelled and concreted. A layer of many pebbles, worn round, was found several feet below, showing the course of the river which had once run there. At some time the river bed had been straightened, making way for the cottages in Valency Row to be built. Lower downstream the course of the river curved slightly, making a place where cattle went down to drink and where man and horses could cross.

After the floods of the 1960s the old bridge was so badly damaged that it was demolished to be replaced by the present bridge. The original one had two arches, one large and a smaller one, to take excess flood water when required. It is not known when this bridge was built but the cottages on either side of it appear to have been there before the bridge. They

Island Cottages and the mill house in the 1920s.

The Old Mill wheel which provided power to grind corn and later electricity for the Wellington Hotel.

Bridge, 1894. Valency Fields, in the centre of this picture, became the tourist car park in the 1970s.

Mr and Mrs Ambrose Pearn, whose house was demolished to allow for the widening of the bridge.

Ward's stores can be seen in the centre behind the electricity pole.

The houses on either side are below the level of the road, providing an indication to the site of the original crossing by the ford.

are well below the level of the road in 2004, in fact the one on the western side had the road almost level with its ground-floor windows. This cottage was demolished to make way for the new widened bridge. When this was being done, well-worn wheel tracks were found in the river bed cut by countless cartwheels. These were lost when the river bed was lowered as part of the flood-prevention scheme. The work on the new bridge was carried out by Hendersons of Newquay who engaged local workmen, including a young Mike Webber who used his carpentry skills to fashion the wooden, curved shuttering needed to make the arch. During this time the lower bridge carried the traffic.

At its height in the nineteenth century, Bridge contained the warehousing and support services for Quaytown and the rest of the village. The main merchants at this time were T.R. Avery, Charles Benoke, Jabez Brown, Richard Burnard, Claudius Hawker, William Sloggatt Hawker, Robert Robinson Langford and Thomas Pope Rosevear. Brothers-in-law Rosevear and Sloggatt formed a partnership at the beginning of the nineteenth century. They used Launceston Cellars, now the Cobweb Inn, as a storehouse. As well as importing wines, spirits, beer, tea and groceries they owned North Delabole and Bowithick Slate Quarry in Tintagel.

William Sloggatt lived at Penally House which is set back from the main Boscastle to Bude road on the eastern side of the village. Surrounded by three and a half acres of land it enjoys some privacy from the hustle and bustle of the lower village. It was built in 1836 by William Sloggatt and, although built during the reign of Queen Victoria, it owes much of its design to the Georgian period. Originally it had 17 rooms, but over the years this has been reduced to 16. William Sloggatt lived there with his family and two house servants. He was a man of some importance in Boscastle and Cornwall: he was a magistrate for Cornwall, a general dealer in iron, coal and gin, and a wine and spirits merchant. He owned the vessels involved in his import and export business and, together with his partner Thomas Rosevear of Barn Park House, owned several warehouses and stores. They were also agents at Lloyds.

Together with Thomas Rickard Avery they were trading during Boscastle's heyday as a port. The three of them had a virtual monopoly on the import and export business. In 1830 they had entered into an agreement in an attempt to rationalise trade in the port. In later years Rosevear was to refer to Avery as 'that violent and wicked man Thomas Rickard Avery' when Avery came to an arrangement with his partner and brother-in-law William Sloggatt. Trading at this time was fraught with dangers. Merchants were forced into deals and partnerships, sometimes against their better judgement. They also had to deal with the treacherous seas. On 4 July 1845 the sloop *Jane*, owned by Sloggatt and Rosevear, left Boscastle for Trebarwith Strand Creek to load slate. Her master was Nicholas Couch. In the night the crew laid to in Port Isaac Bay and the captain went below to sleep. The mate on deck also fell asleep and the vessel drifted on to shore and was wrecked. Rosevear described the incident as 'a good vessel thrown away by or through the unpardonable carelessness of a worthless crew.'

There are many myths, legends and stories concerning Boscastle, the disappearing hurlers on the cliffs, the eating of Boscastle babies and the 'Silent Bells of Botreaux' amongst them. There are also many stories about Penally House and its grounds. These tales are contemporary with the people who lived there and with those associated with the house and its owners. It is rumoured that Sloggatt was involved in smuggling and used the house to store the smuggled goods. It is certainly documented that a sailing ship owned by Rosevear and Sloggatt was involved with piracy. It was ambushed by a French pirate vessel. The cargo ship was carrying wines and spirits and managed to slip behind Meachard Rock at the entrance to the harbour. The pirates giving chase were unaware of Boscastle's hidden entrance and thought the cargo ship had foundered on the rocks. They sailed away empty handed. Thomas Rosevear records the incident in his diaries. In thanksgiving for the deliverance of the ship and cargo he built the original Methodist chapel in Fore Street.

William Sloggatt was responsible for the building of Private Path and vehicles using it were able to avoid the steep Penally Hill. The hill above Private Path was cultivated and had an ideal south-facing aspect in an otherwise deep valley. Well into the twentieth century potatoes were still being grown there. These Boscastle potatoes were well known as being the earliest potato crop in the country. In 1861 the port was said to have been considerably improved by the vast quantities of iron ore from Trebursye being shipped out. The manager, Mr Martin, talked of having steam engines to convey trucks of ore on the common roads and had engaged to use Private Path and other premises of Messrs Sloggatt and Rosevear on the north side of the harbour in order to avoid the steep hill into Boscastle. The following year this engine, with two iron carriages capable of carrying seven tons each, travelled from its Lincoln manufacturers, Messrs Taplin & Co., to Tavistock by rail. It then travelled under its own steam to Trebursye, a journey which took three and a half days. It suffered from bad road conditions which were not up to its 10-ton weight, but eventually it arrived in Boscastle on 17 April 1863, making its first journey with a single truck as a fuel tender. During this journey it was said to have caused a pair of horses to bolt with their plough and to have set fire to the shirt of a man working in the fields. It was then laid up for several months 'for repairs'. When the overhaul was completed it successfully carried 15 tons of ore to Boscastle. The following morning the two trucks were loaded with coal for the return journey to Trebursye. A good start was made but within half a mile one of the wheels slid off the road into the marshy ground and the machinery was dislocated,

A Richard Webber postcard of Pentargon Caves, Boscastle.

The Hawker family and staff on the lawn of Penally House.

leaving the engine lying like a fallen giant beside the road. Two months later the engine was back at work. It made trips three times a week, loaded with 20 tons of ore for Boscastle and 14 tons of coal on its return to Trebursye. When the mine closed and there was no more work the engine became redundant.

There are tales of smuggling connected to Penally House involving a series of caves under Penally Head. The house is only 350 yards from the cliff edge. Stories tell of a shaft that was sunk below the house, running down to the caves. Small boats loaded with wines and spirits would enter the caves in secrecy to unload. The contraband would then be taken via Penally House and the Private Path to the warehouses and added to the legitimate stock. There is some evidence to support the existence of the secret shaft. The original Penally House was square and the ground floor consisted of four square rooms. One of those rooms had an additional stone wall built into it, making it rectangular in shape. Was that to hide the evidence of the shaft? Other tales about the caves are more recent.

During the First World War, people walking the cliff path reported hearing German voices below the cliffs, and it has been supposed that German submarines were using the area to surface and recharge their batteries and air supplies.

When William Sloggatt died his only daughter Mary inherited Penally House. She had married Claudius Crigan Hawker on 4 February 1837. Claudius was the brother of Revd Robert Steven Hawker, the famous vicar of Morwenstow who wrote the Cornish anthem 'Trelawney'. Revd Hawker was a frequent visitor to Penally and had in fact visited there only a few days before his death. Claudius Hawker was another important person of the village. As well as being a merchant and dealer he was an attorney at law, clerk to the Camelford Union and Superintendant Registrar. On his death Claudius Hawker left Penally and his business to his son, Colonel William Sloggatt Hawker. Things were not so easy for the Colonel. The pattern of life was rapidly changing. The shipping trade that had made Boscastle an important port was now being challenged by the coming of the railway. Indeed the railway company suggested that Boscastle be linked to the main Waterloo–Padstow line by the building of a branch line from Otterham to a station in the Valency Valley. However, those involved in shipping vehemently opposed the plan. But the railway came anyway, to Camelford Station in the parish of Minster.

In the same way that William Sloggatt had formed a partnership with Thomas Rosevear, William Sloggatt Hawker went into partnership with Harry Bowering. On 7 May 1904 an indenture was signed taking Harry Bowering into partnership in the trade or business of coal, grain, wine, spirit and general merchandise. The business, however, was in decline and Colonel Hawker committed suicide shortly after. Penally House was repossessed by the mortgage company and bought from them by Boscastle Manor. When the manor was put up for sale Penally House was being run as a guest-house by Mrs B.L. Mendez. It was described in the sale prospectus as an 'attractive and picturesquely placed regency residence with ornamental grounds, kitchen garden and woodland.' It had seven bedrooms, bathroom and toilet, three reception rooms, kitchen, offices and conservatory. On the opposite side of the road it had a walled kitchen garden.

In 1953 the house was bought by Miss Frances Baxter, an aunt of television personality Raymond Baxter. She was a retired RAF Flight Lieutenant, where she had worked as a welfare officer. With this background in welfare she was always willing to help people in hard times and she took them in as lodgers.

Thomas Pope Rosevear lived at Barn Park. Originally the name Barn Park was ascribed to the area around what is now Barn Park House. It was known as Barn Park or Barn Park Village. The area belonged in the late 1700s to James Bastard of Michaelstow and consisted of a house and large barn, a cottage to the west, adjoining stable, three meadows and three gardens. When the original buildings were erected is not known. The remains of the cottage were demolished to build the housing estate which is still under construction at the time of writing.

What is variously called Barn Park House, Barn Park Gallery and Glenfield was, in its early stages, a house on the eastern side with a later addition to the west, possibly created by the conversion of a barn with gig house underneath. A study of the western elevation shows a miss-match of windows. The centre upstairs window could well have been a door, approached by a set of external stone steps and used as a hayloft to store the produce from the surrounding meadows.

In 1873 Sir John Maclean described Barn Park House as:

> *... a comfortable old house, now the residence of Mr. Tuke, surgeon, it was formerly the property of Mr. James Bastard of Michaelstow who sold it to the late Mrs Sorrell of Hengar and together with the Hengar Estate it was devolved upon Sir Mathew Onslow, Baronet. Adjoining this is a convenient residence erected by the late Thomas Pope Rosevear which is now occupied by his nephew and heir William Sloggatt Rosevear.*

Thomas Pope Rosevear was in partnership with William Sloggatt of Penally House, he was a merchant, shipowner, agent at Lloyds and proprietor of North Delabole Slate Quarry. He was also a Methodist local preacher and reformer. In January 1830 a notice was placed in the *West Britain,* advertising:

Barn Park House.

The west wing of Barn Park House was built as the home of Thomas Pope Rosevear

> *At less than half price of imported Hollands, and at the highest strength allowed, Rosevear and Sloggatt beg to inform their friends and the public, that they have received a further supply of this unrivalled spirit, being the same wholesome, unadulterrated article produced in Holland (liable to a duty on importation of 22s.6d per gallon) and held in such deserved estimation on the continent, as well as the rest of Europe, Asia and America and now introduced to the public at a British duty, by sanction of the Government in order to extirpate smuggling.*

Rosevear and Sloggatt, like many merchants at the time, were shipowners and owned the smack *Affo,* which had been built by and was launched on 5 September 1826 from the yard of Mr J. Tredwen at Padstow.

Rosevear was a substantial landowner in Boscastle, owning the Pelly or Penally estate with the Mansion House, offices, buildings, cottages, warehouses, yards, sheds, courtlages and gardens. The Pelly estate was part of the manor of Trewannot, anciently part of the possession of the

Doctor Charlie Wade at the wheel of his Sunbeam Witch, 1892. This was the first car to arrive in Boscastle.

Botreaux family. In the eighteenth century it belonged to Sir James Laroche, derived most probably from the Robartes family, and was purchased in 1794 by Sir Jonathan Phillipps who, in 1821, sold it to Messrs Rosevear and Sloggatt. Rosevear also owned Millets Meadow, two pieces on Forrabury Common, Pentargin Hill, Higher and Lower Pentargin Fields, Tresuck, Trebyla, Great Welltown and Little Welltown. Outside Boscastle he owned Garron or Trewarmett Down and North Delabole or Bowithick Quarries. He had property at Trebarwith Strand and King Arthur's Castle, where he had shipping wharves. Within the village he owned the Ship Inn and much of Dunn Street, including a garden at the rear of the Ebenezer Chapel and the Wesleyan Chapel building.

Rosevear kept a journal which survives to this day. In it he recorded the daily happenings in his life. There are details of his family, travels, business dealings, the shipping trade, political and religious developments, and all sorts of day-to-day 'trivia'. It gives a very vivid picture of daily life in Boscastle in the first half of the nineteenth century. Rosevear purchased the land at Barn Park in about 1820 from Thomas Dymond. On part of it he built his house by adding a western wing to the existing eastern wing, which he leased from Sir Henry Onslow. The house consisted of a converted gig house, chamber over a lobby, a kitchen and two storerooms (one of which was over a pump), one shed house, one dining-room and two bedrooms on the attic storey. The wall

INFECTIOUS DISEASE (NOTIFICATION) ACT, 1889.

The Camelford Rural Sanitary Authority
for the District of Boscastle

Dr. to C. Wade
of Boscastle.

For FEES as under in respect of Certificates furnished under the above Act during the ~~Quarter~~ month ending December 14th 1894.

	Number of Certificates forwarded during the Months of			TOTAL Number during the ~~QUARTER~~ Month	Fee payable in respect of each Case.		Amount at each Rate of Payment.		
		December			s.	d.	£	s.	d.
I. Certificates in respect of Private Patients ...		1		1	2	6		2	6
II. Certificates in respect of cases attended as Medical Officer of any Public Body or Institution					1	0			
TOTALS		1		1				2	6

I have examined this Account, and Certify the same to be correct as regards the total number of Certificates sent in to me.

C. Wade M. O. H.

Received *of the* Camelford Rural *Sanitary Authority for the District of* Boscastle. *the amount of the above Account, this* 15th *day of* December 1894.

Charles Wade

London: KNIGHT & Co., Local Government Publishers, 90 Fleet Street.—(S 1331-91)
Infectious Diseases, 6.

Receipted bill for monies received by Dr Wade in connection with a notifiable disease.

dividing the east and west wings was built by Rosevear and contained the water-storage tank. There was, and still is in 2004, a deep well beneath the pathway between Barn Park and Corentin, and water could be pumped into water tanks in both houses.

Rosevear lived in the house with his wife Letitia and his brother John Rosevear. They had live-in servants and often had guests. These guests were visiting family members, business associates or accredited preachers. Many of the original features of Rosevear's house still survive at the time of writing. It is a listed building and the house is built of slate stone rubble, which is rendered and stuccoed on the front. The roof is slate with a gable-end on the front left and a hipped end on the front right. There are two storeys and a basement. The house has an L-shaped plan with the entrance on the right leading to an entrance hall, reception rooms on the left, central hall and staircase. The main reception room was across the back of the right-hand side. The house also had a dairy and cellar. The interior features from the 1800s include moulded cornices, doors and doorcases with reeded architrave, there is a marble chimney-piece in the main room downstairs and above the staircase is an ornate plaster rose. The room above the gig house is panelled and of early-Georgian appearance.

When Rosevear died in 1854 he left the house to his wife Letitia for her lifetime and then to his nephew William Sloggatt Rosevear. William lived in the west wing of Barn Park. He was deputy lieutenant of Cornwall and a County Magistrate. The east wing of the house was occupied by John Tuke, surgeon.

At the end of the 1800s Barn Park became the home of Charles Wade, GP. He lived there with two servants, Margaret Stone and Lillie Wivell. Dr Wade was a colourful young man and was reputedly the first man in Boscastle to own a motor car. He was the son of Arthur and Helen Wade. Arthur Wade was a surgeon.

At the beginning of the twentieth century Barn Park House became the property of George Bellamy who was the lord of the manor, and it was let to manor tenants. In the 1940s, on their return from India, the Harrison family lived there. When the manor was sold in 1956 Barn Park House was included as lot 104. It was described as:

... a detached residence known as Barnpark House, Tintagel Road. Tenancy Miss M.I. Harrison. Yearly rent at Michaelmas £25 p.a. Accommodation: Four bedrooms, bathroom & wc, three reception rooms, kitchen and offices.

In a separate lot numbered 128 was Barn Park and Barn Park Cottage. These were described as:

... a choice parcel of accommodation and building land called and known as Barn Park with cottage and outbuildings as now occupied by (1) Messrs T & M Sharrock at an apportioned rental of £11.7s.0d p.a. as yearly Michaelmas tenants; (2) as to cottage by Mr. W.H. Piper as a monthly tenant at a rental of £6.12s.2d p.a.

When the manor was sold in 1956 the house was bought by Joseph Ivor Snowdon. Ivor Snowdon carried out work on the property and it became known as Barn Park and Glenfield. He lived there with his family and his grandchildren. When Ivor Snowdon died the property was bought by G.W. Colburn and sold as two separate properties in 1986. The following year Glenfield received Grade II listing.

Ivor and Kathleen Snowdon and their sons Eric, Basil and Alan, c.1963.

Thomas Rickard Avery lived at Valency House which was next door to the Ship Inn brew house and part of Valency Row. It was given a new frontage to incorporate the architecture fashionable in Georgian times. Avery, like his fellow merchants, was a shipowner and part owner of Delabole Slate Quarry. He traded in hemp, tallow, tea, groceries, iron, coal, beer and porter. He had a large sloop-rigged smack, the *Canadian*, built at Padstow by Mr Carter's yard especially for his timber trade. She was launched at Padstow on 30 July 1839. Avery also built vessels in his yard at Boscastle, the last one being the *Thomasine and Mary* which was named for his mentally handicapped daughter. Avery was not always popular with his competitors. Revd Hawker of Morwenstow described him as a 'notorious wrecker and receiver of contraband goods', and Thomas Rosevear referred to him in his journal on 23 April and 3 June 1844:

My partner and brother in law Mr Wm Sloggat came to an arrangement and agreement with that violent and wicked man Thos Rickard Avery in regard to the Benoke

Trust Estate in which I have been vexationally involved from the year 1828 to this – i.e. at a sacrifice of several hundred pounds – Benoke wife and son having turned around and joined the enemy of both themselves and their trustees. The son, Cotton Amy Benoke having been induced, most probably, by Avery to file a bill in Chancery against I his Trustee whose money had been expended for 15 years and upward in keeping all these persons from starvation and from Gaol.

Avery's reputation as a wrecker may have come from the fact that he was officially a Receiver of Wrecks, a position which gave him salvage rights. To Robert R. Langford he was 'a staff which would ever fail all but self. A man of worthless promises.' He had been in dispute with Rosevear. When the lord of the manor, Cotton Amy, died in 1766 his daughter Ann inherited. Ann was unfortunately a lunatic. She remained unmarried and had no children. When she died in 1819 her interests in the manor passed to Catherine Amy Francis and Catherine's sister Rebecca Amy Benoke. Rebecca's husband Richard Benoke got into financial difficulties and mortgaged his wife's inheritance to Rosevear on 22 February 1828. However, in 1844 he sold the premises involved to Avery, leaving Rosevear to launch a long and expensive lawsuit to try to recover his money. On the death of Catherine, Avery became lord of the manor.

Avery did much for Boscastle's prosperity and he was quick to bring mechanisation to the quarry at Delabole. Believing that he could make it much more profitable he bought out the quarrymen who were the leaseholders of Landwork Quarry. He erected horse whims and a water-wheel for pumping. In 1836 Avery bought out that part of Delabole Quarry owned by the Bake family. His activities were again controversial – he made life difficult for the other men working in nearby quarries. There were several lawsuits between Avery and his competitors. In 1841 he erected several cottages for his workmen and he introduced a large steam engine in addition to the horse whims. The village of Medrose grew up largely due to his efforts. Avery sold his interests in the quarry some time after 1848 for what was said to be a very high price.

Avery had interests in other quarries, of which several were much closer to Boscastle. An important quarry industry existed in the eighteenth and nineteenth centuries along the coast. The earliest quarrying was done entirely with hand tools until the use of gunpowder became common in the late-eighteenth century. Cliff quarries had no difficulty in disposing of their waste – they simply dropped it into the sea below – and huge blocks of waste slate litter the shoreline. With the waste slate disposed of the usable slate could be extracted for flooring and roofing material. Once the slate had been split into manageable blocks it was hoisted to the cliff top with hand winches. The guide chains by which the blocks were raised were fastened to the seabed. The blocks were then taken to the splitting sheds and split according to suitability. Some would be used for gateposts and water tanks, some for hedging slabs or flooring. The finer slate was split for roofing.

Once gunpowder became readily available it was used to full advantage. Deep holes were drilled into the slate beds close to a fault or edge by two men, one using a long-handled sledgehammer and the other holding and rotating a long iron bar known as a jumper, which acted like a drill bit. These holes would be set close together in a row. Some can still be clearly seen where rock cutting took place in Boscastle. Small quantities of powder were dropped into the holes, a fuse was added and the hole tamped with ground-up slate dust. Alternative fuses were sometimes made from goose quills filled with firing powder. There was always the danger of premature explosions when firing took place.

East Delabole Quarry was at Buckator, Beeny, just to the north of Boscastle. Slate would be lowered from the quarry directly onto ships moored below if the sea was calm. This slate was particularly fine and was used for billiard and snooker tables. The slate step into Top School and the slabs outside Trehayne House all came from Buckator. At the quarry there was a miniature railway along the level area over-

Working with slate are Charlie Kinsman, John Sandercock and Eric Fearnley.

looking the sea, together with a stables and a smithy. The wooden props in the cliff used to secure the ropes can still be seen in the early-twenty-first century. The quarrymen descended down these ropes to the quarry face. A large slate slab, still present at the time of writing at Buckator, is inscribed with the date 1709.

Further west is Pentargon Quarry, exploited mainly for building stone. Extraction was fairly easy due to the erosion in this area. Removal was along specially cut tracks in the cliffside, along which the carts travelled. The two-storey powder house was at nearby Tresuck Farm and was used for the storage of gunpowder below and for sleeping accommodation above. The powder house was demolished by the National Trust and the stone used to build the Coastguard vehicle store. It had been a prominent feature on the landscape, particularly when approaching Boscastle from Camelford. Stone from Pentargon and Tresuck was used to build the substantial hedges on the Bude road between Penally House and Hillsborough. The stones cost one farthing each.

To the west of Willapark are the quarries of Swanser, Welltown, Growa and Trevalga. Swanser or California Quarry can be identified by an impressive, strongly built wall overhanging the cliff. On this was a wooden platform supporting a crane or gantry which was operated by horse and used to hoist blocks to the top. There are various ruined buildings along the cliff tops. Some were used as overnight shelter and others were splitting sheds, where men would sit all day producing thin roofing slates. Old photographs show that there was a small railway with iron wagons here. The men working these quarries were in constant danger from their working conditions, the weather being their worst enemy. If gales or frosty weather stopped them working they did not get paid. One man, Mr Dangar from Tintagel, who was captain of Growa Quarry on Trevalga cliffs, was killed when he was blown over the cliff and into the sea during a gale. The skills the men acquired descending the cliffs in these conditions made them a valuable addition to the Coastguard cliff-rescue service. A good workman could split 100 dozen roofing slates in a day. His hours were 7.30a.m. to 5.30p.m. with half an hour lunch break. Rag slates were from 6ft by 2ft and some 18 inches square and sold at 2s.6d. a dozen in 1888. The slates were known by names which related to their size, which were (in inches): Queens 36 x 7, Duchess 24 x 14, Countesses 20 x 10, Ladies 16 x 9 and Doubles 12 x 7. Scantle slates were made by boys in sizes 9 x 5, 8 x 6, 7 x 7 and 6 x 3. Cisterns up to 2,000 gallons were made along with corn chests, pig troughs, mangers, pump troughs, baths, salting troughs, milk coolers, larders, chimney tops, mantelpieces, window-sills, garden edging and hedging, room skirtings, lintels, quoins, rolling-pins, candlesticks and ashtrays. Every Cornish churchyard has examples of slate headstones. Thomas Rickard Avery was a tough and competitive businessman.

Even in death Thomas Rickard Avery was surrounded by legend and superstition, as recorded by Revd Hawker in his journal on 26 December 1858:

> *The whole countryside is excited by these storms and the people connect them with the death of a Mr Avery, a merchant of Boscastle and a notorious wrecker. As soon as a ship was seen he used to mount his horse and never leave her out of his sight until she came ashore when he would take possession, then he would make enormous profit by charging salvage... Ten days ago a man named Jabez Brown living at Boscastle was returning at night when he saw sailing up the valley from the sea a cloud filled with a bright fiery light. All the sailors also saw it. It glided over Avery's house and passed inland up the glen until it reached a church to which he belonged and his family vault is.*

Jabez Brown was obviously very taken with the sighting because he wrote an account of it which appeared in the *Times* newspaper.

On the evening of his death Avery had gone out on to the cliffs and was seen watching the sea. He returned home and retired to bed as normal. A servant heard him walking about his room at five the following morning. At six o'clock one of his vessels broke loose from its moorings in the harbour and when the servant went up to tell him he found Avery dead.

Jabez Brown, who saw the fiery cloud, had emigrated from Bude to Canada at the age of 18 in 1848. He and his father walked to Stratton where Jabez caught the carrier's van to Rock. From there he took the ferry to Padstow and boarded Avery's barque, the *Clio,* as a cabin passenger. On his return to Cornwall he set himself up in business in Boscastle. By 1861 he was a corn and spirit merchant and had his sister Lydia and brother William living with him.

In 1880 he was trading in coal which he was shipping to Boscastle in his own trading vessels. He lost one vessel that was not insured. The smack, *Bottreaux Castle,* with its master Sharrock, drifted on to rocks under Willapark in a southerly wind. She was totally wrecked. Her crew was saved but in launching their boat the boy got jammed and had one of his legs broken. He had to be brought ashore in the hobbling boat. They were unable to save the cargo of coal which had been loaded at Newport. Jabez Brown's store which he leased from the manor was right in the centre of lower Boscastle next to where the visitor car park is at the time of writing, on the site of a row of small modern shops. It was known as the New Stores and the lease taken out in 1887 was for the New Stores, dwelling-house, coal yards and hereditaments. The lease was renewed in

The brig TPC, *built in 1860 at Appledore, was bought in 1863 by Thomas Webb Ward of Boscastle.*

1891, this time for 14 years, but in 1898 the premises were taken over by the Ward family. Ward's store was similar in size and shape to Fox's Cellar. The store housed all manner of wholesale goods that were shipped in through the harbour, until the last trip made by the *Francis Beddoe* in 1916. From then on their goods were brought in by rail to a shed at Otterham Station. Daniel Fulford Ward took cargoes of coal from Wales, wood from Cannons Marsh, and iron, galvanise and gravel from Bristol, together with what were termed 'Bristol Goods'. The store held almost everything you might want from a local shop.

Daniel Ward was born in Boscastle on 26 January 1857. His father Thomas Webb Ward married Gertrude Richards Fulford on 6 April 1854. Thomas Webb Ward was the owner of the brig *TPC*. The *TPC* was built in 1860 at Appledore by her first owner and master, Thomas Peter Cook of Bideford, after whom she was named. She was registered at 58 tons. In 1863 she was bought by T.W. Ward of Boscastle and registered at Padstow. That same year J.W. Jenkyns became managing owner and master. The *TPC* was lost in September 1869 on passage from St Ives to Plymouth. Daniel started life as a draper's assistant before becoming a commercial traveller in general goods, a sound basis for his life as a storekeeper. He became a JP later in life and lived at Lynwood in New Road. His sister, Sybella de la Tour Ward, was also a draper and had her shop at Sunnyside opposite the school in Fore Street.

Daniel Ward was a local Methodist preacher. He married Sarah Louise Rowlett of Holsworthy where her family were in the plumbing trade. Sarah was fully involved in the business and, as her recipe book shows, she kept detailed notes of her catering. For example, she has a recipe for St Martin's Fair on 22 November 1909, involving 48½lbs of boiled beef and 28½lbs of roast beef. Quarterly meetings and social teas for perhaps 40 people were catered for and included splits, saffron buns (using 6lbs of flour), boiled ham, ribs of beef, ox tongues, biscuits, bread and butter, and tea. Daniel and Sarah had three sons – Frank Fulford, Archie and Harold Wilfred, who was born in 1897.

Harold joined the Royal Navy from school and was a signalman on a minesweeper in the First World War. He joined the Merchant Navy in 1918 and studied for his Board of Trade Masters certificate, which he got in 1926. During the Second World War he was in the Home Guard and later the Royal Naval Volunteer Reserve. He married Irene Grace Batley of Corsham in Wiltshire and they settled in Boscastle, where he worked as a secretary to the business. Their son Michael was born in the nursing home at Corentin and went on to marry Pamela Gard who was also born there.

When the Wards took over from Jabez Brown the store was part of the manor and included Riverside, where they lived, and the coal store immediately opposite the bridge. There was a weighbridge to weigh carts as they arrived with coal from the harbour. The coal that was shipped in by sea was stored in layers in the store. As the layers grew higher, planks would be placed up them for the delivering carts to go up and add further layers. The coal store was given up when Daniel died. The warehouse continued until it was demolished in the 1970s to widen the road, along with several other smaller buildings for storage on the river side which were open-fronted and the ancient candle store which stood nearby, where wicks were dipped in tallow. Candles were exported in substantial numbers through the harbour. This building later became a match house with Ward's oil store beneath. It was the Wards with whom Sir John McLean stayed in the late 1860s when gathering information for his *Parochial and Family History of Forrabury and Minster.*

When the store was bought by the County Council in anticipation of the road widening, the Wards, who had been living at Penrowan in New Road, had already built their house Lynley for their retirement.

The coal store was taken over in 1923 by Richard Webber who came to Boscastle as a carpenter in 1906. He set up as a photographer and had a darkroom and workshop in the garden of the Ship Inn. He produced and sold postcards at his shop. During the 1920s he had 25 varieties of cards. He would order 1,000 of each and sometimes re-order during the season. He was manager of Boscastle Golf Club which had a nine-hole links course on Hillsborough Farm beside Penally House. When the golf course closed Richard Webber bought the clubhouse shed and used it for his darkroom. In 1922 he started a taxi business which developed into the first bus service in and out of the village. Initially this was a trailing wicker basket mounted on a pair of wheels which was towed behind his bicycle and used to transport people about. One day during the First World War he was returning to Boscastle with serviceman Bill Ferrett, when the fastening of this trailing carriage came adrift as they approached the bridge where

Above: *Ward's storemen, Jack Allen and Cecil Beadon.*

Right: *Harold and Daniel Ward.*

Below left: *Irene Grace Batley, wife of Harold Ward.*

Below right: *Harold Wilfred Ward, Lieutenant RNR, 1939.*

B-Type ERA belonging to Prince Bira.

The Webber family. Pictured are: *Mike, Trixie and their father Norman.*

Norman Webber's Gift Shop, 1950.

several people were awaiting their arrival. Richard Webber rode on unaware that his passenger had been deposited unceremoniously in the road! He had the contract to carry all passengers and goods to and from Camelford Station. He used an open-top charabanc and garaged it in what had been both Jabez Brown's and later Ward's coal store. Customers were able to garage their vehicles in the building. One such person was Juswant Rikh, a minor Indian potentate who garaged his white Rolls Royce there in the 1920s whilst living at Penagar on The Avenue.

When Richard died in 1938 aged 63 his son Norman took over and continued running it as a garage. During the Second World War the garage closed down because petrol was unobtainable, and Norman took employment as a bus driver. Amongst other jobs he ferried builders to work on the airfields at St Eval and St Merryn. During this period the garage was used to store a racing car belonging to Prince Bira of Thailand. Bira drove a variety of cars but achieved his most notable victories with ERA. He eventually had three of them – two B-types, named Romulus and Remus, and a C-type, Hanuman, named after the Siamese monkey god. It was Romulus of White Mouse Racing which was stored in a large pantechnicon in Webber's garage. When the manor was sold after the war Norman Webber bought the building next to his garage. The building had been the manor estate office and became a gift shop.

In 1950 Norman's son Michael joined the business as an apprentice mechanic, carrying out engine repairs, maintenance, panel beating and spraying. He later went on to drive the firm's taxis. Michael had no interest in taking over the business so his father sold it to a Mr Turner as a going concern. Mr and Mrs Turner lived in the flat behind and continued to run the garage for a couple of years before their son David began to help out. However, David's interest was more electrical than mechanical and gradually he changed the business over to an electrical retailers, selling every conceivable electrical household appliance. He set up the famous 'Turners Line' – an early form of cable television. He erected an aerial above the shop behind Private Path, high on the hillside. From it he ran miles of co-axial cable to every home willing to pay to receive his signal. This was practically every house as the hilly nature of the village made reception from the BBCs transmitter at North Hessary Tor on Dartmoor a hit-and-miss affair, especially with roof-top aerials. Unfortunately the line was very vulnerable to the weather as well as hedge trimmers and the odd high-sided vehicle. It was a regular occurrence at the beginning of winter to miss the last episode of your favourite serial because the first storms of the year had blown the line apart. It was a great relief to all when Boscastle received its own relay transmitter on the 'stitches' in the 1970s.

The main grocery outlet at Bridge was known as Scantlebury House, later to become Burnard's Stores. It stood on the opposite side of the road to Ward's, facing the bridge. Robert Robinson Langford had a draper's and grocer's there. He and his wife Francis had three children, Frances Thomazine, Elizabeth Avery and Robert Robinson. In 1844 Langford was the owner of a barn and mow hay, Barn Meadow and Long Meadow, two 'stitches' on the common, a block of houses and yards, and the house and shop at Bridge. He was also the owner of several trading vessels. The *Alarm* was built for him at Padstow by Sloggatt. It was a 48-ton smack with W. Darke and J. Haynes as masters. It was lost on 3 November 1862. The *Elizabeth* was a 98-ton schooner built in Plymouth in 1839 with B. Carter and J. Bellamy as masters. The *Jane Lowden* was a 500-ton barque built at Mirimanchi, New Brunswick in 1841. She was registered in Padstow in 1848 and acquired an Ottoman pass to trade to the Black Sea in 1851, but her main trading was to North America with emigrants and returning from Quebec with timber. She was lost at sea on 31 December 1865. The *Mary* was a 51-ton smack built in 1840 at Barnstaple and captained by Phillips. The *Valency* was built at Plymouth in 1838. She was a 37-ton smack built especially for Robert Langford. The *Zarah* was built in Sunderland in 1846. She was a 310-ton barque and Langford became her managing owner in 1865. She traded from Falmouth and Padstow to Quebec, Nova Scotia and the Mediterranean.

Scantlebury House became Bridge House in the second half of the nineteenth century when the shop front was added. It had been built in the carpenter's shop which is Harbour Café in 2004. Robert Langford transferred the registry of his ships to Plymouth in the early 1850s. R. Couch took over the business. He was the only son of Mr and Mrs John Couch of Lewarne in the parish of North Hill. He was educated at North Hill National School and later went to work on the farm owned by his grandfather, Mr Richard Horrell. At the age of 17 he joined the engineering staff of the celebrated Phoenix Mine, a position he held for 14 years. His next appointment was as manager of a large Co-operative Society at Upton, Linkinhorne. After filling this vacancy for nearly nine years, in 1880 he purchased a general drapery and grocery business at Delabole, before purchasing a similar business in Boscastle. The death in 1883 of manor agent Mr Richard created a vacancy in the agency of Boscastle Manor and Mr Couch was selected to fill it. He was a staunch member of the Weslyan Methodist Church and was a lay preacher. His preaching was of a sound evangelical type. He held several offices in the Church including society steward, class leader and superintendant of the Sunday school. Outside the Church he was chairman of the old School Board, a member of the Parish Council (as both vice-chairman and chairman), and

Michael and Denise Webber's wedding. In the background are: *Rodney Knight and Denise's daughter Clare Siford.*

Mike Webber Collection

Phone: "BOSCASTLE 47"

473

REPAIRS, TYRES ETC.
CARS FOR HIRE

HIGH PRESSURE, WASHING

N. H. WEBBER
THE GARAGE
BOSCASTLE

CARS, MOTOR CYCLES, STORED OR DRIVEN AT OWNERS RISK AND RESPONSIBILITY.

Mrs Lockwood   Sept   1950

June 6th	4 galls of Petrol		12	5
12th	4 " " "		12	5
July 4th	4 " " "		12	5
20th	4 " " "		12	5
27th	6 " " "		18	7½
Aug 3rd	4 " " "		12	5
9th	4 " " "		12	5
18th	4 " " "		12	5
	1 Puncture		3	0
	1-40 gallon Barrel Shell Talpa oil	9	16	
	1 Barrel	1	5	0
		£16	7	6½

A billhead from Norman Webber, 1950.

Outside in the sunshine at Burnard's Stores.

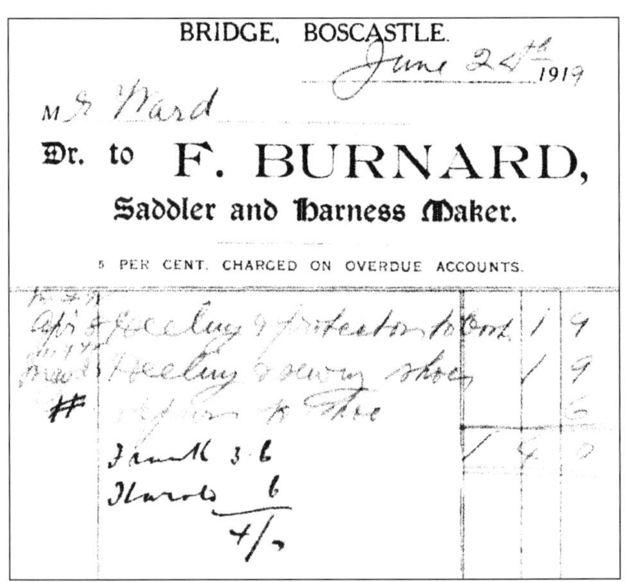

BRIDGE, BOSCASTLE. June 24th 1919

Mr Ward

Dr. to F. BURNARD,

Saddler and Harness Maker.

5 PER CENT. CHARGED ON OVERDUE ACCOUNTS.

A billhead from F. Burnard, 1919.

he represented the parishes on Camelford Rural District Council and the Board of Guardians. After leaving Bridge House he lived in the last villa in New Road at Lewarne, named after the parish he had moved from.

Bridge House had a wooden beam projecting over the front yard which enabled goods to be hoisted to the first floor, and it also had a cellar beneath. It was a prominent business which passed to Daniel Ferrett who traded as D.T. Ferret & Son. Both Daniel and his son Reg were also local Methodist preachers. They passed the business to another branch of the family.

William Francis Allen Burnard was born in Newquay. On 23 March 1903 he married a Boscastle girl, Tryphena Ferrett, the daughter of Daniel Ferrett. William was a saddler and had a saddler's shop next to Valency House. When his son Stanley was born in 1910 he and Tryphena were living at Lynwood House, New Road, in one of the villas. He was still a saddler but had become a fancy-goods dealer by the 1930s and moved to Valency House. He used his skill as a saddler to continue working with leather in the Old Bellows Shop and his wife ran Valency House as a boarding-house.

Stanley took over and also became the owner of Burnard's Stores, which was the main supplier of

Bowering's Bakery.

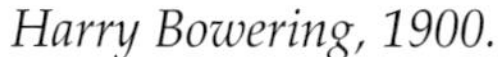

Harry Bowering, 1900.

Lilian Bowering, 1900.

groceries and other goods at Bridge. Stan retired in the 1960s and the shop was converted into flats shortly afterwards, by the new owner, Francis Munden. Stan continued to trade at the Old Bellows Gift Shop for several years until finally retiring to Okeford on Forrabury Hill.

Before its closure, Burnard's was the only grocery shop at Bridge, although there were several in the main village. Like several other buildings in the Bridge area, when Bridge House was sold, covenants were placed on it to prevent the use of the land or any building on it for any noxious or offensive purpose, and to prevent anything being done which might be detrimental to surrounding properties.

At the rear of Bridge House is Valency Row, referred to locally as Back Alley. This was at one time part of the main road from Bude as it came down to the ford over the Valency where the modern road bridge stands in 2004. When the manor was sold the five small houses in Valency Row were sold with their small gardens at the rear and half of the adjoining roadway, subject to a 'right of way over such moiety for... and other purposes at all times and for all purposes... .' Footpaths used to lead up from the back of the properties to Private Path, and because the gardens were so small the women would spread out their washing to dry on the thorn bushes near the path. On a ground-floor window of Robin Cottage were inscribed the initials JA and the date 1789.

The other retail outlet in Bridge was the bakery of Harry Bowering in the Cobweb buildings. By the

Boscastle, Octr. 30th 1920.

Messrs Ward & Sons. Boscastle

Dr. to H. Bowering,

LATE W. S. HAWKER & Co.

General Merchant

STORES AT CAMELFORD AND OTTERHAM STATIONS.

A billhead from Harry Bowering, 1920.

time the Cobweb was established as an inn Harry Bowering was trading from the building to the left where Boscastle Pottery is situated at the time of writing. After his tragic motorcycle accident at the top of the village, the premises were bought by Elizabeth Whitehouse (now Bluett) where she started a pottery business in 1957 making traditional slipwares. Roger Irving Little started his own studio pottery in 1962 and when she gave up the pottery to get married and pursue her interests in horses and hunting he purchased Boscastle Pottery from her in 1967. Roger and his wife Nanette and son Tim produce a unique form of Mochaware. They closely guard the secret of how it is done but say that in order to achieve the delicate tree and fern pattern on the pottery they use a 'certain herb' which possesses curious properties. The extracted essence of this herb is applied to a freshly slipped pot. The secret brew runs rapidly, spreading miraculously into trees and bushes before your eyes like smoke rising from a Havana cigar.

They continue a long history of potters. The seventeenth-century port lists for Barnstaple show us that John Burnard shipped into Botrix Castle and again Boatcastle 243 tons of clay and 12 tons of raw lead ore (for glazing) over a period of 18 years from 1661 to 1679. One sailing coaster, *The Grace*, had a 30-ton burden weight and, with master Humphrey French, is recorded as making 14 voyages. Six other vessels are named as sharing the delivery of potters' materials to Boscastle at that time.

Many, many years later, in the 1940s, the now-famous potter Bernard Leach and his family were living in the village.

Boscastle men in the 1930s. The back row includes: *Dick Kernick* (centre back), *Walter Knight* (back right); front row: *Fernley Honey, Scober Cann, Les Beard, Claude Knight, ?, ?, ?, Jack Beard, ?, Frank Symons.*

Chapter Six

Entertainment

Bands, Broomsticks and Breakdowns

It is easy to see that Cornwall has a strong and individual sense of place and that Cornish people have a distinctive personality and strength. Everybody can recognise Cornwall's separateness and its difference as soon as they cross the Tamar.

It has a great similarity to Pembroke and Cardigan in South West Wales and to Brittany. The similarity is striking in the types of houses, particularly the granite houses of Penwith and those of Finistere. These similarities reflect both race and way of life and create the temperament in which heredity is stronger than anything. You can see the Celtic temperament in the Cornish – warm and generous if not hurt or offended, touchy and quick, easily resentful and not likely to forget, sensitive, reserved and mistrustful. It is a deep, individual and clannish personality which sticks strongly and proudly together and looks after its own.

Cornwall and its people have remained remarkably close to Nature – to the land and the sea from which a hard and often perilous living has been won, and to the different seasons of the year. Seasonal changes made different demands and the year was seen as a constant cycle of birth, death and rebirth. Before the regulation of time by clocks, watches and chronometers, man used a rudimentary calendar based on festivals to keep abreast of the seasonal demands on his time. These festivals acted as a reminder of when to sow and when to harvest, and were associated with revelry and singing. It is a tradition stretching far back into the past and yet extending into modern times.

Remnants of these festivals were seen until the last half of the twentieth century in the annual carnival, the band festival, carol singing through the village, the summer Flora Dance and maypole dancing, and earlier in the century the annual celebration of darkie days and beating the bounds. In June the days from Sunday through to Wednesday preceding Ascension Thursday are known as Rogation days or as 'beating the bounds'. The word 'Rogation' comes from the latin 'rogare', meaning to ask. In pre-Christian times this was when the gods were called upon to grant a good harvest. Even today special prayers are offered on Rogation Sunday asking God for his blessing.

This pagan tradition was later incorporated into the Roman festival of Termanalia, held in honour of the god of the fields and boundaries. He was represented by square blocks of stone which stood at the edges of fields or estates to mark the boundaries. It was the custom to walk these boundaries annually to fix their perimeters and to remind and teach people where they were in the days before maps. Another custom was to beat the ground with sticks to frighten off the spirits of winter and to reinforce the memory. These customs developed into 'beating the bounds' of the parish which took place on Rogation days when villagers would walk in procession around the boundary, singing and dancing along the way. The Boscastle party would meet outside the manor office early in the morning and then proceed to Hillsborough and on to Mousehole, Newmills, Hellamellin, over church bridge and across country to Trekeek, Slaughterbridge, Cockcrowing, Condolden, Waterpit Down, Highgates, Trehane, Welltown, Western Blackapit, Willapark and back through the harbour to the manor estate office where sweets and copper coins would be distributed for the children to scramble for.

Beating the bounds in 1922. Pictured are, standing: *Mr A.G. Norman (Deputy Steward), Mr E.W. Couch (Manor Agent), James Sandercock, W.F.A. Burnard, James Bath, Fred Pearn;* kneeling: *Fred and Frank Ferrett.*

A week or so before Christmas the arrival of carol singers was eagerly awaited and, although English carols could be heard in church, the traditional Cornish carols would be sung in the pubs and in homes and even carried abroad by emigrants. The old singers always sang in four parts – air (treble), seconds (alto), counter (tenor) and bass. The Bible Christian chapel at the corner of High Street and Mount Pleasant had a tradition of singing hymns and carols in this way and, through the foresight of Arthur Biddick, three handwritten hymn books, one

Bible Christian hymn books from 1876.

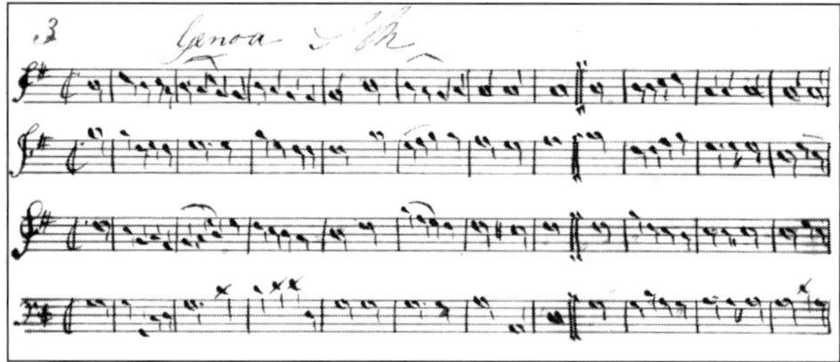
Example of the music score from the Bible Christian hymn books of 1876, belonging to E. Hoskin.

The oldest known photograph of Boscastle Brass and Reed Band, 1899. Bandmaster Prout is pictured centre front. The second man from the left in the front row is William Hockin, who later became bandmaster.

Boscastle Brass and Reed Band, 1912.

of which belonged to E. Hoskin and is dated 1876, have survived, written in all four parts.

It was at this time that Boscastle Brass and Reed Band was formed. Many bands of the period were formed by or with the help of employers or landowners as a means of providing music for festivals and local events. Boscastle Band was no exception. It provided music for the annual carnival, various fêtes, such as those of the Boscastle Friendly Society, and open-air dancing on the lawn opposite Manor House where waltzes, quicksteps and valetas were played. Engagements were carried out away from the village and horse-drawn vehicles were hired to transport the bandsmen and their instruments to and from their destinations. But this was not always without incident. In June 1906, in the early hours of the morning, the band was returning from an engagement with the Holsworthy Temperance Society. Some miles out of Holsworthy one of the horses in the brake driven by Mr J. Edwards began to kick. It smashed the splinter bar and damaged the front of the carriage. The horse had to be taken out and the journey continued with the other horse, making it necessary for some of the band members to walk part of the way. One of the men rode the kicking horse and they eventually reached Boscastle at 3a.m.

During one of the summer Flora Dances Richard Webber, who played bass trombone, gave vent to a particularly fierce blast, just as the band was passing Sharrock's shop in Fore Street. Tom Sharrock's dog was sitting on the doorstep and ran inside in terror. Shortly afterwards the poor thing died of fright!

At the end of the 1800s the bandmaster was Mr Prout. He was a carpenter and had previously been the bandmaster of the City of Bath Band. He was succeeded by William Hockin, a local postman. Bill Hockin lived at Rosebank Cottage, Paradise Lane, with his wife May and daughter Iris. Later they moved into High Street, opposite the Napoleon Inn. Whenever his post round allowed he would meet the Bude coach at the valley gate and play the coach horn as they drove into the Wellington Hotel yard.

In 1920 a loan of £170 was taken out to buy new instruments and the village joined together to help raise the money needed to repay the loan. Under the management of Harry Bowering and Ernest Couch a 'splendid variety entertainment' was put on in the public hall. There was an opening sketch entitled 'Bang goes the Bell', performed by J.W. Rea. This was followed by what was described as a musical absurdity, 'King Kopandeatemall', which was arranged by Harry Bowering who had composed the words of the solos and speeches in topical rhyme. The characters included Lord Motheaten (Tom Sharrock), Lady Motheaten (Bill Honey), ladies of the noble families (Misses Lobb, Bartley, Mitchell and Mitchell), King Kopandeatemall (Harry Bowering), Queen (Mr C.E. Beadon), and Princes of the Royal Blood (Messrs

Above: *The band leading the Flora Dance over the bridge.*

Right: *Bandmaster William (Bill) Hockin, 1912.*

Below: *Harry Bowering's orchestra.*

F. Pearn, B. Webber and H. Rush). The scene depicted a cannibal isle on which the Motheatens' yacht became stranded.

This was followed by a 'laughable farce' entitled 'My Turn Next' and included a hilarious performance by Mr E.W. Couch, the manor agent, as Tarixicum Twitters. His performance was so well received he was known for many years afterwards as Twitters Couch.

Part of the proceeds from the band engagements were shared out between the bandsmen who numbered about 14. With the coming of the First World War they disbanded, re-forming after the war.

Bill Hockin was a greatly appreciated bandmaster and in June 1922 he was presented with an ebony conductor's baton with three engraved silver mounts in a velvet-lined box. An inscription was included which read: 'Presented to Mr W. Hockin by the members of the Band as an appreciation of their gratitude and respect for his services as Bandmaster of Boscastle Brass Band.' Mr Hockin had got the band together after the war and had spent 'no end of time and patience' in training boys and working the band up.

They were again disbanded at the outbreak of the Second World War. After 1945 several of the villagers got together and re-formed the band with as many of the old instruments as could be gathered together. Quite a few had ended up at the bottom of Pentargon cliff, which was the village dump at this time. Ennis Caven Band, originally a fife and drum band, was one of many which disbanded during the war years and postwar their uniforms were advertised for sale in the local newspaper. The smart brown and gold

Boscastle Brass Band in 1947, after winning the Exeter Band Contest. The conductor was Mr Grigg.

Boscastle Band, 1957. Left to right, back row: *G. Pascoe, C. Jose, K. Dymond, B. Wickett, D. Ferrett, M. Webber, G. Wickett, M. Beard, W. Gard, J. Beard, M. Ferrett, F. Pridham, R. Dymond, PC Perry, L. Beard, J. Hancock, bandmaster Charlie Berryman;* front row: *E. Snowdon, R. Sandercock, M. McDonald, A. Fry, P. Kinsman, R. Ferrett, R. Stedman, G. Honey, J. Kinsman, D. Stedman.*

outfits were bought for the new Boscastle Silver Band under bandmaster Grigg. Boys were encouraged to join the men of the band and practice commenced in the Top School in Fore Street. The younger members had the same uniform as the men but the trousers were cut to make shorts that every boy wore until he left school. Mr Grigg had been a member of St Dennis band in his youth and was a great believer in bringing on younger members who were to be the band of the future.

Michael Webber recalls how he first joined the youth band and then the proper band. He tells how they entered the Exeter band contest and spent many hours rehearsing the music to 'Village Feast'. When the great day dawned they set off for Exeter in two buses hired for the occasion. Near Okehampton one of the buses caught fire and the bandsmen had to evacuate the vehicle whilst the driver dealt with an electrical fault. It was fortunate that the supporters' coach was following behind and they were able to flag it down, getting the supporters to change buses, and the band continued on to the contest where they took to the stage playing well until the final section of the test piece. Then restraint was abandoned and the bandmaster lost control, costing them first prize. When they were awarded second prize he refused to collect the cup which resembled an eggcup, saying he had won a bigger prizes for playing solo.

After the usual celebratory drinks the band returned home. Arriving at Bottreaux Cross in the early hours of the morning the men decided to announce their victory to the village. They unpacked their instruments and selected the march and off they went down Fore Street, playing with enough verve and volume to wake the dead.

Mr Grigg continued to conduct the band until 1953 when he retired. He was succeeded by Charles Berryman who was also conductor of Boscastle Male Voice Choir, many of whose members also played in the band. In 1947 the band members included: Les Hewitt, Albert Philp, Gordon Wickett, Gill Biddick, Bill Perry, Stan Sandercock, Mike Webber, Dennis Hancock, Jim Cory, Charlie Jose, Gus Moyles, Sim Grigg, Stuart Biddick, Brian Honey, John Hancock, Charlie Berryman, Fernley Honey, Les Beard, Frank Pridham, George Pascall, Jack Beard, Sam Heard, Les Martin, Bob Biddick and Arthur Biddick.

Ten years later in 1957 band members included: Jack Beard, Walter Gard, Reg Berry, John Dymond, Michael Ferrett, Charlie Jose, George Pascall, Les Beard, Ken Dymond, Michael Webber, Gordon Wickett, Mervyn Beard, Brian Wickett, David Ferrett, John Hancock, Richard Stedman, Frank Pridham, Dr Hillier, Percy Nicholls, Arthur Biddick, Charles Berryman, Bernard Rush (secretary of the band committee), Arthur Nicholls, Tommy Pascall, Rodney Sandercock, Eric Snowdon, John Kinsman, Malcolm McDonald, Richard Ferrett, Alan Fry, Derek Stedman, Graham Honey and Peter Kinsman.

Boscastle Mixed Choir, 1978. Left to right, back row: *Bill Bradley, Dick Pethick, Stuart Biddick, Harry Gates, David Knight, Sam Broad, Michael Webber, Cyril Biddick, Jack Beard, Dennis Wade, Wilfred Binns, Bill Boundy;* front row: *Sally Biddick, Gwen Knight, Joan Dyke, Chris Heard, Maria Nicholls, Doreen Hancock, Nan Gates, Val Callaway, Mrs Carr, Irene Wade, Rosemary Orme, Dorothy Biddick, Sue Cape, Jean Biddick;* seated: *Arthur Biddick, ?.*

They played a total of 25 brass and two percussion instruments.

Many boys were recruited and formed a boys' band with their own uniform. When they reached an acceptable playing level they were introduced into the parent band. At least two of these youngsters found places in service bands when they took up their National Service. The band was playing to a good standard supporting local dances and the weekly summer Flora Dances. The Flora Dances were particularly successful and during the dancing it was found necessary to place some of the dancers ahead of the band, and the crowd would stretch as far as the eye could see.

The Flora Dance assembled at the top of the village at the crossroads of Mount Pleasant and High Street. Advertising posters invited locals and visitors alike to 'forget their corns and join in'. The band would strike up on the hour and proceed at the head of the dancers down through High Street, Fore Street, Dunn Street and Old Road, finally ending up in Cobweb Field. The dancers would dress especially for the occasion with the children wearing flowers in their hair. People would gather from miles around to join a foursome and hop, skip and twirl down the hill, a deceptively simple-looking dance which could get many a visitor in a muddle. Those not taking part would line the streets or stand in their doorways enjoying the sights and sounds of one of the most popular village occasions.

August Bank Holiday was Band Fête Day when the village gathered in Valency Fields. The band would give a concert and refreshments were served. The school put on a display of maypole dancing and

The Flora Dance at Dunn Street, 1949.

The Flora Dance gets under way in High Street, 1949.

various stalls were put up including hoop-la, Aunt Sally skittle alley, lucky dip and a coconut shy. Men competed at tossing a sheaf (later a bale) of hay over a high bar with pitchforks and a live pig was given as a prize.

On 3 June 1958 disaster struck the village. After a day of torrential rain the River Valency had become a raging torrent. The whole valley floor became full of fast-moving, brown, swirling water which flooded many of the riverside properties. People were trapped in shop doorways and had to be rescued. The lower village was cut in two as the water swept over the bridge, taking part of the parapet with it. It was only seven years since the area had been flooded previously. At that time people described how trees in the valley that were 20 feet high had been uprooted and carried away to pile up against the bridge, causing the water to swirl around either side of it.

This time the consequences were far more tragic. The Valency rose 15 feet above its normal level. Water rushed into Norman Webber's garage, and the gift shop next door was flooded. One elderly lady who had taken refuge in an empty shop by smashing the glass of a locked door was in state of collapse when rescue arrived. Burnard's Store and its cellar were filled with water and Beadon's guest-house and café at Riverside had the river running right through the premises, carrying out tables, chairs and even the washing machine.

Miss Rachel Beadon was trapped in the telephone kiosk next to the bridge as she tried to raise the alarm. The rising water trapped her inside and the water pressure firmly jammed the door closed, sealing her in. The torrent was so fierce that the box with Miss Beadon inside was in danger of being swept away. In an effort to save her a local fisherman with the help of two of his friends took a rope across the bridge, by walking barefoot along the top of what was left of the parapet, against the pressure of the torrent, and tied the telephone kiosk to an adjacent telegraph pole to stop it being swept away before returning to safety across the bridge parapet. Miss Beadon was eventually released in a state of shock when the flood waters subsided. Further down towards the harbour the Harbour Light, or as it was then the Pixie Shop, had its refrigerator swept from its fittings. Harbour Light still has a mark on it, showing where the flood water reached.

After the first tremendous rush of water villagers hurried out to try to help their neighbours and to salvage what they could, including the items that had been swept out of Riverside, before they could be carried out to sea. Bandmaster Charlie Berryman was one of this group. Unfortunately, whilst trying to free a branch trapped in the arch of the bridge, he was swept off his feet and carried downriver towards the harbour. Along the way people tried to grab him but could not get a firm hold on him and he was swept under the lower bridge. He was alive all the way down the river but was sucked under the water at the harbour. His 20-year-old son Tracy, along with George Pridham and Roy Pickard, put out in a boat in an attempt to effect a rescue, but they could not find him despite the search continuing until dark. His body was not recovered until midnight when, at low tide, it was found lying between two boats. A relief fund was set up afterwards. The money raised was distributed to those who had lost furniture and goods in the flood.

The death of their bandmaster was felt keenly by the band. Arthur Biddick took over at short notice and kept the band together during this critical time. When they felt able to again enter contests they asked Mr L. Prout to take over their training, and during his leadership they achieved considerable success, winning first prize in 1963 at the Exeter contest.

By the 1970s there were demands being made on the village which conflicted with the type of life that the villagers had led during the band's heyday. Houses were being bought as second homes and holiday businesses. Youngsters unable to find housing in the village were moving away. The field long used for the village fêtes and concerts was turned into a car park to accommodate the tourist trade and the amount of cars parking in High Street, Fore Street, Dunn Street and Old Hill during the summer months made it impossible for the Flora Dance to proceed safely through the village. With youngsters leaving the village and older players retiring, the band numbers dwindled. For a time

Cleaning up at Lower Bridge following the 1950 floods.

Lower Bridge flooded in 1963.

Boscastle Football Team, 1910/11. Left to right, back row: ?, *Arthur Gard, ?, Richard Kernick, ?;* middle row: *Jack Beazley, ?, Bill Hockin;* front row: *John Brown, Tom Sharrock, ?, Phil Gard, Alan Ferrett* (behind), *?.*

Boscastle and St Gennys bands exchanged players to enable them to fulfill their engagements, but in the end the struggle became too much and at a public meeting in 1973 it was decided to disband after over a century of playing and entertaining. The bank balance of over £6,000 was divided between Boscastle Football Club and Boscastle Snooker Club.

The band had been part of a musical heritage which took various forms. In the early 1900s some members of Boscastle Band were also members of

Bowering's Orchestra. This was a string orchestra which played regularly at the town hall, now Harbour Café. Members of the band included Cyril Biddick who later went on to form his own band. There were a pair of mandolin players, one of whom was Mabel Sharrock. Richard Webber played the trombone, which he was reputed to have learnt in four weeks. He was said to be the man who introduced the waltz to Boscastle and gave instruction to many at the weekly dances. He was known to some as 'Old Waltzy'. The band played popular dance music, waltzes, quicksteps, Paul Jones and the like, but it also gave concert performances and supported other local entertainments. A trio of players who played at concerts and in the public houses on cello, fiddle and concertina were Cyril Biddick, William Hockin and George Bone. They also played in the town hall for dances. George Bone played an English duet concertina which he lost when his ship HMS *Triumph* was torpedoed and sunk in the Dardanelles in the First World War. His shipmates had raised the money to buy him a replacement. George lived in High Street and in 1923 married Elizabeth Jane Garland of Tubbs Ground.

Stephen Burley dancing the Boscastle Breakdown, 1999.

The Boscastle Breakdown. Music as played by Beatrice Beer and collected by Jon Mills in 1974. She played it in the key of F.

Biddick, Hockin and Bone were amongst those that came together at the Wellington Hotel on 9 October 1943 at the request of the BBC. Richard Dimbleby was the recording engineer under the direction of Reginald Redman. Little relevant information is to be found in the BBC's archives but the resulting LP included William Hockin (leader and fiddle), Percy Hoskins (fiddle), George Bone (English concertina), Cyril Biddick (cello), and Arthur and Bob Biddick (piano accordians). Bill Hockin's wife May said that her husband, George Bone and Cyril Biddick were the main musicians and were in great demand for social events locally.

Bill Hockin played the lead fiddle in the 'Boscastle Breakdown', the music played to accompany the traditional step dancing which was danced by people like Paddy Donelly, Mrs Amos Philp and later Charlie Jose. The four-hand reel is one of the step dances that comprise the Boscastle Breakdown. As its name implies it is a dance for four dancers. Four-hand and three-hand reels are found throughout Cornwall. The dancers are distributed in a line (not a circle, as you might expect) and dance in a sort of figure of eight around one another. Three- and four-hand reels were popular in houses and pubs where there was not a lot of space to dance, because they don't require much room.

The dances that were 'broken' together included a step dance for couples facing one another, a waltz and a step dance for soloists to show off their skill. Step dances of the Boscastle Breakdown type were originally clog dances. Fishermen in Cornwall wore clogs, usually with a buckle, as recently as the first half of the twentieth century. Clogs were replaced by leather shoes with metal scoots. In Cornwall step dances are frequently referred to as scoot dances. By the 1960s, the Boscastle Breakdown was danced with soft-soled shoes.

The tunes of the Boscastle Breakdown are in 4/4 time and are very similar to the hornpipes collected from gypsy harpists in South Wales. It seems plausible that there was an interchange of folk music and dance culture via the coal trade with Wales through Boscastle harbour.

Beside the roadway, just before Minster Church, is a derelict cottage known as Shepherds Cottage which was used in the 1940s by some of the village's young men like Ron Hancock, Cyril Biddick and Charlie Jose. They would gather wood from nearby to get a roaring fire going and then play and dance the night away.

According to some, the local term 'breakdown' is said to come from the tradition where the musicians had to carry on playing until the dancers broke down. Although the *Concise Oxford Dictionary* defines 'breakdown' as a negro dance, perhaps indicating that the Boscastle Breakdown had its origins further afield and had been brought to Boscastle through the shipping industry, it is more likely the breakdown was exported to America from Britain, where it has been part of British folk tradition. It was not just a single tune but a series of hornpipes and one waltz, the barn-door waltz, played one after the other or broken together, as can be seen in the music collected by Jon Mills. In the early 1900s there were still enough folk-dancers in the village to form a team which joined with other teams like those from Davidstow, Tintagel and Delabole to put on public displays. In the 1920s the breakdown was being played on the bones by W. Perry, in the '60s by Beatrice Beer on the piano and in the '80s by Arthur Biddick, amongst others.

Another very local piece of music, well known across the British Isles, was the 'Boscastle Broomstick Dance'. It was played to accompany a dancer who danced skilfully around and over a broomstick. Broom dances are to be found throughout the South West peninsula. These were performed by a solo dancer with either a broom or just a broom handle. However, what distinguishes the Boscastle Broomstick Dance is that it is a dance for two dancers, one at either end of the broomstick. One such performer was Mrs Amos Philp. It was still being performed in the Cobweb Inn in the 1960s.

'Here's to the Devil'. Music collected in the 1960s by Jon Mills.

William Bottrell, in his *Traditions and Hearthside Stories* (1870, p.186), wrote:

> *... many a merry jig and three-handed reel was kept agoing by the tune being sung to such old catches as*
>
> *Here's to the devil*
> *With his wooden spade and shovel*
> *Digging tin by the bushel*
> *With his tail cocked up.*

'Here's to the Devil' was being sung in Boscastle as late as the 1960s and '70s with the words:

> *Here's to the devil*
> *With his wooden spade and shovel*
> *Digging taties by the bushel*
> *With his tail cocked up.*

Bill Hockin's nephew Claude Knight was born in Boscastle in 1909. Like many young men of his day he was musical and sang in the choir at Forrabury Church. He was one of 'Lowe's Angels', trained and conducted by Revd Bernard S. Lowe. Other 'angels' included Horace Pridham, Cyril Russell, Ronald Symons, William Hilton and Percy Nicholls. During his formative years many black musicians visited this country from the United States. Their music had a great effect here and was reflected in the singing of negro spiritual songs such as 'Coal Black Mammy', and in the setting up of jazz bands. Claude Knight, together with Percy Nicholls, Charlie Hiscock and Beatrice Folley, formed the 'Bottreaux Syncopators'. They had a uniform of black trousers with a blue stripe and short blue jackets and bow ties. Percy Nicholls was organist at Trevalga Church for 45 years and president of Boscastle Band. Claude Knight played washboard and drums, Charlie Hiscock was a baker and played saxaphone, and Beatrice Folley played the piano. Claude went on to play in the Biddick Band, which was formed by Cyril Biddick and included his sons Stuart, Arthur and Bob as well Claude. Cyril Biddick came to Boscastle in 1903 when his father Hart Biddick, who had been a chorister at Egloshayle Church, bought East Beeny Farm. Cyril played the cello, Arthur (who later became a bandsman with the DCLI) played the accordian, Bob was a skillful squeeze-box player and Stuart played the piano. Claude Knight played the drums. When Claude left to play with the Roy Weary dance band his place was taken by Alfie Chaplin, a shoemaker from Tintagel who, as was well as playing the drums, was a singer with a voice reputed to be like that of Bing Crosby. Another occasional player with the Biddicks was Percy Hoskin. Both he and his wife

Lillie were accomplished musicians and, amongst other things, played the organ. They were both the children of farming families. Percy's father Elijah farmed at Pendavey and Lillie's father Henry Brown at Reddivallen.

In November 1922 the Boscastle Carnival included a float entitled 'Jazz Band' which included Claude Knight, Percy Nicholls, Bill Hilton, Mark Olde, Bernard Olde, Alan Ferrett, Willie Bone, Cyril Russell and George Puddyfoot, and a concert in the town hall on Remembrance Day included the 'Boscastle White Minstrels' of T. Hockin, G. Bone, R. Hockin, W. Honey, B. Beasley and W. Perry, giving a rendering of 'Juh Jah Jazz' and 'Down the Swanee River Flows'.

After the Second World War Claude Knight went on to play with the Red Stars Dance Band, but in the 1950s the Biddicks were looking for a drummer and he returned to play with them until his death in 1965. His son Rodney inherited some musical talent from his father and mother who played the piano in her younger days. In his late teens and early twenties he helped form and played in a pop band – this time a band of the 1960s called the 'Echoes'. Rodney played lead guitar with Keith Aldridge from Trethevy on rhythm guitar. Derek Hicks who lived in the Lynhay, Fore Street was bass guitarist, and Simon Mills of Corentin played drums, initially on a set borrowed from Claude Knight before the group could afford to buy their own. When Keith Aldridge joined the RAF in 1965 and the rest of the members also found jobs the group disbanded, but during its lifetime it played in village halls all over Cornwall. During one notable occasion, at an end-of-term dance at Sir James Smith's School in Camelford, there was a near riot when the band was taken offstage because the dancing had become so enthusiastic that the organisers were afraid the wooden floor would become damaged by the girls' stiletto heels, so fashionable at that time.

Boscastle's singing tradition is no less diverse than that of its bands. In addition to the church and chapel choirs there was a male voice choir and many individual performers like Ben Beazley, a man of Irish descent who lived at Penally Terrace and was at one time Boscastle's town crier. He was father of carpenter Jack and Vic, who married Doll Ferrett. Both Jack and Vic lived at Fair Park, Butts Lane. Ben was known for his renditions of Irish folk-songs. On one occasion he gave an impromptu public broadcast when Claude Knight rigged up a loudspeaker in the bushes outside Hillrise, Mount Pleasant and had Bill Beazley inside with a microphone singing his songs. However, public performances were normally given in the town hall, parish hall or in the pubs, all of which had a thriving music scene carrying on right into the twentieth century.

The early and mid-twentieth century saw performers like Charlie Jose recounting the tale of the 'Dogs Meeting' and singing 'Mortal Unlucky Old Chap' in the Napoleon and Cobweb Inns.

Mortal Unlucky Old Chap

As sung by Charlie Jose in the Napoleon Inn, Boscastle, in 1974:

CHORUS:
I'm a mortal, unlucky, old, chap.
Did ee ever hear tell such a case?
From morning 'till night,
Nought ever goes right.
'Tis enough to drive any man maze.

1. I went out t'other day with me gun,
And I traipsed through the mire and the bog.
I blazed away at the rabbits all day,
And didn't shoot nort but me dog.

2. Well, I got me a nice country farm,
But it turned to be a sour bunch of grapes.
The hens wouldn't lay,
So I gived 'em away,
And the chickens all got the gapes.

3. Well, I went down to Boscastle Fair,
And I bought me a fine set of lambs.
But when I got home and sorted 'em out,
I found that the buccas were rams.

Charlie Jose used a wide variety of music, some of which he got from the books beautifully handwritten in copperplate from Cyril Biddick. The books later went to Evan Trick who also used them for his performances. Cyril Biddick's son Stuart set up the scene in the Cobweb in the late 1950s, where he was paid £1 per night to play the piano for the pub sing-alongs.

The Wellington Hotel had its own sing-alongs to the piano accompaniment of Joan Sandercock. Joan was born at Trebursye near Launceston in 1911. She was a talented musician and played the organ at Launceston Chapel before moving to Boscastle to work at the Wellington Hotel, where she met Fred Sandercock whom she married in 1937.

All these musical and performing skills were put to use at carnival time. Boscastle Carnival was a village affair which took place annually in November. It was worked on throughout the year under the auspices of the Carnival Committee. The procession of walkers, bicycles, horses and floats assembled at Mount Pleasant. After the Bible Christian chapel on the corner of Mount Pleasant and High Street closed the ground floor was used to assemble the children. Before the use of electricity on the floats the procession was torchlit. The Youth Club provided the torches which were made from

The 1938 children's entries to the Boscastle Carnival. Left to right: *Phyllis Prout, John Scott, Jean Jose, Hazel Biscombe, Doreen ?, Norman Pickard.*

Children at the Boscastle Carnival in 1936. Left to right, back row: *Vera Pickard and Vi Hicks, Phyllis Masson (Oxo), Monica Pickard (Chorus Girls); Nancy Hockin and Iris Hockin (Hundred Years Between); Iris Philp (Minstrel);* front row: *Margaret Scott (Oranges and Lemons); Jean Scott (Fairy); Hazel Biscombe (Autumn); Phyllis Prout.*

Boscastle Carnival, 1949. Pictured are: *John Rogers, ?, Mary Gard, Julie Olde.*

Boscastle Carnival, 1950s. Dresden Figures.

Boscastle Carnival, 1950s. The Laundry.

Boscastle Carnival, 1950s. Boscastle Minstrels.

Boscastle Carnival, 1950s. Our Seaside Sniffle Group.

Boscastle's last carnival queen, Molly Robbins. Her attendants were: *Wendy Brewer, Odette Fearnley, Gale Rush, Jean Nicholls.*

broken broom handles fixed into syrup tins which had been collected throughout the year. A paraffin-soaked cloth would be put inside the tin and lit to form the torch. These were later to be replaced by Tilley lanterns.

The highlight of the carnival was the crowning of the carnival queen. The Mission Room would be crowded for the ceremony and the carnival queen would be accompanied by her attendants. Following the crowning a variety of entertainment would be given by the local talent – for example, in 1951 Mr R. Pethick sang, accompanied by Mrs Nicholls and Bob Biddick. Violin solos were given by Valerie Stedman, Janet Sleeman, Sheila Hancock, Rosemary Parnell and Yvonne Elford. A piano solo was also given by Kenneth Higgins, who later played a duet with Mary Higgins. The carnival queen that year was Hazel Biscombe and her attendants were Doreen Perry, Jean Hancock, Iris Hancock and Anne Knight.

Boscastle queens have included Peggy Cowling (1936), Mary Cowling (1942), Phyllis Gard (1949), Hazel Biscombe (1951), Doreen Perry (1952), and Molly Robbins was the last in 1955.

Many will remember Eric Fearnley who was carnival secretary for six years in the 1950s and was responsible for the firework display which ended the night.

In January 1980 the late Phyllis Morey of St Clether put her memories of Boscastle Carnival into verse and summed up the atmosphere so well:

Boscastle Carnival

Going down to Boscastle on a cold November night,
No moon is shining, so a brisk walk seems just right;
An air of anticipation is held by the small family group,
As they wend their way along the road, talking and laughing they troop;
Eager expectancy on whom or what they might see,
They are on their way to the carnival, in the days that used to be.

It must be close on thirty years, since those peaceful days,
Yet looking back it seems, they could have been yesterdays;
The children were young, content, and full of life so near the sea,
Time was no object then, and we were so happy and free.
We soon descended the Penally hill; one-in-six its true,

With ancient cottages, and quaint old harbour coming into view;
Past the shops and over the bridge, we took our stand, awaiting with glee,
The arrival of the Carnival Queens, the tableaux, horse and foot entry.

They made their way from the 'Napoleon' at the very top of the town,
And no-one hardly seemed to care, or to wear a frown;
They came down the New Road, led by a horse and rider so smart,

Boscastle Cave of Harmony, 2003. Master of ceremonies, David Whitaker.

Boscastle Cave of Harmony, 2003. 'The Vicar and I will be There', performed by Roger Nicholls and Roger Toy.

Boscastle Cave of Harmony, 2003. 'O Sarah! O Enery', with Roger Nicholls and Tilly James.

Souvenir Programme, 2003. The Boscastle Cave of Harmony's production of The Twinklin' Twenties.

Followed by the local Queen and her retinue, dressed up for the part.

The waiting crowd watched patiently as each entry came into the 'Wellington' square,
To be judged from an upper window, the winners of prizes to share;
A light was put to the bonfire there, and flames shot up so high,
And the multi-coloured fireworks were a sight, shooting into the sky.

After the show was over, and the prizes won,
We met our friends along the harbour, by the sideshows for some fun;
Always taking home a dish, a vase, or something as a souvenir,
A simple evening out, coffee at the Millhouse, for some a pint of beer.

Such pleasant memories are so often tinged with some regret,
For old customs and traditions die hard, and it's not easy to forget;
Many of the older folk have long since moved; or they have passed on,
Strange new faces take their place, and the old days have gone.

No more does the horse and his rider escort the Queen to town,
No more do we walk from Beeny to Boscastle, going down;
Breathing in the salty breath of the deep Atlantic ocean,
No more! No more! Do we hear, the excited crowds' commotion.

Nor do we hear the sounds of music, that on that special night of the year,
Did steal away from those Silver Bands, playing to us so loud so clear;
Boscastle, Launceston, St Gennys and St Breward, were all represented there,
But now it is just a memory, of phantom sights and sounds on the air.

Although there are not so many outlets for the village talents in the early-twenty-first century, there is one very entertaining and much over-subscribed event which has everyone jostling for tickets. This is the annual Boscastle 'Cave of Harmony' which, at the original suggestion of local sculptor Carole Vincent, performs shows as they might have taken place during the period they depict. The first performance in 1997 depicted Queen Victoria's diamond jubilee in 1897 and in subsequent years was followed in 1998 by an Edwardian production set at the time of Edward VII's coronation in 1902, then in 1999 by a Dickensian depiction set in the year of Dickens' death in 1870. A special millenium edition followed in 2000 which was less a music hall and more a review of the history of Boscastle through the ages. The years 2001 to 2003 covered the First World War, a cockney music hall and the 'Twinkling Twenties'.

The productions are designed and directed by Michael Turner who, before taking on this task, had previous music hall experience and spent time with a travelling opera company raising money for Cancer Research. Michael says that originally the aim was to give as good a show as could be put on, striving to present as professional a performance as possible. Some members of the cast are professionals like former 'Black and White Minstrel', John Bolitho, teacher of singing Helen Pincus, and retired music

The Boys' Brigade. Left to right, back row: *Harold Hassler, Peter Olde, Ken Edwards;* middle row: *Len Olde, Percy Nicholls, Dr Hillier, Arthur Olde;* front row: *Raymond Nicholls, Ted Barchard, Arthur Biddick, ?.*

The Boys' Brigade. Left to right, back row: *Eric Masson, Peter Olde, Donald Stephens, Leonard Olde, Geoffrey Warren, Eric Nicholls, Brian Honey;* middle row: *Harold Hoskin, Percy Nicholls, Dr Hillier, Arthur Olde, Colin Nicholls;* front row: *George Paskall, Leonard Pearn, Ken Edwards.*

Above left: *Tintagel and Boscastle Guides, 1958.* Amongst those pictured with Miss Lobb are: *Madeline Fry, Anne Knight, Iris Hancock, Belinda Kinsman, Barbara Sandercock, Gillian Seldon, Jacqueline McDonald, Pam Mugford, Robina Symons, Mary Gard, Norma Piper, Susan Berry, Bridget Olde, Anne Ferrett.*

Above right: *Boscastle Cubs, 1938.* Left to right, back row: *G. Warren, Miss Whitehead, G. Pridham;* front row: *B. Honey, M. Ward, H. Hassler.*

teacher Martin Nash, who is musical director and pianist and a great supporter of the music hall.

According to Michael Turner, one of the great discoveries of these productions was local coal merchant Roger Nicholls. He is a singer of near-professional standard with a great stage presence for both comedy and tragedy. Roger's family has a strong musical tradition – his mother Maria has played the organ at Forrabury, Minster and Trevalga churches for the last 30 years; his grandfather Percy was the organist at Trevalga Church for 45 years; and his father Nicky has sung in a male voice choir since he was 15 – a total of 30 years with Tintagel Male Voice Choir and lately with the County of Cornwall Male Choir. Another tremendous find has been lighting engineer Ross Yates, and more recently a very considerable acting talent has been discovered in Roger Toy from Treknow. These are only a few of those taking part in a production which involves about 30 people who start rehearsals in September, a full five months before production in February. They rehearse twice a week. Most amateur productions start to rehearse about six weeks before production but a great deal of satisfaction is gained from seeing how the cast and crew respond to the challenge. The chairman and master of ceremonies, and one of the founding members, is David Whitaker.

Youngsters in the village were encouraged to join in with the adults' entertainment, but they also had the Boys' Brigade, the Scouts, Guides and Brownies and the Youth Groups. The Boys' Brigade of the early-twentieth century attended a Bible-study group in the Methodist chapel on Sunday afternoons and held their brigade meetings at

Apollo Cinema poster from the 1920s.

The Flower Dance, Boscastle Girls' Club, 1950. Pictured are: *Elizabeth Bowering, Joyce Hancock, ?, Jean Nicholls, Mary Gard, Wendy Brewer.*

Festival of Youth Entertainment, 3 May 1951. Left to right, standing: *Margaret Scott, Jean Scott, Hazel Biscombe, Pamela Gard;* centre: *Hester Kinsman, Jennifer Ferrett, Trixie Webber;* front: *Jean Nicholls, Elizabeth Bowering, Rosemary Parnall.*

Boscastle Girls' Club, 1950. Pictured are: *Jean Scott, Margaret Scott, Hazel Biscombe, Pamela Gard.*

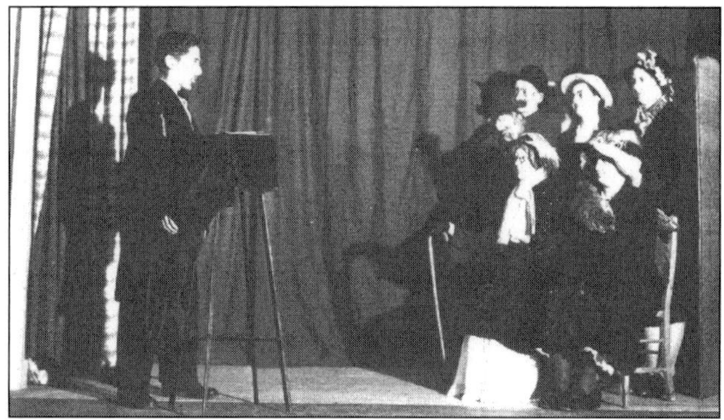

Festival of Youth Entertainment, 3 May 1951. Pictured are, left to right, standing: *Brian Beer, Gordon Wickett, Jean Scott, Margaret Scott;* seated: *Hazel Biscombe, Phyllis Gard.*

Tolcarne House, the home of Dr Hillier, who was their captain. Once a year they gave a gymnastics exhibition in the town hall and each summer they went camping at Polzeath and Porthpean with the likes of Eric Nicholls, Clifton Sandercock and Fearnley and Sid Honey. The Boscastle Girls' Club met under the teaching of Miss Ihse who taught them as a dance group. They put on a concert once a year.

Even at primary school, children have been encouraged to sing. Early in the twentieth century the headmaster, Mr J.S. Elford, was a keen musician. He encouraged the children to sing in the village choir and various musical events he organised. He was an accomplished singer and pianist.

The youngsters of the early-twenty-first century have less provided for them but the playgroup is a long-established registered charity. It was started in 1972 by Marion Ferrett, Joan Kinsman and Mary Nicholls, with Carole Vincent as chairperson. They were later joined by Wanda Larratt and Lyn Partrick and originally met on Tuesdays and Thursdays. Over the years the majority of Boscastle's children have passed through its doors.

Chapter Seven

Butcher, Baker and Blacksmith

Top Town

A wander around the harbour, Quaytown and Bridge is what many visitors to Boscastle think is all there is to see. But it is only the tip of the iceberg. The main village or 'Town', to give it its proper title, is situated in a sheltered valley spreading on to the hills on either side. Traditionally, it contained almost all the houses and shops, although since the rise of the tourist industry most shops have either closed or migrated to Quaytown and Bridge and have diversified into selling gifts and souvenirs. Writing in 1897 John Lloyd Warden Page described the village as follows:

> *The valley of Boscastle is so deep and shadowy that it is almost a ravine. Partly along this valley, and partly up the slope to another valley branching from it, straggles the village. The lower part is uninteresting, not to say dingy, but the upper part is picturesque, the ancient cottages rising one above the other, half hidden in garden and orchard... it has few equals in Cornwall.*

With all its souvenir shops, bright signs and streets crowded with holidaymakers you can hardly describe Bridge and Quaytown as dingy nowadays, but Boscastle Town still retains a calmness and dignity in its cottages, gardens and small green spaces that can be appreciated by those who want to get away from the hustle and bustle for a while.

Town has developed over the centuries since the Botreaux family built their Norman castle at the top of Dunn Street. It has extended northwards down the hill towards Jordan Vale and up Forrabury Hill. It also stretches southwards, up the hill, through Fore Street, Bottreaux Cross, High Street, Mount Pleasant and Paradise. The area at the top of the village is known for obvious reasons as Top Town.

The High Street area of Top Town, as its name suggests, was Boscastle's principle street with houses and shops along both sides and joining straight into Fore Street, until the New Road cut through the two in the 1880s. This construction involved building a complete new section of road from just above Trecarne Gate around a tight right-hand bend into Parade (New Bridge), cutting across the road from Mount Pleasant to Treforda Water and on to create Bottreaux Cross at the junction of High Street and Fore Street. The New Road then carried on past what is Bottreaux Garage in 2004, to Doctors Corner, and then turned down towards the harbour through the Avenue to Keals Hill. On the side of Keals Hill were built at this time, to designs by architect F. Mullett-Ellis, a series of villas, now called Penrowan, Meachard, Lynwood, Lewarne, Belmont, Glenfinart and Valley View. Some years later Valley View had a tower added by the lord of the manor, George Bellamy, as a wedding present for his manor agent Ernest Couch. The road gave good access from the new railway station at Melorne (Camelford Station) to the village, and the prestigious new villas provided quality accommodation to attract incomers. A plantation of young trees was developed on either side of the road at Parade and the Avenue was lined with horse-chestnut trees.

In order to cross High Street and Fore Street several buildings had to be demolished, including a mow hay on the site where Lundy View stands at the time of writing. Several buildings once lined the road from Heigh Ho to Butts Lane, running down Fore Street at the point where Peartree Garden has been built. The surgery, car park and Bottreaux Hotel have replaced a group of buildings which included the Elizabethan Manor House, Market House and associated stables and service buildings.

To complete Bottreaux Cross the market site was set up to the north-west of the crossroads. Markets have been held since the Botreaux family were first granted a market in 1204, giving the area town status. Edward II granted the village the privilege of holding its annual fair at Martin Mass. This tradition was continued into the twentieth century by the manor. On 22 November no work was done, rent was paid, bills settled and festivities took place in the form of a dinner. It was at this time of year that the annual carnival was also held.

The market was held at Talkarn on Wednesdays. Norman markets were usually held in town squares. The square was surrounded by buildings and the streets entering the square were narrowed to assist the collection of tolls. The area associated with Boscastle's market has long been held to have been between the Napoleon Inn and what is now St James' in Minster Parish Hall. Until the beginning of the eighteenth century, roads entering the village converged here. The road from the west came through Gunpool, from the east Butts Lane and from the north down High Street into Fore Street and on to the harbour area. At the entrance to Butts Lane is a house still called Fairfield and on the western end of the modern surgery site was situated the Market House until it was demolished in 1870.

Next to Fairfield is Trehayne House which is named after Trehane Farm and was bought in the mid-1950s by Eric Nicholls, following the deaths of sitting tenants Elsie and Archie Rogers. Eric converted the house into two flats which now belong to his daughter Cynthia. In carrying out the conversion it became obvious that the house had been made larger by adding an extra floor. The original roofline is still visible just above the first-floor windows. The size and shape of the original house and that of the large chimney on the lower end indicates the house was once thatched. Many of the beams are carved on the lower edges and were whitewashed. When the flats were being converted the present entrance was made out of an existing window opening. In doing this work it was discovered that it had been a door previously! The work uncovered in the door linings two coins, one English and one German both dated 1747, and two carved fire surrounds of Delabole slate dating from the 1700s. On the lower window-sills are the initials of two of the former tenants, W. Taylor and Mr Gay, with the date 1897. William Taylor was a farmer and in 1915 his daughter Frances married John Gay, a widower who was a miller at the Wellington Hotel mill. Part of the flooring had to be replaced, some of which was the round wood of old ships' timbers with a painted pattern along the edge. The kitchen contained a small window with a curved arch and iron bars instead of glass and a very large open fireplace, into which a black range had been set beside the cloam oven. When the repairs were completed Eric Nicholls put a time capsule into the cloam oven containing such items as the electoral register, local paper, postcards, money and a map of the area. It was then covered over and sealed in. Beside the fireplace was a small vent which was used to smoke meat and fish.

The renovations also revealed a hidden cavity containing a hare or rabbit's foot and part of a pig's jaw, presumably put there many years before as some sort of charm. Beneath the slate slabs in the outhouse was the pink-coloured mixture of ox blood and lime which was used as a sort of concrete. The slate slabs at the front of Trehayne came from the East Delabole Quarry at Buckator.

Another building which formed part of the eastern side of the town or market square was Sharrock's Shop or North Cornwall Stores. The *West Briton* advertised the shop on 18 March 1814 as follows:

> *To be let by tender, for a term of 14 years, from lady day next with immediate possession all that Merchantile House and Premises situate near the Boscastle Inn in the centre of Boscastle, late in the occupation of Mr Miller deceased. Consisting of a kitchen, small parlour, dairy, coal house, with an underground cellar, a large shop, a dining room. Three bedrooms, two large garrets, a garden with a detached office, pigsties and courtlage.*

In the mid-1800s it was run by Solomon Banbury and his wife Mary Ann. The Banburys had moved to

John Pascoe Sharrock, coastguard and storekeeper.

This postcard of 1905 is entitled 'Motherless'. Tom, John and Mabel Sharrock feed the orphaned piglets.

Tom and Mabel Sharrock outside their North Cornwall Store.

Boscastle from Devon in the 1850s. Their children John, Thomas, Sarah and William were all born in Boscastle. By the mid-1800s the Banburys had left and the store was being run by the Sharrocks. It sold all manner of goods – they had boxes of dried fruit displayed in the windows, a favourite spot for their cats to sleep. Inside were fruit and vegetables, medicines, groceries, slippers and boots, ironmongery, paraffin and methylated spirits, a large bacon slicer and many, many other goods.

John Pascoe Sharrock was born at St Mawes. His brother Joseph was the captain of Jabez Brown's smack, the *Bottreaux Castle,* which was wrecked leaving the harbour with its cargo of slate. John was married in the local church of St Just-in-Roseland. He was a coastguard and a member of the Independent Order of Oddfellows of the Loyal Camel and Bottreaux Lodge for 50 years. After his marriage he was posted to Dorset, returning to Port Isaac in 1850. After serving at Bude he was sent to the Crimea and shortly after his return he came to Boscastle. Whilst serving here he received a silver medal for his part in saving the lives of 16 men and a pilot from the *Defence of Liverpool* which had been wrecked beneath the cliffs of Beeny. He was also given a watch which, instead of numerals on its face, carried his name: J.O.H.N.S.H.A.R.R.O.C.K.

He had five sons, at least three of whom were seamen. One of these sons, himself a seaman, had several sons, two of whom were involved with the stagecoach run from the Wellington Hotel to the Falcon in Bude. A Sharrock drove the last coach from Bude to the Wellington. Eventually, the sons moved with their families from Boscastle to Bude, leaving only the younger John Pascoe Sharrock and his two children at the shop in Boscastle. John junr had been a commercial traveller in his early days until taking the shop. He and his wife had three children including Tom and Mabel. John died in 1923 aged 76 and is buried at Minster Church. Tom and Mabel took over the shop known as Sharrock's Stores, running it until its closure in 1969.

Besides Fairfield, Trehayne and Sharrock's Stores, the eastern side of the town square was completed by a row of buildings running southwards from Butts Lane to join those at the lower end of High Street. They are shown in a print of the area produced in the late 1700s and form houses and outbuildings associated with the Elizabethan manor-house which was situated on the site of the present surgery car park in 2004. This manor-house replaced the earlier mansion-house situated in the castle. It was built by John Hender who was lord of the manor between 1611 and 1656, at the time when the *Mayflower* sailed to America with the Pilgrim Fathers and in the time of the Civil War here. It was a large building for the village with wainscotted rooms and a banqueting hall. In the time when the Cottons were lords of the manor it was known as the Great House. In later years it was occasionally occupied by Sir Jonathan

The sheep market in 1968.

The cattle market in 1968.

John Brown bringing sheep to market in 1960.

Farmer John Brown at the sheep market in 1960.

Phillips who died in 1798. It was partly demolished in 1818 and materials from it were sold at auction by Mr George Harman. Some of the building and stables were still standing on the opposite side of the road in the 1870s. Behind them were gardens and what was described as a gigantic pear tree. When the site was excavated in 1984 in connection with the building of Bottreaux Surgery several pieces of granite were found, including mullioned window frames similar to those still visible at Welltown Manor. A semi-circular granite trough was also uncovered.

The north side of the town square consisted of St James' Chapel and its graveyard, the west side was bounded by the Market House and the south side by a row of cottages running east–west along the Napoleon Inn awkway. In the centre was the market square or fairground known as Fair Park. Boscastle Fair Park consisted of two small enclosures where a sheep fair was held until the 1960s. A cattle market also took place at the western end of the site. These fairs could be quite lively, causing trouble for the nearby landlords. In 1821 the *Royal Cornwall Gazette* carried a report that Boscastle Fair was fully supplied, that sheep and lambs were in request and a good deal of business was done at advanced prices. Things did not always go well. In November 1846 the fair had been well supplied with cattle which sold readily and at good prices, but it was reported that there were a lot of 'the light fingered brigade of both sexes' and a young farmer was relieved of £35. In December 1856 Mr Robbins junr, who had travelled to the fair from Trekestle near Launceston, suffered a serious accident. On his way home his cart had been upset, causing him very serious injury.

The fair would bring much business with the need for immediate refreshments and the purchase of goods for both farm and home. These requirements could be met by the businesses in High Street. Looking up High Street from Bottreaux Cross, you would have seen, on the right-hand side, Bottreaux Stores, the Napoleon Inn with the forge and carpenter's shop behind it, the cobbler's shop, Hilldene House with its malthouse, brewery and slaughterhouse, then a butcher's shop, stabling, the Brig Inn and just along from the junction with Paradise Road was a grocery store and another butcher's shop, which later became a greengrocery and fruiterer.

Looking up the left-hand side of High Street there was a chemist's shop, drapery, an hotel which had also been a grocery store, a police house and at the junction with Mount Pleasant was a Bible Christian chapel. Beside Lundy View was Downings carpenter's shop.

Bottreaux Stores and its close neighbour Lundy View were built alongside the New Road at the turn of the nineteenth century. The lord of the manor Henry Pigé-Leschallas gave the land and materials needed to Messrs Burnard and Bullock to build Lundy View and Bottreaux House respectively on a 20-year lease. At the end of 20 years the property was to revert to the manor.

William Francis Gard Burnard was a carpenter. In 1896 he was the owner of a house and garden, workshop and Peartree Garden. He was said to be a perfectionist. If an apprentice in his building business made a mistake he would receive the sharp end of Mr Burnard's tongue and his shoddy work would be destroyed with some drama. William's wife Elizabeth took the Band of Hope meetings on Sunday evenings. Lundy View had its own grounds and two detached gardens across the road as well as a range of outbuildings. By the 1940s it was being run as a guest-house by Mrs Seabrook and Miss Cowling. It had nine bedrooms and four reception rooms, as well as kitchen, bathroom, toilet and offices. Miss Mary Seabrook was a hairdresser.

Arthur Bullock was also a carpenter and a greengrocer and general merchant. He and his wife Elizabeth lived at Bottreaux House and Stores. The house had eight bedrooms, bathroom and toilet, three reception rooms, kitchen, offices, large shop and storeroom. They emigrated to Canada in the early-twentieth century and the premises were taken over by William Olds. His son, William John Olds, was the builder and proprietor of Bottreaux Garage. He built and lived at Merewells at the end of Paradise Road. The house and shop stayed in the hands of the Olds family until the 1930s when the Rankins took over. George and Loveday Rankin and their daughters Jean and Ella ran both the shop and guest-house. Sydney W. Whateley ran a weekly dental surgery from there on Thursdays and it was also used for family celebrations and wedding receptions, and as a post for the district nurse. At the outbreak of the Second World War the Rankins returned to Australia and the Codd family took over.

After the war the shop was run by the four Misses Smith, Reeves, Davenport and Standing. I can remember my mother telling of some great excitement in the shop one morning. Two of the ladies were relating the tale of a tin of clotted cream that had been sent by post to a relative of one of the shop's regular customers. The customer had received a letter by way of a 'thank you' stating that the recipient had rubbed it in well and was noticing a great improvement!

A family from Liverpool, called Swann, took over in the early 1960s and opened the Copper Kettle, a small tearoom, in the old storeroom below the bay-window of the guest-house lounge, thus making maximum use of the building.

On the opposite corner to Bottreaux Stores is a house known as Heigh Ho, where Mr Whateley had

Left: *Bottreaux Hotel and Stores.*

Below: *Bottreaux Stores and High Street in 1963.*

Grace Brown, 1920.

his surgery before moving into Bottreaux House. This house was lived in by the Scobel family and later the Sleemans and the Smellies. Another occupant of Heigh Ho was Hannah Brown who looked after her mother, Grace. Hannah had to keep a close eye on the old lady who was very forgetful and would wander off into other peoples homes if they left their doors open. Hannah was a servant at the rectory (Westerings) and after her mother died she moved to Rosebank Cottage in Paradise, which is still known in 2004 as Hannah Brown's Cottage.

On the hill above Bottreaux Stores is the Napoleon Inn and on the opposite side of the road are three small terraced cottages. The lower of the three, called Rose Cottage, was the home of the Kernick family. Rose Cottage, like The Cottage further up and the Lynhay in Fore Street and several other houses in the older part of the village, has a tiny square hole built into an upstairs wall which looks northwards towards the sea. One was also discovered under the rendering of Corner House which looked westward. Some people have said they were spy holes to look for customs officials or naval press-gangs, but it seems an ordinary window would serve the purpose better. At the Grange in Torquay are identical holes built into the upper floor away from the entrance doorway. This building was a thirteenth-century monks' residence and the holes were there to admit light and could be blocked at night with a straw-filled sack to keep out the draught.

John Kernick was born in 1845 in Trevalga, and was a blacksmith by trade and lived with his wife Mary and children Emily, William, Lydia and Richard. They had living with them in 1890 a journeyman smith called James Rowe. John's son Richard also became a blacksmith. His forge was just across the road from his house, behind the Napoleon Inn. He was a maker and repairer of agricultural implements and stoves. As well as shoeing horses and doing general smithing he also provided and fitted metal rims for cartwheels, particularly those made at the carpenter's shop just above the forge.

Richard and his wife Susan Alice had a son Dudley who was born at Rose Cottage on 28 August 1921. Dudley developed a great love of football and went on to become a professional player with Torquay, Exeter City, Northampton Town, Birmingham City and Shrewsbury Town. He was one of the country's top non-league managers and played for, managed and was secretary and commercial manager of Nuneaton Borough. He went on to become a radio reporter for the BBC and scripted a successful TV series. He was also a FA coach under Jimmy Hill at Coventry City and a long-service commercial manager of Stoke City. John Motson, BBC TV football commentator, said that 'Dudley was part of football's commercial revolution.'

Behind Rose Cottage, running at right angles to it, were almshouses. Sir John Cotton's will of 1701 mentioned six almshouses then existing. The late Mrs Kernick showed their remains to Revd F.J.W. Maddock in the late 1970s and said that her late husband remembered them and the lady who lived in the house when he was a boy, where part of the wall was still standing.

Sir John Cotton's will stated:

Whereas there is £50 lyeth in my hands, the interest of it yearly hath been paid to the poor living in the almshouses; in lieu thereof I do devise and bequeath 5 shillings weekly, forever to be paid to such people as shall dwell in the said almshouses, in the said parish of Minster, viz 1 shilling weekly to three persons inhabiting in three of the said almshouses and 8d weekly to those that shall inhabit in the other three.

Sir John died in 1703 and it was agreed that, instead of the rent-charge he had provided, the money should be paid by his nephew and heir Mr Edward Amy, who entered into a bond to that effect on 13 December 1711. In 1829 the churchwardens and overseers of Forrabury wrote to the commissioners then investigating charities, saying that they had not had the money for ten years.

It was reported in 1836 that the property was in the hands of three persons, one of whom did not make payments, and this left the income at only £1.17s.6d.

Above: *Mrs Susan Kernick outside Rose Cottage.*

Right: *Richard Kernick in the doorway of his smithy.*

Below left: *A billhead from R.J. Kernick in 1919.*

Below right: *Dudley Kernick at Northampton Town Football Club.*

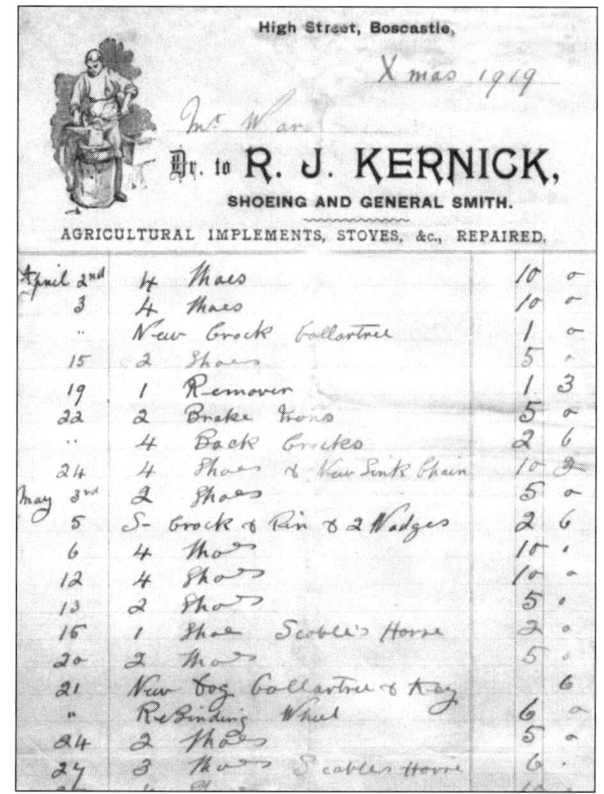

High Street, Boscastle,

Xmas 1919

Mr Ware

Dr. to R. J. KERNICK,

SHOEING AND GENERAL SMITH.

AGRICULTURAL IMPLEMENTS, STOVES, &c., REPAIRED.

April 2nd	4 Shoes	10	0
3	4 Shoes	10	0
"	New Crook Collartree	1	0
15	2 Shoes	5	0
19	1 Remover	1	3
22	2 Brake Irons	5	0
"	4 Back Crooks	2	6
24	4 Shoes & New Sink Chain	10	9
May 3rd	2 Shoes	5	0
5	S- Crook & Pin & 2 Wedges	2	6
6	4 Shoes	10	0
12	4 Shoes	10	0
13	2 Shoes	5	0
16	1 Shoe Scoble's Horse	2	0
20	2 Shoes	5	0
21	New Dog Collartree & Key		6
"	Rebinding Wheel	6	0
24	2 Shoes	5	0
27	3 Shoes Scobles Horse	6	0

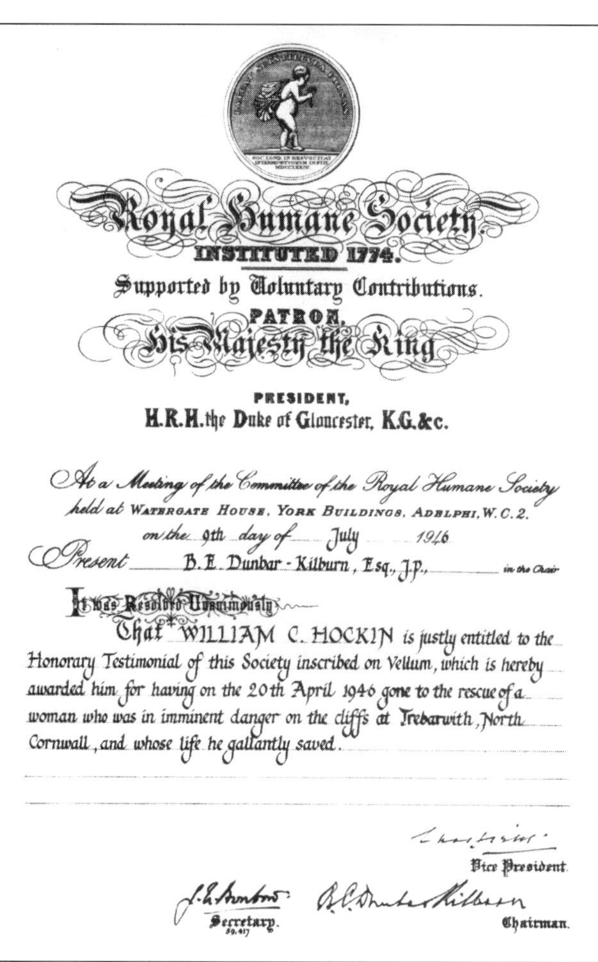

Royal Humane Society
INSTITUTED 1774.
Supported by Voluntary Contributions.
PATRON,
His Majesty the King

PRESIDENT,
H.R.H. the Duke of Gloucester, K.G. &c.

At a Meeting of the Committee of the Royal Humane Society held at Watergate House, York Buildings, Adelphi, W.C.2. on the 9th day of July 1946

Present B. E. Dunbar-Kilburn, Esq., J.P., in the Chair

It was Resolved Unanimously

That WILLIAM C. HOCKIN is justly entitled to the Honorary Testimonial of this Society inscribed on Vellum, which is hereby awarded him for having on the 20th April 1946 gone to the rescue of a woman who was in imminent danger on the cliffs at Trebarwith, North Cornwall, and whose life he gallantly saved.

Vice President.

Secretary.

Chairman.

Royal Humane Society Testimonial on vellum awarded to Bill Hockin in 1946.

Bill Hockin and John Brown, DCLI, Paris, 1917.

Sir Jonathan Phillips of Newport House, Launceston, at one time surgeon in the Navy, gave in his will in 1797, £50 each to the parishes of Minster and Forrabury, for the poor. It was decided to use the interest on the money. In 1836 it was being distributed to the poor of the parishes at Christmas together with the money from Sir John Cotton's charity. Sir Jonathan married Grace, daughter and co-heir of Mr Cotton Amy, and so had part of Sir John Cotton's estate. He was the fifth son of John Phillips of St Teath, who settled in Camelford and took great part in the affairs of that borough. Sir Jonathan was recorder of Camelford in 1775 and MP for a short while in 1784. He died in 1798 and was buried at Minster. In 1863 the trust money was reported lost, except for £2.10s.0d. from the Phillips Charity for Minster, which was being distributed to the poor.

Next door to Rose Cottage are two cottages which were once a single property. Throughout the 1800s it was a chemist's and still has the larger shop window facing on to the street. In the mid-1800s it was run by Francis Hurdon and his wife Grace. Later it became a dressmaker's where Miss Grigg, daughter of the landlord of the Napoleon Inn, carried out her work. This later became divided into the two homes of the Hockin and Honey families, two of the longest resident families in Boscastle. There are a Thomas and John Hocken on the Cornwall Muster Roll for Minster of 1569, together with names that are easy to recognise as still living in the area in 2004, such as Webbe, Symond, Scott, Josling, Pethecke, Yolton, Mugford, Steven and Hamly. A William Hockyn was being taxed for one hearth in 1662 along with Cann, Dangar, Hoskings, Davy, Nicholls, Wickett, Tubb, Blake, Brown, Guard, Jewell and Jolly. There is little doubt they resided in the area long before that. The name Hocken or Hocking originated in Cornwall and is possibly Celtic. It appears frequently in records, in 1523, for example, as Huchyn. The modern noun 'hawker' comes from the German word 'hocken', meaning to carry on one's back.

Henry Hockin was the son of Richard Hockin. He was born in 1851 in Launceston. He married Elizabeth Ann Worden from Truscott on 10 September 1870 and was a merchant wagoner. They had ten children: Richard (1871), Edward (1872), Laura (1875), Thomas (1878), Frank (1881), Florence Lilian (1883), William Claud (1884), Arthur (1887), Daniel (1890) and Annie May (1895).

William 'Bill' Hockin, with his wife and daughter Iris, moved from Rosebank Cottage in Paradise to live in High Street in the 1930s. Edward, known as Ned, married Bessie Philp and lived in Corner House at the top of High Street, and after Florence Lilian married Walter Knight in 1909 they also lived in High Street, as did Annie May, when she married William Honey.

Bill Hockin was born in 1884. He became the village postman and bandmaster and was a beekeeper and accomplished musician. He married

The Hockin family in 1899. Left to right, back row: *William, Richard, Lilian, Daniel, Edward;* front row: *Thomas, Henry, Annie May, Elizabeth.*

Above left: *Postman Bill Hockin and his wife May in the doorway at 3 High Street.*

Above right: *Iris Hockin and her dog on the step of 3 High Street.*

Right: *Cyril Biddick and Bill Hockin.*

Minnie May Phillips Honey on 25 November 1922. They had one daughter called Iris. He and his best mate 'Ginger' Brown joined the Duke of Cornwall's Light Infantry on 3 January 1916 and both served with the expeditionary force in France. He was discharged on 12 March 1918 having been wounded in action. He was described by Colonel Scholes as 'honest, sober, steady and reliable'. He was also a brave man – on 9 June 1946 he was awarded the honorary Testamonial of the Royal Humane Society for saving the life of a woman who was in imminent danger on the cliffs at Trebarwith.

Annie May Hockin was known as Nance. She was born in 1895 and on 21 April 1924 married William Burdon Honey, who was the son of Charles and Emma Teresa Honey. William Honey served with Kitchener's Army in the First World War alongside John Scott, Thomas Symons, Fred Squire, Bertram Davy, S. Martin, Dan Hockin and Sydney Ferrett – all of whom were Boscastle men.

Florence Lilian was always known by her second name, Lilian. She was born in 1883 and went into service at the old rectory (Westerings). She married Walter Knight on 27 March 1909. Walter came to Boscastle from Egloshayle and had three brothers, Samuel, Anthony and Clement, and two sisters, Polly and Jane. Before marrying he had served with the 2nd Battalion the Duke of Cornwall's Light Infantry in South Africa during the Boer War. He saw service in Paardeburg, Dreifontein, Cape Colony and Transvaal, having left Devonport for Cape Town on 29 Novemeber 1899. During the First World War he enlisted again and served with the Grenadier Guards. At the end of the war he signed on with the Territorial Force of the 5th Battalion DCLI. In addition to his Boer War and First World War medals he was awarded a Volunteer Medal, given for long service and good conduct. He was a member of the Boscastle Life-Saving Apparatus team from whom he received a further long-service medal. Walter and Lilian had one son, Claude Arthur.

It might seem that by the 1930s High Street was full of members of the Hockin and Honey families. But this is not so. Next door to the Napoleon Inn was a cottage which has since been incorporated into the Inn. Prior to this it was lived in by Thomas and Annie Mugford. It had two sitting-rooms, three bedrooms and a kitchen. Mrs Mugford ran a boarding-house there. Mr and Mrs Mugford's daughter Vera married Sam Hancock and they continued to live there with their children Charles, Joy and Iris until moving to Orchard House.

On the northern side of Hilldene House was the cobbler's shop where William Force worked. He was the son of Thomas and Elizabeth and like his father he was a cordwainer or shoemaker. He was born in Boscastle in 1850 and married Jane Dennis on 15 March 1877. Jane was the daughter of quarryman Francis Dennis. The couple had nine children:

Walter Knight is sitting on the right. The frying pan has a legend 'Our Best Friend' and to the left above the bunting are inscribed the words (Cornish NIHS DCLI).

Elizabeth, Thomas who died in Toronto in 1913, Edith, Annie, William who married Blanch Batten and became a bakery salesman before his death in 1944 (William's second wife was Jane Stenlake and they had three children, William born in 1910, Jane in 1915 and Bessie in 1916), Alice, Charles, Hilda and John. The cobbler's shop was raised above ground level on stilts and accessed by 12 granite steps, and beneath it in a shed William Honey had an ice-cream business which he ran during the summer months in the 1930s. His son Brian used to help make the ice-cream by turning the handle of the ice-cream maker which was filled with ice that had been brought up from Padstow. The completed ice-cream was sold from a horse-drawn cart. In the winter months the cart was converted to sell fish and chips. It came to an abrupt and dramatic end one carnival night when the chip fryer caught fire, causing the pony to bolt and destroying the cart.

Hilldene House itself, like St Christophers Hotel on the opposite side of the street, is a three-storey Georgian building with classical façades on the foundations of much earlier and smaller cottages. Both houses had flat-fronted shop windows on the left-hand side of the ground floor similar to the one which can still be seen at Hilldene House in 2004. This was the window of Keal's butcher's shop in the late 1800s. William Keal and his wife Grace lived there with their two daughters, Elizabeth and Grace. Later, members of the family had a shop in the bow-fronted premises in Dunn Street which had been the Dolphin Inn. The slaughterhouse was at the rear of Hilldene House. With no refrigeration meat had to be sold quickly and the price was reduced on Saturday evening if any was left unsold. What could not be sold was salted. In Hilldene with the Keals lodged Thomas Moon who was a piano dealer and tuner.

Hilldene House itself was two properties, one of which was owned by William Callaway and occupied by John Rawling. William Callaway was

Eliza Jane, Mary Ann and William Honey, 1895.

Elizabeth Ann Hockin, 1883.

Teresa and Charles Honey, 1896.

Sydney Honey.

William Honey with his pony-drawn ice-cream cart.

William Honey outside the family home at 5 High Street.

Brian Honey and Barbara Scott's wedding at Minster Church. Left to right: *Anne Knight, Arthur Biddick, bridegroom Brian Honey, bride Barbara Scott, Fred Scott, Sandra Knight, Bridget Olde.*

Percy Nicholls, ice-cream seller in Trickle Alley, 1936.

Hilda Nicholls and Mary Hilton on a day out.

Thomas Moyse's brother-in-law. Behind Hilldene House, as well as the slaughterhouse, was the house and brew house of Thomas Moyse. He was a maltster and cordwainer in the first half of the nineteenth century. The Moyse family had been resident in Boscastle since the late 1700s. He was born in 1801 and lived with his wife Mary and their children, Thomas and William (who were twins), Elizabeth and Mary. In 1839 the property measured 31 perches and the rent was one shilling. By the 1840s they had William Rowling, a journeyman shoemaker and Thomas Bastard, an apprentice shoemaker, living with them, as well as a female servant called Esther Bolt and Thomas' mother Elizabeth. Thomas Moyse was a churchwarden and is commemorated on a plaque on the wall of Minster Church. In January 1900 Hilldene was advertised for sale as follows:

> *THREE-STOREYED DWELLING-HOUSE as now occupied by Mrs. Grace Pethick Keals (who is under notice to quit at Lady-Day next), situate in the High Street, at the head of the town of Boscastle and containing two large sitting-rooms, kitchens and pantries, over which there are six bedrooms and a large attic.*
>
> *At the rear there is a large building used as a malt-house, and two cottages, now derelict. Also an extensive garden, well approached from the street overlooking the sea, and which would form a most excellent building site.*
>
> *The whole property stands on about 7,580 square feet, and at a small outlay could be improved and developed, and being situate in one of the most favourable health resorts on the popular North Coast of Cornwall will be found an excellent investment for capitalists and builders.*

When the manor was sold Hilldene House was also sold, together with the semi-detached cottage next door and a garden in Mount Pleasant where the bungalow Morwenna was later built. At that time the main house had seven bedrooms, bathroom and toilet, two reception rooms, kitchen and offices. Thomas Moyse's house and brew house had already been demolished and Hilldene House was being lived in by William Nicholls and his family who also took in guests.

William, known as Nixie, was the son of Thomas and Sarah Nicholls who were living in Corner House at the end of the nineteenth century. Thomas was a mason and a local preacher. He and his wife had nine children. In order to tell if they were all at home one could simply count the pairs of shoes lined up at the top of the stairs, as each child had only one pair.

Nixie was born at Corner House in 1870. He was a carpenter, caretaker of the waterworks and, in 1935, was clerk of works when the new water-supply was brought into Boscastle. He was also a celebrated player of both the spoons and the bones and took part in the celebration of Boscastle's Darkie Days. He ran a carpenter's shop behind the Napoleon Inn immediately above Dick Kernick's forge. He also had a milk-delivery round with which his daughter Jean helped. After he gave this up it was taken over by his son Percy. Percy incorporated this with an ice-cream business which he had bought complete with handcart from William Honey. Nixie married Elizabeth Grace Garland, daughter of Mr and Mrs F. Garland of Tubbs Ground. The Garland family have roots in Boscastle going back at least to the 1500s when Thomas Garland appears in the Muster Rolls for Minster in 1569. Elizabeth Grace Nicholls worked at Penally House for Colonel Hawker and his family. When she married Nixie the Hawker family gave them a blue and white dinner service as a wedding present. Nixie also did carpentry work at Penally House. On one occasion he was making a toilet seat and asked the cook, whose size was a good advertisement for her cooking, to sit on the seat so he could measure it! Whether she saw the funny side of it we do not know. They had four children: Wilfred who went on to work for the GPO and lived in Hayle; Pamela Mary Jean who married Charles Hancock (they had a daughter Pamela and lived at Hilldene Cottage. Charles ran a taxi service, keeping his large black car in the garage under what was at one time the Bible Christian chapel. They moved to Hayle when he went on to work at St Erth creamery); Ernest Colin joined the Royal Navy and was injured when his ship was torpedoed; and James Percy married Hilda Godfrey. He was known by his second name, Percy. He was an active member of the Boscastle Life-Saving Apparatus team and an organiser of the carnival. He also played the accordian with the Bottreaux Syncopators – all this despite him having a weak heart. He worked as a clerk for Olde & Sons at Otterham Station and was organist at Trevalga Church for 45 years, as well as playing regularly at both Forrabury and Minster Churches. He died at the early age of 63 in 1973. He is survived by his two sons Arthur and Nicholas. Nicholas' twin brother Godfrey died in infancy.

At the time of writing Hilldene House is divided into flats in the same way that St Christophers once was. St Christophers has seen various uses over the years. In the 1840s it was a store run by Prudence Wivell and her daughter Joan. Joan and her brother Martyn also had a grocery store which provided a drapery service in Mount Pleasant at what is now called Elderslie. Martyn eventually took over the running of the store in High Street, known then as Providence House, and described himself as a general merchant. Living with him in the late 1860s were his late mother's sister Mary Symons, a domestic servant Mary Ann Brown, and his assistant and commercial clerk Samuel Augustus Finnemore. Later young Francis Finnemore left school in August 1864 to be their shop boy. Martyn Wivell was born in 1829. He married his wife Jemima and they had four daughters, Prudence, Annie, Effie and Jane, and one son William.

On 14 June 1859, Edward Hoare, an aged person, who although living in a very humble way was said to be possessed of considerable property, was brought up in custody under remand before William Sloggatt and Revd R.B. Kinsman. He was charged with stealing about half a gallon of oats, the property of Martyn Wivell, grocer, at Boscastle. Mr Wivell had a mule in a meadow near the village and close to the prisoner's house at Polrunny, and he had been in the habit of carrying it some corn every morning. His suspicions became aroused that the corn was being

High Street in 1898. In the foreground is Granfer Wivell.

stolen and he communicated with PC King. On the Friday morning he carried the corn as usual and left. Directly afterwards, the prisoner came out of his house, went to the box containing the corn and emptied it into a bag and carried it away. The policeman who was watching made his presence known and took the prisoner into custody. He pleaded guilty and was sentenced to 21 days' hard labour in Bodmin Gaol. The prisoner Edward Hoare had a wife Mary and was a retired blacksmith who had been born in Kilkhampton.

Providence House became St Christophers Hotel in the early 1900s. It boasted fresh produce from its own garden, separate tables and a garage, and was recommended by the Civil Service and the Scholastic Holiday Association. It was open to non-residents and served coffees and afternoon teas.

By the time the manor was put up for sale in 1946, St Christophers had been converted into three flats in the tenancies of Mrs C.H. Kerswell, Mr J.I. Snowdon and Mrs K. Garbutt. Mrs Kerswell lived on the ground floor where there were two bedrooms, a sitting-room, kitchen, scullery and toilet. The Snowdons had four bedrooms, sitting-room, kitchen, bathroom and lavatory on the first floor, and Mrs Garbutt had two bedrooms, sitting-room, kitchen, lavatory and two attic storerooms.

Joseph Ivor Snowdon was known as Ivor and came to Boscastle to help put in the supply when mains electricity arrived in the village. The Cornwall Electric Power Company acquired rights through an East Cornwall Special Order passed by Parliament in 1934 to extend the high- and low-voltage mains and to develop the use of electricity in the Camelford Rural District Council area of North Cornwall. By 1936 the 33,000-volt ring overhead main was constructed which fed electricity from the national grid transforming station at Fraddon via Bodmin, Delabole, Launceston, Callington, Liskeard, Lostwithiel and back to Bodmin and Fraddon. At each of these towns the supply was transformed down to 11,000 volts and at each village the supply was again transformed down to the safe voltage of 240 volts. In 1937 three substations provided supply for Boscastle. The Boscastle tariff in 1936 was based on a quarterly fixed charge according to the floor area of the house, plus a unit charge of 1d. per unit. Prior to this Boscastle had no public gas or electricity supply. The Parish Council provided 29 street lights from Penally Hill through Boscastle to High Street and Cambeak. Mr Snowdon was not slow to take advantage of the benefits provided by the new labour-saving devices and he had two electric heaters, a cooker, a wash boiler, kettle and iron installed within the first year, helped no doubt by his staff discount.

Kathleen and Ivor Snowdon.

In 1895 lamplighting had been put out to tender by the Parish Council and they were paying 14s. per light per winter. With the arrival of electric street lighting the old oil-lamps were offered for sale. The lamps were sold to Mr G. Olde for 3s. each and the lamp-posts were used to repair gates on Forrabury Common and a stile at Trehane Farm. Boscastle's last lamplighter was Walter Knight, another resident of High Street.

The next two houses up the hill from St Christophers are the newest additions to High Street and were built at the beginning of the twentieth century. The first one was rented from the manor to Cornwall County Council and used as a police house. The other was rented by Mr Fred Sandercock. Fred was a brother to Clifton Sandercock, of Dunn Street. Fred and his wife had a son, Stanley, and Fred had Paradise Farm as a milking parlour. At the time the manor was offered for sale, each house had two bedrooms, sitting-room, kitchen and offices.

The next house is on the corner of Mount Pleasant and High Street and, as we have already seen, was the home of the Nicholls family and later of Ned and Bessie Hockin. This house, like those at the bottom of High Street, was built as the village developed up the hill from the castle. It is one of the oldest and least-altered houses in the village. At one time the row continued up the hill, with maps of the late 1700s showing a building on the area where there is now a small green and a seat. There are remains of this building under the green and partly under the tarmaced road. Its foundations and the remains of a cloam oven are still in situ at the time of writing.

On the other side of the street above Hilldene House is the small group of houses that formed the Brig Inn and its associated buildings. The Brig Inn was at one time used together with The Cottage next door and Hillside Cottage. At various times rooms have migrated between the Brig Inn and The Cottage. It may seem odd nowadays that behind the front door of the Brig Inn is the kitchen of The Cottage, and above it one of The Cottage's bedrooms. This common use of property is continued in the gardens. Before the advent of inside toilets several properties had their outside earth closets behind the old Brig Inn. Each property also had storage sheds, a pigsty and gardens, but not necessarily next to the relevant house or to each other.

This sort of shared living may not suit everyone today, but if the old ways are understood and neighbours are respected it works as well now as it did in the days of the manor. Until the early 1900s the cottage now called Hillside was part of the same complex as the old Brig Inn and was part stabling and part cart shed. It was only a single storey high and if you study the stonework you can see where the additional storey was added. You can also see, on the front right-hand corner, that the wall is cut back to allow for clearance of the wheel hubs of carts and wagons as they turned the corner.

Whilst decorating the upstairs front room of The Cottage, the owner at the time of writing found a small window in the north-facing wall which at one time looked out to sea. If it were unblocked today it would look into the bedroom of Hillside! Hillside was, from the 1930s–'50s, the home of Walter Jose. Walter had a large wooden shed at the bottom of the gardens where he cut hair and gave the village's young men their 'short back and sides'.

At the junction of High Street and Mount Pleasant next door to Corner House is a building that once housed the Bible Christian chapel. The Bible Christians, or Bryanites as they were known, began preaching in Boscastle in 1817. For 40 years they held their preaching services and prayer meetings in the private house of Moses Pearn. They built the chapel to accommodate 120 people and settled it on trustees. In 1873 it had 20 members and the Sunday school had between 40 and 60 boys and girls. This was one of three chapels in the village. It opened in 1859 and the Bryanites were trying to revive what they believed to be the original form of Methodism.

William Bryant, the Bible Christian founder, was born at Gunwen in Luxulyan in 1778. He was the son of Anglican-Methodist parents who had met in John Pascoe's house at Medrose. William was a deeply religious boy. At the age of 23 he dedicated himself to a career of sustained personal evangelism. In 1803 he married Catherine Cowlin in the old church of St Piran. St Piran's is now buried beneath the sands at Perranporth but it is considered to be one of the oldest Christian buildings in Britain. They were the last couple to be married there. It was said that William Bryant brushed aside the good advice and guidance of others and seemed to equate the will of God with his own inclination. In 1810 he was expelled from the Methodist membership of his chapel which he had helped to build on land he had given to the church. He then spent several years building up a group of societies. He created a livelier, more exuberant form of Methodism. It was said by some that 'they acted more like maniacs than reasonable beings.' Many of Bryant's first helpers were young people in their early

Bess and Ned Hockin in the courtyard of Corner House, High Street.

The Bible Christian chapel, Mount Pleasant, 1880.

twenties. Every day Bryant walked miles over moorland roads, preaching and meeting the classes. After further discord with the church in 1831 he and his family emigrated to America.

In 1816 the Bible Christians had about 100 members, mostly in Cornwall, but this increased until in 1902 when they contributed over 32,000 members to the United Methodist Church, of whom nearly 7,000 were in Cornwall. Several of their preachers were one-time wrestling champions, like the Delabole preacher Abraham Bastard, a member of whose family, William, married into one of Boscastle's oldest families when he wed Elizabeth Ann Gard on 29 November 1879.

For the most part the Bryanites were ordinary Methodists, although they tended to be simpler and plainer than the Wesleyans, but they were often noisier. The chapel in Mount Pleasant had a balcony for the musicians who led the choir, as well as its organ. On Sundays, morning service would be followed by Sunday school in the afternoon. Children visiting from outlying areas would bring their dinner with them. Families who 'supported' the Bible Christian chapel were those of Arthur Bullock, Daniel Ferrett, Daniel Squire, Miss Jewell, Harry Brown, Nicholas Sandercock, the Boneys, Wivells, Honeys, Venners, Hoskins and Suttons. The chapel finally closed in 1915, after which it was used as a garage and carpenter's until being converted into a home by the Nicholls family.

On the same side of Mount Pleasant was the Wivells' grocery and drapery at Elderslie. In the 1930s it was lived in by Henry Drayton, a member of HM Customs and Excise. This later became the property of Miss May Fountain. She was born on 8 May 1888, the fifth daughter of Joseph Septimus and Margaret (née Allen) Fountain of Greenwhich. She was educated there at a private school, the first of the Physical Training Colleges for Women which gave her the idea of taking up her very unusual career. She was principal of Chelsea College of Further Education from 1929 to 1950, where she worked to introduce less formal methods and activities. She lectured for two years in the Teachers' Training College in Truro and at the same time took the qualifying examinations of the Chartered Society of Massage and Medical Gymnastics. She spent two years at the Royal Central Gymnastics Institute in Stockholm and became fluent in Swedish, translating a number of taxing technical works. Miss Fountain retired to Boscastle in 1950 where she was known for her honesty, kindness and generosity. In the 1960s she fought a long and hard campaign against the closure of the railway.

Next door to Miss May Fountain's is a cottage originally known as Rose Cottage that was the home of schoolteacher Miss Miles. At the time of writing it is known as The Cottage, Mount Pleasant, the home of plumber and heating engineer, Mike Hircock. Mike married Vivien Hilton, a Boscastle girl, and they have two grown-up children, Teresa and Anthony. Mike, Vivian and Teresa moved to Boscastle from Taunton in 1967 and set up in business here. Anthony was born in Boscastle. Mike has been a parish councillor for 35 years and chairman for 26 of them. He is also a long-serving school governor, having been on the Board of Governors of Boscastle CP School for 26 years.

On the opposite side of the road at the western end were a group of houses, the remains of which were demolished in the 1960s on the instruction of the County Council for them to hold against any future road-widening scheme. In one of these houses lived the family of James Winnicott. James was born in St Columb in 1812 and married Elizabeth Pearn of Boscastle. He lived with his wife, daughter and granddaughter, all called Elizabeth, at Mount Pleasant at the end of the nineteenth century. At that time they had four children, James, Mary, William and Maria. Many years later the old lady was known as Witchy Winnicott because she kept a frog in a jar on her mantleshelf. Pentecost Symons was another tenant of one of these houses. He had been abroad and was considered quite well off. He was also known for his hair-brained schemes like firing his shotgun off at night, supposedly at rabbits and much to the annoyance of his neighbours. Another of his schemes came to him when exploring an old quarry at the top of Gibbs Lane. Here he discovered what he believed was a seam of coal and persuaded Mr Kernick at the forge that he could deliver coals to him cheaper than he was buying at the time. Although he was highly sceptical Dick Kernick couldn't afford to turn the chance of cheaper coal down, so he told Pentecost he'd try a bag and if it burnt correctly he could supply the forge. Pentecost went off and duly filled a bag with his coal and brought it down to the forge. The lumps were put on to the hot coals and, what was in fact Boscastle black slate, split and flew off in all directions, causing mayhem in the forge, leaving Dick Kernick swearing and threatening to kill him. Needless to say Dick Kernick was not a happy man. After Pentecost the house was lived in by the Sleep family until they moved to Marine Terrace. The final tenant was Albert Perry.

Ellen Paskall, Iris Hockin and Jean Nicholls in front of the old cottages in Mount Pleasant.

Albert was a farm labourer and had married May Chapman. They had five children, Leonard, Bill, George, Betty and Denise. Bill Perry started work, even before he had left school, for the Gard family making early-morning milk deliveries before starting his school day. He went on to work full time on a smallholding and as he was in a reserved occupation he was exempted from military service. After legislation was introduced making it compulsory to pasteurise milk the Gards' milk business ceased and they concentrated on the building side of their business, taking Bill with them. In 1972 Bill and his brother George set up their own building firm. In his spare time Bill played E-flat bass with the Boscastle Band and was a member of the choir. Betty, who was born in 1928, married Harvey Philp in 1952 and spent many years at Trevivian House just around the corner in Upper High Street, where their son William was born, before moving to the Cambeak estate.

Although the author knows of no link with the family of Harvey Philp it is worth noting that on 27 March 1830, 122 years before Harvey and Betty married, William Philp was found guilty of blowing up the sloop *Jane* with 150lbs of gunpowder. No sentence was passed, however, due to some technical error. Gunpowder seems to have been very readily available because on 21 March the following year Thomas Rosevear recorded in his diary that James Medland 'blowed up his house with gunpowder. A poor wretched and adulterous character.'

Also living at Trevivian, but in the latter half of the twentieth century, was Norah Biscombe and her son Wesley. Norah was born at New Mills and married her husband Bill at St Juliot. Bill died in the late 1970s, and having spent most of her life as a farmer's wife at New Mills, Norah then moved to Trevivian.

A small farm at Half Acre was also accessed from Mount Pleasant. During the second half of the nineteenth century it was in the tenancy of the Hockin family who farmed 20 acres. Edward and Ann Hockin lived there with their daughter Mary. At the end of the century the Hockins had moved out and William and Martha Cotton took over. William was a labourer and had a daughter Elizabeth and twins William and Florence. In April 1895 William Cotton appeared before the bench at Camelford charged with stealing a fowl from Mr Forward, who informed the prosecutor that he had reported to the police the loss of a fowl on the previous Sunday. PC Richards telegraphed to Inspector Gill at Camelford. The police immediately visited William Cotton's house and found one or two black feathers, and while searching the premises they saw Mrs Cotton leaving the house with a fowl pie. The prisoner had admitted the offence when charged and his wife said that the feathers had been burned and the head and feet thrown into the river. The pie had been confiscated and produced in court as evidence. Cotton was found guilty and fined £1 and costs.

Half Acre was later farmed by the Cowling family who were Boscastle butchers with a shop in Fore Street. In the late 1940s John Hancock and his wife moved in and their daughter Sheila and son Royston were both born there. The family moved to Tresuck in 1956.

At the time of writing Half Acre is the home and studio of painter and sculptor Carole Vincent. When Carole bought Half Acre in 1961 it was divided into three parts as animal housing, which she converted from pigsty to home. She started work in Boscastle at the primary school, going on to teach PE and art for ten years at Sir James Smith's School in Camelford. After a short break away she returned for another five years of part-time teaching. In 2004 Carole works in concrete using coloured pigments and creating her own unique sculptures. Her large-scale commissions have included the 'Armada Dial' in Plymouth City Centre, the 'Red Carpet' at the entrance to the Centre for the Edinburgh International Festival, the 'Bude Light', a memorial to the Cornish inventor Sir Goldsworthy Gurney, and the 'Blue Circle Garden' which won a bronze medal at the Chelsea Flower Show in 2001 and was based on her own garden at Half Acre. It was the only garden designed by a sculptor and was sponsored by Blue Circle Cement. In an article about Chelsea the *Radio Times* said that 'people who think concrete is brutish, utilitarian or dull will be astonished by its beauty.'

Until the New Road was built Mount Pleasant continued uninterrupted to Treforda Water and on to Minster, Lesnewth, Otterham and beyond. High Street itself continued up the hill beyond its junction with Mount Pleasant with cottages on both sides of the road. On the left-hand corner was Steps or Hillrise Cottage, known as Roundtree Cottage in 2004. In the late-nineteenth century it was occupied by Charles Honey and his wife Emma Teresa, then in the early-twentieth century by Walter and Lilian Knight. On the front of the cottage was an additional building which extended right to the edge of the road and was where Digory Downing stabled his donkey. Next door, Trevivian House was the home of Harry Brown and his wife Jane. Harry was a farmer at Reddivallen and had two children, Lillie and John. Lillie married another farmer's son, John Percy Hoskin. Both of them were members of the nearby Bible Christian chapel.

John Brown was known affectionately as 'Ginger'. He became a farmer like his father. He kept cattle and owned the shippen at Bridge. He and his wife Serena also lived at the old Ship Inn, which in their time was called Atlantic Farm and Guest House. John, like many Boscastle men, served in France with the DCLI in the First World War.

The road leading westwards from Mount Pleasant (called Paradise Road in 2004) was once known as Trickle Alley, corrupted to Treacle Alley. It was referred to as Trickle Alley because a spring, together with water taken from the Jordan under Tubbs

John Brown returning from the shippen, 1958.

Jane Brown outside her home at Trevivian House.

John (Ginger) Brown outside Atlantic Farm and Guest House in 1958.

John and Serena Brown.

Ground, fed a leat to the Napoleon Inn stables and Dick Kernick's forge, and trickled across it. The first building on the south side of Trickle Alley was small and built of stone. It stood at the entrance to what is Summer Winds at the time of writing. In the late-nineteenth and early-twentieth centuries it was a pork, mutton and lamb butcher's and later became the greengrocer's shop of Noel Joyce and his wife Evelyn. Noel also worked as village postman and was a colourful character who enjoyed singing and entertaining visitors in the local pubs. The building was demolished in 1968.

The first house on this side of the road was Rosebank. Once it was the end of a row of terraced houses. In the early-twentieth century it was lived in by Bill and May Hockin and their daughter Iris. In the 1930s the Hockins moved to High Street and Hannah Brown moved here from High Street, following the death of her mother Grace. The rest of the terrace had gone by the end of the eighteenth century, to be replaced by a house with a pigsty and cowhouse attached, two cottages and gardens. A century later Grace Hallett was living there with her daughter Sarah and brother William Honey. Prior to the sale of the manor Sarah was still living in one of the cottages – the other, Rosebank, had Hannah Brown living in it, and in the two separate parts of the main house were Susan Allen and Amos Philp.

Following the manor sale the new owner of the main house was Bill Codd, a baker's assistant. He bought it for £800 with the help of a loan from his employer, S. Radcliffe, County Baker and Confectioner. The Codds remained in the house for 20 years, calling it Seaview. In the 1960s it was bought by a family from away and gradually its land was sold off.

The northern side of Paradise contains a different type of buildings, with the appearance of a later style. On the corner of High Street and Paradise, Minster Cottage has rendered stonework and sash windows. Until fairly recently, when renovation was carried out, the inside had many original Regency features including a shallow but wide staircase opening to right and left at the top. Like many of the houses in High Street and Fore Street it has a detached garden on the south side of Paradise where its tenants could keep a pig and grow their own flowers and vegetables. Although many of these gardens have disappeared Minster Cottage still retains this fascinating legacy of times past.

Next door is Dolphins, which until the mid-1960s was one of Top Town's general stores. In the nineteenth century it was a fruit and vegetable shop in the hands of first a Miss Jewell and then the Symons family. It later became a grocery and general store. By the late 1930s it was being run by Claude Knight. Claude was born in Boscastle in 1909 and was the son of Walter and Lilian Knight. He left school at 14 and before going into the grocery trade had been a cycle agent. He used to charge people's radio accumulators. During the Second World War he joined the Royal Air Force and his wife Muriel took over running the shop. Claude was demobbed in 1946 and became a postman in Boscastle before transferring to Camelford. Besides having the shop and being a postman he sold and repaired wireless sets and later televisions. He was a radio ham, spending hours on his transmitter contacting people all over the world by Morse code. He was also a keen musician and played drums with the Biddick Band. All this combined to take its toll on him. His work with the Post Office, radio and television business, the shop and the band eventually combined to affect his health. He owned a Jaguar car and on his way to work early one winter's morning he became stuck in a snowdrift and tried to push the heavy vehicle out, straining his heart in the process. He died of a stroke soon afterwards at the young age of 57.

Claude's wife Muriel lived in Delabole before they married. She was the granddaughter of Joseph Hamlyn. The Hamlyns were considerable landowners in south-east Devon and their ancestry goes back to the Norman invasion. Hamlyn (Hamelyn) was the second son of Robert of Mortain

Muriel and daughter Elizabeth Knight outside Knight's shop in 1960.

Knight's shop window in the 1960s.

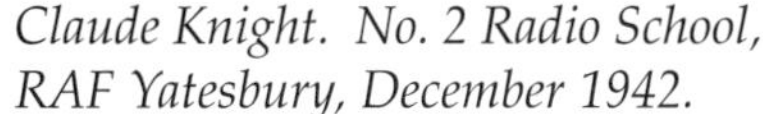

Claude Knight. No. 2 Radio School, RAF Yatesbury, December 1942.

Rodney, Anne and Sandra Knight at school in 1958.

Rodney Knight, Royal Observer Corps, 1968.

who raised an army in Brittany to support his half-brother, William the Conqueror. Hamlyn became Earl of Surrey with the family seat at Hapstead. He was granted 22 manors in Cornwall and three in south-east Devon for his support of William. His descendant Joseph Hamlyn worked in Buckfastleigh in the family tanning business and decided on a career change, training as a carpenter. He took up coach building at a time when there was a great expansion in the transport business and obtained a contract to supply and maintain horse-drawn omnibuses for the City of Plymouth. Unfortunately, the city decided to embrace the new-fangled internal combustion engine in the form of motor buses and Joseph was left to bear the cost of the materials and tools he had purchased. This forced him into bankruptcy and he came to Delabole where he continued to build horse-drawn coaches.

Two beautiful stone houses adjoin Dolphins which are believed to date back to the early-eighteenth century and are built in the Queen Anne style. The first one, Hartland View, was home of draper and grocer Frederick Jewell. He married Frances in the 1840s and lived there with their four children, Elizabeth, William, Phillipa and Mary. William became a butcher and had the pork and butcher's shop opposite the house. They lived next door to an elderly naval pensioner called Jane Stone. Her house called Ivy Cottage was later renamed Trelawney. At the beginning of the twentieth century it was the home of the Downings. John Downing was a carpenter and he worked from his shop behind Lundy View. He also kept a few cows in fields at the western end of Paradise. The Downings had lived at the Brig Inn and by the 1930s were in partnership as Downing and Beazley. The house in Paradise had a large garden to the side and rear and joined a plat which extended down to Hilldene House. Beside the plat stood a row of seven cottages built back to back, five or six steps below road level. A Thomas Hopper lived in one of them with his wife Mary and daughter Harriet. In 1900 Thomas put a notice in the local newspaper which read:

> *I hereby give notice that I will not be responsible for any debts which have been incurred (if any) since 1898 by Mary Hopper... who has disgracefully absconded.*

Whether his wife's misdemeanors went to his head or not Thomas Hopper was brought before the Camelford Police Court in September 1901, charged with unlawfully and maliciously shooting at William Nicholls. The complainant, a carpenter, said he was

Maria Nicholls and her mother Annie Pridham.

walking to work and outside Hopper's house he shouted 'Is Mousey at home?' Hopper shouted 'If you don't go away I'll put a bullet through your head.' Nicholls replied 'Get out you old whoremaster', and walked away. About ten yards on he heard the report of a gun and something whizzed through the bushes, although he could not say whether it was a bullet or shot. The chairman said the evidence was sufficient to commit Hopper for trial. Many local families were housed in Paradise Row, including those of William Rogers, Thomas Kellow, William Sloggatt, Bill Chapman, Bill Couch, Tom Pascoe, Fred Beer, Frank Pridham and the Cotton family who were there in the 1930s.

On the opposite side of the road are the substantial buildings of Paradise Farm. These buildings have been converted into a home and are lived in by Sam and Delia Hancock in 2004. The Hancocks are another well-established family in Boscastle. Sam's grandfather originally came from Port Isaac, moving to Fenterleigh at Bossiney and then taking a farm at Tresparrett. Sam's father William was one of 13 children. He left home to take his own farm at Lesnewth. William and his wife Mary had seven children: Sam, Mary, Leonard, Den, John, Charles and Ronald. John farmed Half Acre before moving to Tresuck. Ronald farmed at Tintagel and Trafalgar and Den farmed at Treworld. William and Mary were known to everyone in the village as Granfer and Mammy. Granfer recalled how he worked a 12-hour day as a young man and then needed to collect 50 faggots of wood for use at home. Each faggot was tied with a twisted stick called a beam and was burnt in the cloam oven. When the oven was sufficiently hot the ash would be raked out into the fireplace below, food put into the oven and the cloam door sealed in place. The Hancocks were one of the families involved in the celebrations for the opening of the new railway line through Camelford Station. They supplied potatoes for the celebrations in August 1893. After they retired Granfer and Mammy lived in High Street in The Cottage. Granfer Hancock was a gentleman in every sense of the word. His front door was always open and he could be seen on his front doorstep, inside the distinctive slate porch from early morning until he came out to eat his bedtime apple in the evening. Eric Nicholls, one time village postman, recalls that he once delivered a letter to Granfer addressed to 'the house with the door that is always open.'

The land around Sam and Delia Hancock's Paradise Farmyard is bounded on the west by the River Jordan. On the opposite side of the river is Paradise House or The Rookery. In 1819 Richard Martin was tenant of 'Parradice' and in about 1820 Richard Benoke built the present house for himself after he received his share of the Amy estates. It was afterwards purchased by Mr William Cole, who on his death aged 83 on 3 January 1839 left it to his daughter Nancy Cole, who lived there for many years with servants Catherine Jose, Elizabeth Force, Susan Brown and Edmond Brown the stable boy. Nancy also owned two stitches on Forrabury Common and fields at Lower Paradise, Caters Meadow, two fields at Shortstones, Swinster and an orchard. She was also the owner of Tregatherall Farm until she sold it to Eldred Brown of Plymouth. On her death it was all left to her brother Revd Francis Cole, vicar of St Issey, from whom it passed to his son William Cole who had served in the Bombay Civil Service. William's wife Anne lived in the house with five children, all of whom had been born in Bombay, and a servant called Mary Prior.

Mammy and Granfer Hancock.

In the 1870s Paradise was bought by civil engineer Charles Sparke and he renamed the house The Rookery. He and his wife Mary Ann had their sons Charles and Trethoza and daughters Madeline and Mary living with them, and kept one servant called Elizabeth Enson.

Ten years later the retired hotel keeper from the Wellington Hotel moved there. William Scott had his sister-in-law Jane Louis and servant Mary Stacey with him.

The early years of the twentieth century saw the

Paradise House in 1913. On the left-hand side is an oil-lit lamp and post.

house still called The Rookery in the hands of Oliver Gwynn Perry. In 1953 Norman Hicks came to the house and once again it was called Paradise. With him were his wife Joyce and children Sarah and Jeremy. He lived in Paradise for the next 33 years. During and after the war Norman had worked for the Milk Marketing Board and the Fatstock Marketing Corporation, and so it was a natural progression for his career to become an agricultural journalist with the *Farmers' Weekly*. He combined this with farming pigs, beef cattle and the famous Boscastle early potatoes. Norman and Joyce created the beautiful gardens around the house, Norman taking care of the landscaping and the water garden alongside the Jordan and Joyce looking after the shrubs and plants. Norman served on the Parish Council for eight years until 1986 and he was chairman of the Cornwall Family History Society. He and Joyce moved to Philleigh in 1986 but their son Jeremy still lives in the village.

Opposite Paradise House was an area of gardens and orchard known as Gunpool Meadow. The word 'Gunpool' comes from the Celtic words 'Gun' (Goon meaning Downland or heath) and 'Pol' (Pool), or pool on the down, giving testament to its potential for being very watery. Until the drought of 1976 this area acted as a sponge during the very wet weather, soaking up excess water from the surrounding fields and releasing it slowly, thus preventing the area from flooding. Some of this land has been developed, particularly at the northern end near Gunpool. Excavations at Bottreaux Garage to install new petrol-storage tanks ran into problems when they rapidly filled with water.

This marshy ground made a very fertile area for growing fruit and vegatables and was divided into gardens and rented by some of the tenants of premises in High Street and Paradise. The remainder of Gunpool Meadow is the area now covered by Bottreaux Garage and forecourt.

At the far western end of Paradise is a large detached house which was set in its own mature gardens with an orchard on its eastern side. Originally known as Osford, the house was built for Kate Austin who, despite the different spelling of their surnames, was an aunt of Jane Austen. She paid £1,950 for the property and on her death left the house to Major and Mrs Noel Streatfield, who were children's authors. The house, which sits on the junction of Paradise Road and Barn Park Road, was renamed Windrush by Mr and Mrs Wintle who lived there at the beginning of the 1960s. Along Barn Park Road are three large houses. Barn Park House was the home of merchant Thomas Pope Rosevear. Next door lies Corentin and further eastwards Tolcarne House.

Corentin was previously called Belvedere House. It was built by Alfred Moore Thomas at the end of the 1800s. The architect was Thomas Hardy

The north-facing side of Corentin, 1958.

and the building work was carried out by the Gard family. No expense was spared in its specification and it was built to a very high standard. The roofing timbers alone were cut from expensive heart wood. Alfred Thomas was born in Boscastle on 30 June 1826 and he and his wife May moved to London, where he became the wealthy proprietor of a sawmill. They lived in Belvedere Road, Lambeth. When he retired he returned to Boscastle and built Belvedere House, now known as Corentin, with a carriage house, stables and accomodation for his employees. At the time of writing these buildings are Pentargon, the Old Coach House and Jonhurst Cottage. At the end of the stable building Mr Thomas incorporated a circular recess to bear his name. Unfortunately, before this could be realised he became bankrupt.

Richard Webber lived at Pentargon after he left the garage at Bridge. The building was converted to a dwelling by his second wife's father, William Burnard. Richard Webber built a wood annex adjoining Pentargon for Clifton Sandercock who worked for him from 1935 until Richard's death in 1938. A shed in the garden next to Pentargon housed charge accumulators used to power radios. Richard also had a deep-litter chicken house in a field above Pentargon. Later he built The Nest as a chicken house, designing it to be a dwelling should the chickens become unprofitable. It stood until the beginning of the twenty-first century and the nest boxes could still be seen on the side.

Corentin had its own well, two cellars, servants' quarters and three large reception rooms. The interior designed by Hardy had marble and cast-iron fireplaces complete with overmantel mirrors. The rooms all had matching plaster mouldings on the ceilings. From the front hall the main staircase rose on your right-hand side. At the rear of the hall a door led down to the kitchen below and the servants' staircase to the floors above. The large kitchen was slate-flagged with a slate-shelved pantry and stairs down to a cellar. A second cellar was located at the back of the building below the wash-house. The owners of Corentin in 2004 tell the tale that when they moved in and went into the kitchen the floor

The Mills family in 1949. Pictured are: *Simon, Joe, Anne, June with Hugh on her knee.*

Above: *Jon Mills in 1962.*

Above left: *Joe and June Mills with their youngest daughters Sally and Frances outside Corentin.*

Left: *Sally and Frances Mills in trousers as usual!*

was moving like water, and they discovered that the flagged floor had been removed and grass was growing in its place. The stained glass in the entrance porch matched the Minton tiles on the floor. Heavy cast-iron railings surrounded the front garden with a pair of double cast-iron gates at the entrance. Almost all of these architectural features were stripped out and sold in the early 1990s.

At the beginning of the twentieth century Corentin became a private nursing and maternity home where operations and dental work were carried out and children were born. The matron was Miss Tipple. The large old-fashioned X-ray machine was housed in what is now Jonhurst Cottage, and its concrete base is still there at the time of writing.

During the Second World War Corentin was used by the Ginner Mawer School of Greek Deportment and Dancing, which had been evacuated from London. Ruby Ginner was a dancer and teacher and lived at Corentin with her brother Charles, an artist who exhibited at the Royal Academy. Ruby's partner, Irene Mawer, lived at Bourne Stream, overlooking the harbour. Many local girls attended the dance and deportment lessons and amongst the young ladies attending the classes were Jessamine and Eleanor, the daughters of the potter Bernard Leach who was living at Harbour Terrace in the 1940s.

Ruby Ginner first visited Boscastle in 1911 and said in 1962 that she had spent a good part of every year there since. She was here thoughout both world wars. She founded her school of dancing in 1923 when she was aged 37. One of her pupils, Nancy Shearwood, later became principal teacher at the school. She was born Nancy Koppuck in 1908. Her father left his family and went to Canada, so Nancy was brought up by her aunt and her mother and changed her name to Shearwood. Her aunt was interested in dancing and Nancy attended the Margaret Morris School of Dancing.

Nancy joined Ruby Ginner's school in 1925 and five years later, in 1930, the whole school went to Greece to study Greek dance. That same year Nancy came to Boscastle and stayed with Ruby at Bourne Stream. Ruby was now married and called Dyer. In the spring of 1932 Ruby and Nancy went to Greece. They travelled on the Orient Express and by boat to Athens, where they spent four weeks studying the monuments and taking a Cook's tour. They were looking at dance in the theatre and studying and recording dance scenes from the pots and friezes in Athens' archaeological museum, making a collection of new dance positions. Through the 1930s Nancy progressed from student to assistant. With the outbreak of the Second World War the School of Greek Deportment and Dancing evacuated to Boscastle and lodged at Corentin, using the parish hall for dancing activities. Later, Nancy bought Trenance, 3 Penally Cottages, and moved from her room at Corentin to live there with her mother and aunt. She finally sold the cottage in 1955/6. Nancy died in 1995 aged 87.

Nancy Shearwood – Ginner Mawer School of Dance.

Ruby Ginner Dyer's brother Charles Ginner was a painter. He was part of the Camden School and exhibited at the Royal Academy. He visited Boscastle from time to time and painted several pictures of the village, including Hillside, showing the Wellington Millhouse in 1913 and Millets Meadow in 1949, painted from an upstairs window at Corentin. Charles died in 1953 aged 72. The following year there was an Arts Council exhibition of his work. Ruby died in 1978 aged 92.

In the late 1950s Commander Joe Mills bought the house and lived there with his wife and six children, Anne, Simon, Hugh, Jonathan, Sally and Frances. They moved to Boscastle from Rustington in Sussex where Joe had lived after leaving the Fleet Air Arm. The Mills family itself comes originally from St Day.

The gardens surrounding the house were set out in Victorian style. To the right of the house slate steps led down between two yew trees to a lawn surrounded by a shrubbery. The rear garden was a productive fruit and vegetable garden with heavy double wooden gates to the stables. There were trained apple and pear trees and a large greenhouse containing three dessert grapevines, the whole enclosed by a tall stone wall. A third garden was on the opposite side of the road from the front of the house. This was again accessed by slate steps and surrounded by cast-iron railings. The plot was compulsorily purchased in the 1960s when the Tintagel road was widened.

Chapter Eight

Tinker, Tailor, Soldier, Sailor

Northwards from Bottreaux Cross, Top Town becomes Town as the hill descends through Fore Street, Dunn Street and Old Hill or Oxen Road to Bridge. As its name suggests, Fore Street was one of the village's main streets and it developed southwards up the hill. Where we now see Bottreaux crossroads was the Elizabethan manor-house, the market, Market House and St James' Chapel, the site of the current Mission Rooms used as the village hall. Next to the village hall is the Old Post House. During the mid- to late 1800s the Old Post House was the home of James Parsons and his family. James was born at Tremaine near Egloskerry. He was a cordwainer or shoemaker. He and his wife Betsy Ann had seven children living with them at the Old Post House – Lydia (1866), Mary (1868), Richard (1870), James (1872), Arthur (1874), Annie (1876) and Catherine (1877).

The Old Posting House, as it became known, was for many years the home of the Symons family. William Symons of Lesnewth was married in 1689 to Mary Jose. They had five children and through their son Pentecost, who was born in 1703, they had eight grandchildren. All of them were born in Lesnewth. One of the grandchildren, Edward, married Catherine Jowel of Lesnewth on 20 February 1773 and they moved to Boscastle where their seven children were born – Mary (1773), Catherine (1776), Joan (1779), Edward (1782), Pentecost (1784), Sarah (1788) and Anne (1791). Pentecost's son Thomas was born in 1812 and he married Frances Rowe on 12 September 1839. Frances was the daughter of Francis Drake Rowe, landlord of the Brig Inn. Thomas, like his father, was a farmer, and they farmed over 300 acres at Tredorne and had fields at Higher and Middle Paradise. He and Frances also ran a fruiterer business in High Street. The Symons family as a whole were both landowners and manor tenants.

Thomas and Frances had nine children – John Rowe (1851), Pentecost, Thomas, Margaret, Sarah,

The Symons family. Left to right, back row: *Elvina, John, Frances, Pentecost;* sitting, front row: *Adeline, Kate, Tommy, Nan, Daisy.*

Cowling & Sons butcher's shop, Fore Street, 1967.

Bob Cowling heads the Boscastle Carnival.

Kitty, Anne, Frances and Tamsin. John Rowe Symons married Catherine Maria Dorcas Emms in 1878 and they lived first in High Street and then at the Old Post House at the beginning of the twentieth century. John was a carriage proprietor. He transported goods to and from the harbour as they were loaded and unloaded from the ships. He was also a horse-drawn-coach owner and one of his many jobs was to carry people on village outings.

John and Catherine had nine children – John (1880), Annie (1882), Pentecost (1884), Mary (1889), Elvina (1891), Daisy (1893), Thomas (1895), Adeline (1877) and Kate. The eldest son John was involved in the family carriage business as well as occupying land at Tubbs Ground. Many descendants of the Symons family still live in the area in 2004, some being still involved in farming.

Opposite the Old Post House, on the eastern side of the street, is Myrtle Cottage, which was at one time in the occupation of the Cowling family who established their butchery business in 1860. One of the earliest references to a Cowling in Boscastle is in an entry on 17 June 1830 in T.P. Rosevear's journal, in which he reports that John Cowling junr had, in vain, solicited the overseer of Minster parish to pay the passage of himself and family to Quebec by the *Springflower.* At that time the ship was waiting to sail from Boscastle. The monies were not forthcoming and so he had gone on board the vessel as it was leaving port, deserting his family. The parish officers had pursued the vessel to Padstow but John Cowling ran up the rigging and prevented them from bringing him ashore.

Thomas Cowling was born in 1826 and was a farmer and farmed Tredorne, as well as becoming a butcher. He and his wife Eliza had four children – Eliza (1855), James Voden (1859), Elizabeth (1862) and Thomas. James Voden Cowling, like his father, was a farmer and butcher. He married Sarah Jane Banbury on 7 November 1881. She was the daughter of Solomon Banbury who had the neighbouring grocery store. James and Sarah had five children – Mabel (1884), Nellie (1886), James Thomas (1887), Dennis (1888) and Mildred (1895).

The Cowlings occupied the castle site known as Higher and Lower Jordans and James Cowling would keep sheep there before taking them to be slaughtered in the slaughterhouse behind his butcher's shop. The sheep would be bought at Camelford market and driven to Boscastle by specially employed drovers like Mr Cobbledick. James continued to build on his father's farming and butchery business and kept a pony and trap. He would park the trap in the side entrance by Myrtle Cottage and unhitch the pony, which would be led through the passageway between Lynhay and Kiddlywink to the stabling behind. His unfortunate brother Thomas, who had lived at Paradise Cottages, was known to have more than a liking for drink and died in the Camelford Workhouse, at Sportsmans.

James married Catherine Taylor on 7 November 1906. He was also a butcher living first at Bridge and then in High Street. During the First World War he used his livestock skills to buy horses for HM Government. He had been badly burned just before the outbreak of war when a methylated-spirit lamp had exploded in his face. James and Catherine had four children – Dennis, Violet, William James and Ivy. Violet married John Beasley, a petty officer in the Royal Navy, on 27 September 1921; and Ivy married

Harold Henry Seabrook and lived at Lundy View. Harold was a bank agent in Camelford. Dennis married Christine Treleaven. He continued to farm both Tredorne and Half Acre, as well as running the butchery business in Fore Street. Dennis would get meat from the ships and he delivered it on horseback at a time when steak could be bought at a shilling (5p) a pound. The shop was open from 9a.m. to 9p.m. At Christmas a bullock would be purchased from Wadebridge market and paraded around the village so that everyone could see their Christmas beef before slaughter.

Dennis inherited his father's love of horses and each year he would head the Boscastle Carnival mounted on his horse. The family had a horse called Peggy who was entered successfully in local point-to-point races and ridden by Kitchener Fry. Both Dennis and his son Bob were skilled pianists and played in the local pubs, and Dennis was an overseer of the poor, helping to administer the Cotton Trust. He also helped with the annual Strawberry Treat and Sunday school outings. Strawberry Treat and games took place in Valency Fields.

Dennis and Christine had six children – Christine, Gwendoline, Dennis Treleaven, Sylvia Blanch, Mary and Constance Patricia. Christine was known as Peggy and was Boscastle's first carnival queen in 1936, when she was 19 years old. Her sister Mary was crowned carnival queen by Mrs Bellamy in 1942. During the war Mary served in Falmouth as one of the first police women. She was WPC No. 6. Mary married William Smee, MSM, who became a major in the REME. Dennis Treleaven Cowling was known as Bob and he kept up the family tradition of being a butcher until his death in 1971.

Bob had been able to buy the butchery premises when the manor was sold together with the house, yards, shippen and outbuildings. By this time the slaughterhouse was no longer being used. The business continued for a few years after his death in the hands of both Michael Webber and John Adams but, like many local shops, was unable to survive as more and more homes became holiday lets. Michael Webber closed the butchery side of the business and in 1975 it was revived by John Adams, and continued until its final closure in the late 1980s.

The next house down the hill from the butcher's shop is Harwood Cottage. At one time, in around 1910, it was the home of schoolmistress Miss Adams. Later it was lived in by William Mugford and his wife Myrtle, who were there at the time of the manor sale. William was a gardener. Next door to the Mugfords was Top School.

At the beginning of Queen Victoria's reign Cornwall had 27 national and British day-schools and 120 dame-schools. Just over half of the county's children received some form of education. In 1840 fees were charged at between one and two pence a week, although this was often paid in kind. One penny was equal to three miners' candles, two rooty bakers or two eggs. Two pence equated to one pound of cream. Often bigger children taught the smaller children. In 1867 the Commission on Employment of Children, Young Persons and Women in Agriculture reported that children were taken into farm service from age ten and their hours of work were from 6.30a.m. until 8 or 9p.m.

In 1843 Revd Kirkness, rector of Forrabury and Minster, was instrumental in setting aside the land for Top School for the education of poor children in the parishes of Forrabury, Minster and Trevalga, in accordance with the principles of the established Church. The school was under the management of the Archdeacon of Cornwall, the rectors of Forrabury, Minster and Trevalga and Revd Richard Stephens, a clerk living in Culverhouse, Devon, and Thomas Rickard Avery, lord of the manor at Valency House. Together they were responsible for appointing the schoolmaster or mistress and for their dismissal if necessary. The land conveyed was described as about 12 perches and next to land belonging to Mr Rosevear's chapel.

Until the provision of this elementary school many people thought education of the poor was not only unnecessary but dangerous. One member of parliament had blamed the French revolution on books! By the 1830s this attitude was changing and some were becoming afraid, in the background of the industrial revolution, of letting education fall into dangerous hands. In order to enforce social discipline and instill a work ethic in working-class children the State took responsibility for education. At this time schooling competed with children's work time. Laws were introduced to shorten working hours and prohibit child labour. Trade unions campaigned for reform in the working conditions and schooling for all children.

Those parents who could afford it had previously sent their children to private or dame-schools. Boscastle had at least one such school at Tower House in Dunn Street. Its dame in 1840 was Mrs Burden. Boscastle had had a schoolmaster, Thomas Waring, and a schoolmistress, Rebecca Tink, at the beginning of the 1800s. At one time Tower House had a remnant of the dame-school in a louvred bell tower which was removed from its roof in the 1970s. In 1841 the census for Minster shows Boscastle as having schoolmasters called William Venning and Thomas Warren, and a schoolmistress called Jane Moyse. Ten years later Jane Bellamy was a schoolmistress and receiver at the Post Office where she lived, at 3 Jordan Row. Other Victorian schoolmistresses were Mary Bath, Mary Ann James, Sarah Keals and Catherine Trewyn.

Elementary schooling for most of the Victorian period lasted six hours a day. The morning session ran from 9a.m. to 12 noon, with two hours for lunch. This was necessary because many children had to walk back to their homes for lunch. Children from the outlying farms who could not walk home brought their lunch with them. The afternoon session ran from 2p.m. to 5p.m.

Twenty years after its opening in 1863 Boscastle School's managers were Revd Symons of Trevalga, R.B. Hellyar and Revd W. Kirkness, and the headmaster was John Adams of Harwood House. In 1864 his daughter Sarah was appointed as an assistant teacher. John Adams and his family came from Somerset. He and his wife Janet lived in Boscastle with their four children, Mary, Joanna, Samuel and Sarah, and when John retired in the late 1870s he continued to live here. In his time children were still helping at home and absences were recorded for blackberrying, potato picking and planting, and harvesting. Children also suffered numerous throat complaints and chills at such convenient times as Tintagel Revel, Boscastle Fair and Shrove Tuesday, and could be absent in the week before Christmas when many of the poorer children went around the village soliciting alms. It seems this church school suffered many absences in the year for Methodist celebrations and tea treats.

In 1870 the Education Act provided for the setting up of publicly elected school boards. Schools set up under this act were separate from the established Church and received rate aid, which meant they could be built to a scale and standard found difficult by the voluntary societies. Boscastle's National School was built in 1878 to the design of architect

Right: *Boscastle School staff in 1985.* Left to right, standing: *Joan Kinsman, Mary Nicholls, Linda Ferrett, Barbara Scott;* seated: *Marion Ferrett, Susan Sweeman, Doreen Jones (teacher), headmaster David Pinn.*

Below: *Boscastle School, 1894. Schoolmaster Mr Fenn has his hands on Bill Hockin's shoulders. George Olde has his hand on Tom Sharrock who is holding the chalk board.*

Sylvanus Trevail. He was born in 1851 and died in 1903. During his life he was designer, developer, Mayor of Truro, County Councillor and President of the Society of Architects. He was a leader in the field of tourism and his enterprises included the Atlantic Hotel at Newquay and the Free Library in Truro. As a child he had a bent for model construction and it was a natural progression for him to become apprenticed to an architect. Trevail took opportunity when it was presented to him and, after the 1870 Education Act, decreed that education should be available to every child, he became one of the first in the field of school architecture.

Top School became the Girls' School and later the Junior School. In 1891 the school suffered the tragic death of their headmaster James Pooley, who died at the age of 33. The schoolchildren headed the cortége. It was not unusual for children to take part in the funerals of the more important members of Victorian Boscastle. They were present at Mr Sloggatt's funeral and the funerals of the lords of the manor.

Some people in the village today can still remember being taught by 'Boss' Elford. Joseph Sibley Elford had taught at public school and came to Boscastle for his health. His wife came from Delabole. As headmaster at Boscastle he taught the full range of subjects including music. He was the chapel organist and played in other churches. Other teachers at this time included Mrs Geake, Mrs Olde and Miss Jane Lobb, who retired in August 1960 after 40 years as a teacher. Discipline was strict and enforced with the stick or strap which was said to be in constant use during the week.

The 1878 school building is still in use at the time of writing, along with Top School when necessary. The main school has a strong attendance and has been modernised to include a new library. As it still does in 2004, the school has taken part in village activities and been the provider of many entertainments including the annual Christmas Nativity play. The school put on shows in the public hall during the 1920s and '30s. It kept alive the tradition of folk-songs and dances, such as 'John Crook', 'All Through the Night', 'Long Ago', 'Come Back to Erin', 'Big Moon', 'The Twelve Days of Christmas', 'Dashing Away with the Smoothing Iron' and 'Who's That Tapping at the Garden Gate?' Dances included 'Three Meet', 'Peascods', 'Sellengers', 'Rufty Tufty', 'Jamaica' and 'Butterflies'. They were trained by ladies like Phyllis Lorraine, Miss Mary Ginner and Miss Armstrong. The local newspaper reported the dances in 1922 were:

> ... [of the] *Old Folk variety, which, after all, are more picturesque than some of the present day gambols, which might be taken for anything and make one wonder what the latest phase, the camel trot, resembles.*

The school playground surrounds the building and it was quite common for a stray football to land in the neighbouring gardens of the old 'fourteenth century cottages', called Smugglers and Tinkers. These two cottages stand within the outer boundary of the castle site and it has been presumed that they are some of the earliest surviving houses. A survey of the roof timbers undertaken by the Moore family dated them to the 1500s. They are an example of Boscastle's distinctive style of building, with slate roofs that use differing sizes of slate, lean-to porch roofs, massive stone chimney-stacks, some of which are located on lateral walls, and gabled dormers over small-pane windows. The plot originally contained three houses – Vulcan Cottage next to the school and called Tinkers in the early-twenty-first century, and two houses now converted into one and called Smugglers. Like Tinkers, Smugglers has a coffin drop in the upstairs passage. Boards can be removed to allow a coffin to be lowered instead of carried down the very narrow stairs. Upstairs the roof has supporting timbers which came from a ship. The lading of the vessel is carved into the timbers.

In the earlier twentieth century Vulcan Cottage was occupied by Mrs Warne and her son. They were tinkers or tinsmiths who mended pots and pans and generally worked in metal. An item which needed to be mended was often carried by children on their way to school and left outside the Warnes' house. After being repaired the pot or pan was collected after school by the child and carried home.

The lower of the two cottages was a grocery and sweetshop in Victorian times. The shop counter ran the full length of the corridor and the front shop window held an enticing selection of Mrs Sandercock's confectionery.

In about 1910 Mr Frank Hilton returned from Army service in India and called this cottage Zillebeke. Frank married Teresa Honey and their son William was a chauffeur and gardener who worked for Drs Davies and Chavasse at Tintagel. His wife Mary Ann came from Par, where she had been a maid and a nursemaid. Zillebeke was sold to Kate Garbutt when the manor was put up for sale and the name changed to Smugglers. She also bought the neighbouring cottage, Vulcan Cottage, and renamed it Tinkers. In the late 1950s Tinkers was bought from Mrs Garbutt by John and Joan Moore. They used it for family holidays when they visited with their daughters Ann, Jenny and Sue. The house also had a small caretaker's flat to the right of the front door so the house could be looked after and made ready for paying holidaymakers. John Moore joined the Royal Army Medical Corps as a stretcher-bearer at the age of 14. He saw service in Africa and Palestine during the Second World War and was involved in the Suez crisis in the 1950s and in Aden in the 1960s. He was still serving when he died as a colonel at the age of 62 in 1969. He had met his wife in West Africa. Joan Hunter Bates, as she was then, had been a nurse

William (Bill) Hilton.

Marjorie, Laura and Doris Walker outside Zillabeke, Fore Street.

Granny Hilton with her grandson William.

Colonel John Moore joined the Army as a stretcher-bearer at the age of 14.

Joan Moore and her daughters Ann, Jenny and Sue.

Thomas Pope Rosevear, 1781–1853.

before the war and joined Queen Alexandra's Royal Army Nursing Corps. On her way home from West Africa the ship she was travelling in was torpedoed. A convoy of 40 ships had left Freetown for Britain at the end of October 1942, dangerously under-escorted by only four corvettes spared from Operation Torch. They were attacked almost at once. Joan was on board SS *Stentor* (Alfred Holt and Blue Star Line). Their vessel was the first to be hit on the twelfth night out. A torpedo had found the cargo of manganese and there was a huge explosion. Prepared for all eventualities Joan, like the other passengers and crew, was carrying her panic bag and wearing her lifebelt. A consignment of palm oil in one of the holds was leaking into the ship and the sea. The ship was on fire and the fire was being fed by the spreading palm oil. When she reached her allotted lifeboat Joan found it had already been launched and so she jumped nearly 40 feet into the oil-covered water to be rescued by HMS *Woodruffe,* one of the accompanying corvettes. The SS *Stentor* sank within six minutes of being torpedoed and the survivors were put up in the captain's cabin of HMS *Woodruffe,* where they were packed in like sardines and Mrs Moore says they were treated to a four-course meal described by the steward as baked beans, baked beans, baked beans and baked beans.

On the opposite side of Fore Street just below Top School is the United Methodist chapel. The chapel was built in 1800 by Mr Thomas Rosevear as a votive offering to commemorate the escape of a vessel belonging to his firm of Rosevear and Sloggatt. The vessel, laden with a valuable cargo, was chased by a French privateer but eluded her pursuer by unexpectedly disappearing behind Meachard and into the hidden harbour of Boscastle. Mr Rosevear gave the chapel as a free gift to the Wesleyan connexion, of

Right: *Methodist church organist Marion Ferrett, 1993.*

Below: *The Methodist church, Fore Street, 1995.*

The Methodist schoolroom kitchen in 1993. The ladies of the chapel are famous for their delicious home-made teas. Pictured are: *Iris Olde, Edna Edwards, Barbara Kenyon.*

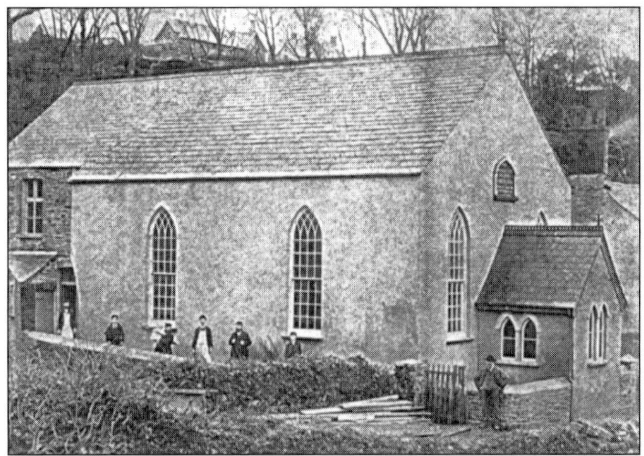

Boscastle Wesleyan Chapel, 1897. This chapel was sometimes known as 'Mr Brown's Chapel' or 'Jabez Brown's Chapel'.

which he was a member. It was opened on 12 April 1801 by John Kingston. In 1823 Thomas Pope Rosevear, son of Thomas Rosevear, pulled down the original building which was too small and rebuilt a new larger one on the same site. This became the United Methodist Reform chapel, capable of holding 400 people. Those who sat in the new pews were expected to pay seat rent of 15d., and this was not to the satisfaction of many. William Gard began to collect the seat rent for 1 January to 31 March 1825 on 29 January that year, and reported to Mr Rosevear that people appeared to be dissatisfied at having to pay. The following day Rosevear noted in his diary that people had annoyed him so much about the pews in the chapel that he had spoken to them after service and in short had told them it was 'now in their power to please themselves.'

Thomas Pope Rosevear was no stranger to controversy. He was a reader of John Stephens' Nonconformist newspaper *The Christian Advocate*, and he adopted, more and more, its radical views. At a Camelford circuit meeting he put forward a set of resolutions incorporating some of these radical ideas. Aquila Barber, the circuit superintendent, ruled them out of order and dissolved the meeting. Rosevear, however, had support, and the meeting continued, illegally, under another chairman. Barber then acted too quickly and undiplomatically by expelling Rosevear who wrote to him:

I have just received your canting, impertinent note of yesterdays date... Put one of your injurious fingers through the loop-hole of your priestly castle, ON MY REPUTATION, a man of long established civil, commercial and moral character, and I will, without further notice, open the Kings Bench battery on you.

Popular support was given to Rosevear who was well known as a local preacher, as well as being trustee of many local chapels. The reform movement gathered pace and Aquila Barber found himself locked out of many of his chapels.

The new Providence chapel was officially opened by Mr Beal of Devonport on Tuesday 1 February 1825 and dedicated to the Redeemer. In 1893 the old pulpit in the chapel was replaced by a 'very neat and convenient rostrum'. The large pew for the choir was put up in one side of the chapel, together with two additional seats for the congregation. The candles were replaced by two 'splendid' chandeliers lit by three lamps in each. The whole cost of the renovation was £23, which was raised by the anniversary and Whitsuntide bazaar. The chapel was going through somewhat of a revival at the time.

A few years later, in 1904, further thorough renovations were carried out involving the renewal of the ceiling which had fallen in and refurbishments to the organ. The total cost this time was between £500–600. Following the work the reopening was carried out by Mr J. Smith.

Supporters of this chapel included William Davey and his parents, William B. Gard, carpenter William Burnard, saddler William Burnard, the Smith family, the Callaways, Dora Mably, the Forces, the Boneys, John P. Sharrock, Jack Symons and Bert Davey from Welltown, J. Sandercock from Polrunny and Frank Garland from Tubbs Ground. Mrs Liz Burnard took the Band of Hope evening meetings. The Band of Hope Festival in June was a big village occasion with a parade from chapel through the village. It was headed by the Town Band. The children took part in a programme of sports and afterwards had their own tea treat, which was followed later in the day by a public tea. Jack Symons and William 'Saddler' Burnard took the boys' Sunday school and later Dr Hillier took the boys in his Bible class and in the Boys' Brigade.

Sunday school anniversaries were held in May when the services were especially addressed to the children. Most of the girls and boys gave recitations at the Sunday school which were repeated on

Dr Hillier with Mr and Mrs Daniel Ferrett.

Monday evening when the scholars received a free tea. Sunday school outings went as far afield as Perranporth, Newquay, Looe, Polperro and St Ives. Often these trips were the only time the children travelled out of the village. Regular attendance at Sunday school was rewarded with a small gift, usually a book. William 'Saddler' Burnard took prayer meetings outside the chapel, in particular at the Wellington Hotel.

This chapel had co-existed with several others in the local area, all of which flourished during Victoria's reign. To the east of Boscastle at Treworld there was a small chapel which was opened on 25 October 1838 and attended by families from outlying farms such as Tregatherall, Copplestone and Tregrylls. At the beginning of the twentieth century Revd A. Unwin was the preacher and Miss Mildred Stephens the organist. Mildred Stephens lived at Tregrylls and later married Tom Sleeman. The chapel closed just after the First World War and passed into the hands of John Boney after his father's death in 1918. After its closure the chapel's datestone was removed to Boscastle's United Methodist chapel.

In the village, as well as the United Methodist Reform chapel (Providence) in Fore Street and the Bible Christian chapel (Siloam) in Mount Pleasant there was the Wesleyan chapel (Ebenezer) in Dunn Street. This chapel was managed by trustees, Samuel Wills, Ralph Wade and merchant Jabez Brown, and is often referred to as 'Jabez Brown's chapel'. It opened in 1837 and could seat 250 people. The popular image of a Methodist as a non-drinker and non-gambler is of fairly recent origin. Neither drinking nor smoking were forbidden by society rules but gambling was regarded as morally wrong. Jabez Brown, however, did not regard lotteries as wrong. He put 50s. on the Frankfurt Lottery in 1853 on the premise that if he won a large prize he would be able to help many good causes. Even into the 1920s village Methodists frowned upon any form of betting, and when the Sports Committee admitted bookmakers to an event letters of protest were received from both Weslyan and United Methodists.

In the middle of the 1800s Jabez Brown was expressing his disappointment at attendance levels and wrote 'O that the spirit of the Lord would draw more near to hear his word.'

This chapel, like the United Methodist one in Fore Street, had its celebrations and annual events. The annual Strawberry Treat took place in Valency Valley. The valley farmers grew large amounts of strawberries and the crops were sent to London by train. Even in the 1960s Mrs Piper at the Harbour Café would send her daughter Norma through the valley to collect fruit for the café. The Wesleyan Sunday schoolchildren were at the whim of the weather for their Strawberry Treat tea and it was not unknown for the treat to be delayed so long that the strawberry crop was over and they had a cherry and banana treat instead!

Harvest Festivals in October were followed by a tea, a Dutch auction of the fruit, vegetables and flowers and a coffee evening. Jabez Brown helped to fund major refurbishments in the 1890s when a porch was added to the front of the chapel. It was re-opened on 1 January 1897, fitted with pitch-pine seats, tables, chairs and new lamps. All these were sold at auction on 27 April 1933 after the closure of the chapel. The sale also included a small pipe-organ which had been played by Ernest 'Twitters' Couch. The organ went to Launcells Parish Church. This chapel, like the others, was well supported by families such as the Wards, Tippetts, Oldes, Pethericks, Ferretts and Couchs. Daniel Ward was one of the preachers together with Richard Couch, Daniel Ferrett and his son Reg.

Boscastle's oldest known Methodist chapel was at Jordan House on the opposite side of Dunn Street. An application was made on 1 July 1793 for a large room in the house to be registered for worship, as was required by Act of Parliament. It was signed by David Parsons, Samuel May, Thomas Pearse and Richard Mabyn, who described themselves as Protestant Dissenters from the Church of England. Registration was granted on 27 July that same year. Jordan House was described as part of the Jordan estate in the parish of Minster.

It was inevitable that, with falling attendances after the First World War, some chapels would face closure. In addition to Boscastle's three chapels and the one at Treworld the area was served by two others, one at the far end of Minster parish at Melorne which opened in 1901, and a Bible Christian chapel in the neighbouring parish of Trevalga which was built on the site of some 'poor' houses with gardens on the opposite side of the road. It opened on 25 July 1872 and was known as Providence Chapel.

Until 1837 marriages were only possible in the established churches but they became possible in Methodist chapels and in registry offices after 1 March 1837. Many Methodists still continued to go

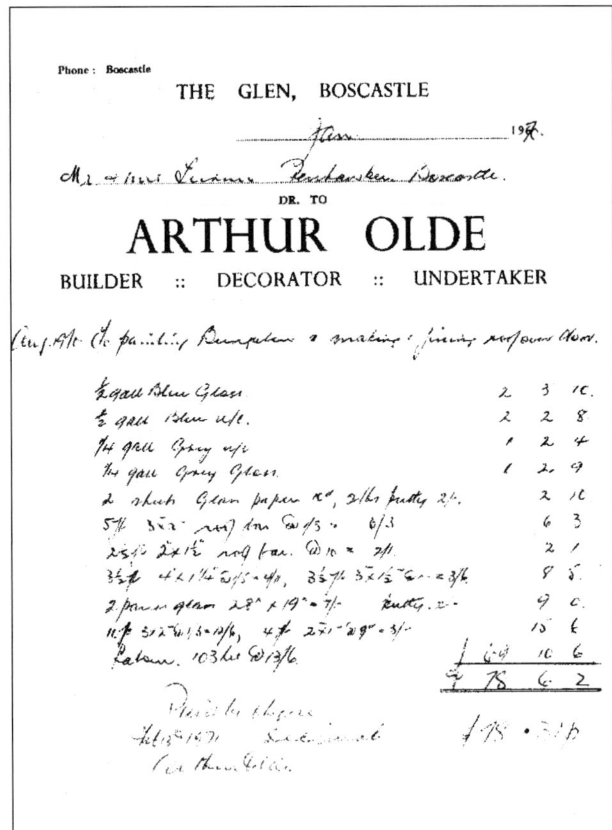

Phone : Boscastle

THE GLEN, BOSCASTLE

DR. TO

ARTHUR OLDE

BUILDER :: DECORATOR :: UNDERTAKER

½ gall Blue Gloss	2	3	10
½ gall Blue u/c.	2	2	8
¼ gall Grey u/c	1	2	4
¼ gall Grey Gloss	1	2	9
2 sheets Glass paper		2	10
		6	3
		2	1
		8	5
		9	0
		15	6
Labour	69	10	6
	78	6	2

A billhead from Arthur Olde.

Iris Hockin in WAAF uniform in 1946.

to the parish church, as had been the custom, but according to the Weslyan Methodist Association Forum there was an early wedding at the registry office in Boscastle in December 1837.

Next to Fore Street chapel is a cottage lived in for many years by Arthur Olde and his family. This building is similar in style and structure to many of the early houses in High Street and Fore Street. It was once part of a terrace of such houses which ran to Elm Cottage beside the castle site. There was a raised roadway running in front of them above the current lie of Fore Street. The Glen, as it is known in 2004, has been extended at the rear and its garden runs down to the River Butts in the form of a long, thin burgage plot, set out originally to maximise the frontal area for rental purposes.

The late Arthur Olde was one of Boscastle's best-known and much-loved residents. He was born in the village in 1921 and lived there all his life, except for his national service during the Second World War when he served in both the Royal Air Force and the Army. Arthur was a carpenter and served his apprenticeship in Tintagel. After the war he worked for Fred Pearn before setting up his own business, which included undertaking. Fred Pearn was the carpenter to the manor at that time. Arthur married local girl Iris, the daughter of Bill and May Hockin, in 1947 in the chapel next door to the house that was to be their family home for their whole married life. Arthur's brother Leonard was best man and his other brother was an usher, as was Brian Honey. The bridesmaids were Faith Duke and Julie Olde and the pageboy Rodney Knight. The marriage brought local family names together. The wedding reception was held at Bottreaux House. Arthur and Iris had grown up together – they went to the same school and attended chapel and both sang in the choir, and both went off to war. After leaving school Iris worked in a grocery shop in Bossiney, owned by Mrs Harold Rush, and she would cycle to work every day. Arthur worked for Howard Irons in Tintagel, where he served his carpentry apprenticeship. Arthur and Iris had two daughters, Bridget and Deborah.

It was very clear that Arthur loved Boscastle and he played football, supported the British Legion throughout his life, served with the Coastguard, and was a member of the Men's Club, the Parish Council and the chapel, where he was a steward. He used his carpentry skills to help maintain the chapel, giving many hours of his time. He played a large part in the rebuilding of the chapel's Sunday schoolroom. His work as both carpenter and undertaker took him into most houses in the village and he was always willing to talk and help people in a way which is not so common in the early-twenty-first century.

Working with Arthur was Ken Edwards from High Street. Arthur had made a handcart for them to carry around their tools, and they were a familiar sight around Boscastle pulling the cart loaded with tools, ladders, paint and wood.

Arthur's wife Iris served in the WAAF during the Second World War. Like many of the young people in the village she thought about fighting for the defence of her country, and she and her schoolfriend June Jose joined the Womens Auxiliary Air Force at the Camelford recruiting office. Their induction was at Torpoint in 1943 and together they trained as carpenters. Like Arthur, Iris has a great love of the village and listening to her talk about what has gone on in Boscastle during her lifetime has provided much of the details of the twentieth century contained in this book. She has been responsible for providing a great many of the photographs and for identifying names and faces associated with them.

The buildings between The Glen where Iris and Arthur have lived and Elm Cottage are newer. Immediately next door is Chy-men (Stone House), previously called Sunnyside, which was, like so many other homes in High Street and Fore Street, a shop. At one time in the early 1900s it was the drapery of Sybella Ward and later the premises of Mr White, watchmaker. Mr White was a sub-tenant of the Wards until the manor was sold and he purchased the property. The premises were also used in his time, in the 1960s, as a sub-branch of the National Provincial Bank.

Whilst Sybella Ward was in the house in December 1923 she had an accident involving her oil stove, which she had lit at about 7.30 in the morning in order to make herself a cup of tea. For some reason the stove exploded and ignited both the bed and the bedroom floor. In trying to put out the flames she received serious burns. Fortunately she was helped by Charlie Joyce of Elm Cottage and a Mr Jenkyn, who got her out of the room at great risk to their own lives.

The steps outside the gates are the remnants of granite cider-presses. Next door, Tremorvah is one of the later additions to Fore Street. It was built by the manor in the twentieth century and was previously known as Glenroy. The first tenants in the house were the Scott family. In 1947 it was described as a modern house known as Tremorvah in the tenancy of Miss E.G. Price. It then had six bedrooms, bathroom and toilet, two reception rooms, kitchen, scullery and a further toilet.

When Mary Smee came back to the village with her husband William in 1958 they took over Tremorvah, which Mary ran as a guest-house. They remained there until William's death 14 years later,

Mr Leonard White, watchmaker, outside his shop in Fore Street.

Remembrance Day parade at the war memorial. Postman Warren is holding the flag.

Freddie Sandercock, DCLI, at Corfe Castle Camp, Swanage, 1939.

William Honey.

Jack Beasley RN.

Daniel Hockin.

Stretcher-bearer Charlie Ferrett died in France of wounds received on the Western Front in September 1918.

Sidney Ferrett who later became a railway fireman.

Jim Ferrett and Douglas Olde at Newhaven, Sussex, in July 1940.

after which Mary moved to Norwood House in Dunn Street, previously the home of Captain Sydney Scott of the Army Education Corps. A small cottage and a modern house stand beside Tremorvah, the last house in the row being Elm Cottage where the Bartlett family lived before emigrating to America. All these houses have gardens running down to the River Butts in the form of burgage plots. Elm Cottage, now a holiday let, was previously the home of Noel Joyce and before that his mother and father Charles. Noel moved there after closing his greengrocery business in Paradise when his mother and father died.

The River Butts is known as Butts Water locally, or anciently as a 'small Butts Brook'. Ordnance Survey have caused some confusion in recent years by transposing the names of the Rivers Butts and Jordan on their maps. The River Jordan flows northwards from its source to the west of Polrunny through Paradise and Jordan Marshes and forms the boundary between the parishes of Forrabury and Minster. The Butts flows from its source to the east of Polrunny, through New Bridge plantation past Treforda Water, on to what is now called Trebutts and the site of the Norman castle butts (a butt was an early shooting range or a mound behind a target). The two rivers are more streams than rivers and connect below the castle site. The united streams run under the Wellington Hotel, leading to the saying that a guest could dine in Minster and sleep in Forrabury. The streams then join the River Valency to flow into the harbour.

Where Fore Street curves around the castle site to join Dunn Street, near the point where the two streams join, is the village war memorial. It was built after the First World War by the Gard family and completed in 1920. In order to bring the site to street level and to get footings for the memorial the masons had to dig deeply and in doing so found several large pieces of dressed granite from the Norman Castle. Some of these pieces have been incorporated in the step up to the site. The original memorial held the names of men who died in the First World War. They were: Privates R. Allen, J. Brown, J.W. Fuge, C. Ferrett and H. Sandercock, all of the Duke of Cornwall's Light Infantry; Trooper R.S. Bowering 8th ALH, Tpr H. Hoskin 8th ALH, Cpl E. Gard CEF, Pte J.S.Olde CEF, Lt Cdr J.I. Harrison RN Maj RAF, Lt F.I. Harrison Royal West Kent Regt, Rfm W.J.Honey 21st LR, PO2 F. Lamerton RN, CM L. Pearn RN, and Pte C.J. Prout 2nd MR. Of a total male population of 336, 133 served in the First World War, and all their names have also been included.

The Second World War also took its toll and Boscastle lost nine men: Boy 1st Class G.R. Alford RN, Flt Sgt S.R. Allen RAF, L. Sgt J.H. Bennett Recce Regt, J.H. Haslar RN, 1st Off J. Kenworthy MN, Bosun J. Masson MN, PO W.J. Olde RAF, FO J.F. Stock RAF and CPO J.C. Wivell RN.

Walter Knight, Grenadier Guardsman, with his wife Lilian and son Claude at Basingstoke in 1914.

The war memorial dressed for Remembrance Day.

Bill Ferrett RN in 1920.

One woman from the village, Jean Metherall, lost her life serving with the Womens Auxiliary Air Force. The village itself saw little enemy action during the Second World War, although precautions had to be taken which included black-out curtains and the organisation of the Home Guard. The harbour was subjected to closure, with a metal boom fixed to the inner pier to prevent enemy landing-craft entering the harbour. The two slipways were secured with pyramid-shaped, concrete tank traps. Slit trenches were cut into the cliffs to enable defenders to fire on approaching boats as they entered the harbour.

After the frequent bombing raids on industrial South Wales and Bristol the German bombers would occasionally discharge unused bombs into the sea. Two such bombs went into Hennett Marsh and sank without exploding. Another bomb exploded near the flagstaff at Penally Head, creating a large hole. Several pieces of shrapnel are still kept as souveniers in the village in 2004. As we have seen, a sea mine exploded in the mouth of the harbour, damaging the outer pier. The Coastguard were armed with rifles and patrolled the coastline.

Local people were lucky to have skills which helped them supplement their larders. Most men had shotguns and local farmers gave them permission to shoot rabbits, which were strung in pairs by the feet and loaded on to lorries to be sent to market by train. The 4p.m. up train from Padstow, which called at all stations including Camelford and Otterham, was known as the 'bunny special'. Small birds were also shot – rooks, starlings and plover were put into pies. There was one occasion when seals were shot, the meat eaten and the blubber rendered down to provide fat for frying. Large eels were taken from the rivers using rabbits' intestines tied on a string. A net was put across the harbour and a barrelful of assorted fish caught. The airmen at RAF Davidstow Moor provided game for the Wellington Hotel which they shot on the moor.

There were young women and schoolchildren evacuated to the village, including the young David Whitaker, and many people had their first experience of American soldiers in jeeps, one of which tried to drive up to Queen's Head. A small black market existed in such things as blankets and orange juice. A fund-raising convoy visited the village with a torpedo on a trailer. There was a gun turret from a bomber fixed on a trailer which could be operated by the schoolchildren, who were able to shoot their teacher.

Italian prisoners of war worked on local farms. They wore grey boiler suits with yellow patches on one leg and on the back. Rationing made life hard, especially for the children who had no Christmas presents or sweets. They helped the war effort by collecting tins, bottles and rags and taking them to stores in the old cottages in Paradise Row or the old blacksmith's shop near the limekiln. This smithy had closed before the war, leaving only the one near the Napoleon Inn operating.

Remembrance Sunday church parades and wreath laying started at the top of High Street at 10 or 10.30a.m. They were attended by members of the Boscastle branch of the British Legion, the ex-servicemen and the Town Band. The parade would march to either Forrabury or Minster Church and then on to the war memorial. This parade continued from the opening of the war memorial until the mid-1990s, although for some years without the band. Members of HM Coastguard were attached to the British Legion and took part in the parade, as well as being responsible, on occasion, for dressing the war memorial. After the First World War the chairman of the Boscastle branch of the British Legion was Mr Juswant Rikh and the president was Mr Mullington. At this time the British Legion used to give local children a Christmas Treat in the Public Hall. The children from the council school would be given a free tea, crackers and a Christmas present from Father Christmas, who would arrive complete with sleigh. Mary Smee remembers the huge Christmas tree, illuminated by lots of coloured candles, which was provided through the generosity of Juswant Rikh. The children's tea would be followed by an evening dance for the adults.

Located in the war memorial garden at the time of writing is a stone vessel that was once in Potters Lane, before the road was widened, where it was being used as a water trough. It is very similar to a stone corn measure in the Market House at Bodmin, with the same type of opening and lip at the bottom. It is between 21 and 22 inches in diameter and 12 inches deep, with the capacity to hold 16 gallons or two Winchester bushels, which was the local measure of capacity for corn, fruit and so on. It has been said that it was used as a measure in the castle but it is more likely that it came from Boscastle's own Market House, like the one in Bodmin, where it formed the standard measure.

Across the road from the war memorial is the new Boscastle Community Centre, opened in 2001 under chairman Malcolm Biddick. This replaced the older building of the Boscastle Men's Club. The Men's Club, or Men's Institute as it was known in its early days, started in what is called Kiddlywink in 2004, and the Lynhay part of the building previously used as the Boscastle Inn. Mr Juswant Rikh was instrumental in going to see James Cowling of Tredorn Farm who was the occupier of the whole property which he rented from the manor. Juswant Rikh stood guarantor for the rent required of 10s. a year. A billiard table was put into the room of Lynhay nearest the road, where it projects out into the street.

Having established support for the club, funds were raised to erect a dedicated building on the site in Dunn Street. In the usual way, money was raised through whist drives, village sales and concerts.

The Men's Club Hut was built in the early 1920s and is illustrated here by A.J. Hinksman in 1924.

THE PUBLIC HALL,
BOSCASTLE.

PROGRAMME

OF GRAND

Entertainment

In aid of

The Boscastle Men's Club,

Feb. 14th, 1924.

PRICE 2d.

Accompanists :

Mrs. H. BOWERING, Miss N. MITCHELL,
Mr. E. W. COUCH.

WAKEFIELD, PRINTER, CAMELFORD.

Entertainment programme for St Valentine's Day, 1924, to raise money for the Boscastle Men's Club. It included an item of a topical Egyptian theme entitled 'Toot and come in'.

Officers were elected to oversee the running of the club and in its early days included George Bellamy, the lord of the manor, and Juswant Rikh, who were president and chairman respectively. Richard Webber was vice-chairman and committee members included J.C. Warren, W. Metherall, J. Allen, F. Hilton, A. Ferrett, W. Honey, W. Ferrett senr, C. Ferrett, F. Pearn, F. Warren, Frank Pearn, R. Tippet and secretary Mr G. Olde. At this time the village also had the Mission Rooms in Gunpool Lane and the public hall at Bridge, as well as the Methodist schoolroom.

Next to the site of the Men's Club was the Wesleyan chapel until its closure in 1933. It was to become the village Post Office, as it still is in 2004. The original Post Office was at Jordan Terrace, where, just after 1900, the telegraph and telephone exchange was installed. Mrs Molly Nicholls was postmistress there, having taken over with her husband Albert from his parents Victor and Annie Nicholls. The very first General Post Office deliveries and collections to and from Boscastle were through Camelford sorting office. This is shown clearly on the only known letter sent from Boscastle by T.R. Avery in 1840, which was franked at Camelford. As mail became more common and heavier a local sub-office was opened to sort, deliver and collect the mails. With the popularity of the telephone a local exchange was needed. By the 1950s the telephone system had outgrown the old building. Automation was replacing the more personal manual exchanges. A new fully automatic exchange was built and installed below Bottreaux Garage, where it still operates at the time of writing. The Post Office moved from Jordan Terrace to the old Wesleyan chapel building under the jurisdiction of postmaster Bob Symons.

Dunn Street gets its name from its proximity to the castle – dyn, dun, dinas being Celtic for a hill-fort or castle, a word that certainly goes back to pre-Norman times, to that of the native Celtic population. As well as having a Wesleyan chapel at its southern end and Jordan House Meeting Room, Dunn Street had at least two public houses – the Commercial Inn on the western side and the Dolphin on the eastern. Almost opposite the Dolphin was the Victorian police house and village lock-up. Like High Street and Fore Street, Dunn Street had its share of shops. The Keal family had a butchery business in the premises that also became the Dolphin Inn. Just below that was Symons' grocery store. The Symons were part of the same family that had the fruiterers in High Street in the late 1800s and in Fore Street at the beginning of the 1900s. Symons' grocery store moved to bigger premises at Tower House and they then sold the business to the Co-operative Society, much to the consternation of other shopkeepers in the village who feared the Co-op would put them out of business.

In the late 1700s and early 1800s Dunn Street was also the home of the Ruse family, one of whom came to be greatly honoured in Australia. Transportation in the eighteenth century was a serious sentence and was often handed out for quite trivial offences. Such was the lot of James Ruse, who was born in Boscastle in 1760 and whose brother Digory Ruse is buried in Minster churchyard. Digory was the father-in-law of Captain John Ballamy after whom the Ballamy Islands are named and who shares the family grave at Minster with his wife Sarah, Captain John and his wife Ann, who was Digory's daughter, and their unmarried daughter Sarah.

James Ruse, however, never returned to England. He was sentenced to transportation for sheep stealing at Bodmin Assizes in July 1782. He arrived at Sydney Cove with the first fleet of convicts to sail to Australia in 1789. He was granted land, tools, seed and stock to enable him to start life as a farmer. This would not be easy. It was the general opinion that a man could not live off the poor soil around Sydney. James, however, used the knowledge he had gained in his early years as a farmer at Boscastle. He burnt the trees and scrub covering his land, dug in the ash, and allowed the clods to weather. He dug in the weeds and grass and left the elements to work on the soil before digging it again and sowing his crop. This method was so successful that by 1791 he was able to give up government-aided stores and become self-sufficient. As a reward for his industry, Governor Phillips gave him a further 30 acres of land. James had married Elizabeth Percy who had arrived on HMS *Neptune*. By July 1792 James was maintaining his wife and their first child. By 1810 he had 100 acres in the Bankstown area near Sydney. He died in 1837 and is buried at St John's, Campbelltown. Children in Australia are taught that Australia's first farmer was James Ruse of Boscastle.

Another James, this time James Pickard, was born in 1830 in Clovelly. He and his wife Ann were living in Penally Terrace in 1871 with their children James aged seven, Susanna aged six, Ruth aged five and Richard aged six months. James was working as an agricultural labourer. Ten years later his son James had become a shoemaker and his daughter Ruth, at 16 years old, was a pupil teacher. When Richard left school he became a tailor. He married his wife Elizabeth and they lived together at High Water beside the quay.

James junr had married his wife Eliza Warren and they lived in Old Road at Frogapits with their children James P., Alice and Charles. James P. married Edith Annie and he, like his father, was a bootmaker. They lived at Wren Cottage in Fore Street at the very beginning of the 1900s. He had a large black shed outside where he carried on his business.

After collecting them on his motorbike from Camelford Station Luxon Pickard sold newspapers at his shop in Dunn Street. He later moved to Tower House which had been a sweetshop where the Misses Murley made sweets and where he also sold fish and chips. In his later years he lived at Jordan House, previously the home of Granny Keals. Luxon had worked at the Falcon Hotel in Bude and whilst there was offered a job by Juswant Rikh, who was living at Penagar at the time. He accompanied Mr Rikh on shooting expeditions, went rabbiting on the cliffs and acted as Mr Rikh's gilly. Luxon could also turn his hand to shoemaking and took over the Symons' premises after they moved to Tower House.

Opposite Luxon Pickard's paper shop are Clifton House, Claremont, The Nook and Norwood House, which, together with Pillar House, were the homes of members of the Olde family.

Mark Olde was the son of Mr J. Olde of Prestacott Farm, Launcells. He came to Boscastle in 1865 and was a saddler by trade. He married Miss Moyse, the daughter of an accountant, and they had nine children. They had their saddlery business at the Green Shop on the bank opposite their home at Pillar House. The original Green Shop was built in the late 1860s before New Road was built. Mark Olde made his products on the premises and sold them from there. He was also the mail carrier, taking the mail and occasional passengers to Camelford. The Green Shop was demolished to make way for Cory's Cott. Mark Olde suffered a tragic death in 1906 at the age of 52 years. He was driving a waggonette with two lady passengers to Camelford and when they got to Tredorn he complained of stomach pains. By the time they had travelled a few hundred yards to Highgate he had become so ill that he fell from the driving seat onto the road. He suffered severe head injuries and when Dr Wade arrived he was already dead.

His son John took over the saddlery business and later his daughter Marie turned it into a haberdashery, selling wool, knitting patterns and equipment. She also sold china, cigarettes and postcards, and from the lower part of the building, which fronted Old Road, she sold paraffin, which

Olde's saddlery, New Road. Pictured are: *Mark Olde and family.*

A Richard Webber portrait of Granny Keals, taken on the lawn of Jordan House in 1905.

Luxon Pickard's paper shop, Dunn Street, 1935.

Symons' shop in Dunn Street was said to sell everything the other shops didn't.

Luxon Pickard and his daughter Monica outside the Harbour Café in the 1960s.

Gran Pickard with Freddie and Jim.

Emily and Luxon Pickard entertain a young listener at the gate of Jordan House.

The oxen pulling the van in this picture were used to advertise Hugo's suet.

Monica Olde at the wheel of the family car.

was stored in a large tank just inside her door. In the 1930s the building was extended with the help of a cricket hut which was bought ready made from Plymouth. Marie used the extra space to add a lending library and during the Second World War lent books to the personnel at the airfield at RAF Davidstow Moor. Marie was also the person who delivered the local rate demands and people could make payments at the Green Shop. She carried on the business until the early 1960s. The shop remained empty for several years and then went through various changes of use as an antiques and bric-a-brac shop, bread and cake shop, craft shop, fish shop and finally an electrical retailers and store for David Scott.

Mark's son George was in South Africa, where he had been for three years, at the time of his father's death. He returned home to help his mother in carrying out the posting business. George later moved to The Nook.

John Moyse Olde lived at Clifton House. He bought Home Farm when the manor was sold in the 1950s. John was a dairyman and married Tryphena, and in November 1911 their son Mark was born. Mark lived at Claremont and was a newsagent, and he is remembered by all who went to Sir James Smith's School in Camelford in the 1950s, as they travelled in his school bus.

William Symons Moyse Olde, another son of saddler Mark Olde and his wife Violet (née Fisher), lived at Norwood House beside The Nook. William was a merchant's manager and buyer. Their son William James was born in 1917. By the time the manor was sold there were members of the family living at Claremont, The Nook, Belmont in New Road and the Glen in Fore Street.

Opposite Mark Olde senr's Green Shop on the western side of New Road at the foot of Forrabury Hill is Melbourne House. Originally called Melbourne Villa it was built in the 1850s by merchant Francis Dingle. He dealt in coal, iron, timber and spirits. The Dingle family came to Boscastle from Australia. Francis and his wife Georgina had two children. The eldest, Francis junr, was born in Melbourne, Australia. They had two live-in servants – Thomas Parsons who was apprenticed to Mr Dingle and housemaid Mary Chubb. By the 1870s Melbourne House was the home of Ralph Wade and his wife Ann. At the same time, living at Orchard House in Gunpool Lane, was Dr Arthur Wade who was in partnership with John Henry Tuke, surgeon of Barn Park. He was mentioned in the *Devon and Cornwall Directory* of 1871. The chemist and druggist at this time was Francis Hurdon. Arthur Wade was born in Tintagel and was a member of the Royal College of Surgeons. He married Boscastle girl Helen and they had four children – Arthur, Stephen, Helen and Charles. Charles succeeded his father in practice as the local doctor. He was known as 'doctor', whereas his father had been known as 'surgeon'. Other village doctors who succeeded the Wades were Doctors Chevasse and Fairchild, Dr Davis, Dr Lucas

Hillier of Tolcarne House and Doctors Watson, Weir and Young.

The Wades at Melbourne House had land running up Forrabury Hill to the corner of Potters Lane where they had a coach-house and staff quarters. Built privately, the house was never part of the manor. By the 1920s the house was lived in by Arthur Harris and his family. Arthur died in 1902. Mrs Susie Harris was Ralph Wade's sister. She had married Arthur Venning Harris in 1908/9. She took an active role in the village, donating the use of the house for village activities. She was a school governor and regarded as a lady in very much the old-fashioned sense of the word. In the 1950s Melbourne House became Melbourne Hotel and it was run by the Marchant family. Since then the house has had several owners, including Wombwell, Burnett, Higgs and the owners at the time of writing, Robert and Teresa Lloyd, who, like the original owners, are local business people. Over a period of years the land and stables have been sold and developed to provide new housing.

Elizabeth Ann Gard.

Opposite Melbourne Stables on the western corner of Potters Lane and Forrabury Hill is Sunnyside Corner, home of the Gard family. The Gards like the Hockins, the Honeys and the Symons are a family who have lived for generations in the village. An inventory of the goods and chattels of John Gard of Minster taken on 30 January 1638 shows him to have been a man of substance. In addition to his household items his workshop contained the timber and tools of a joiner and his house had the addition of a porch and porch chamber, and a chamber over the hall. Through village records Gards have been recorded as glaziers, master masons, builders, stone masons and plasterers. Another branch of the family went into cooperage and were maltsters, shopkeepers and innkeepers. The family name is continuous in the parish records, which include the marriage of Richard Garde and Agatha Hawkins in 1632; Nicholas Gard and Christine Panter in 1789 (the Panters were involved in the brewery and inn-keeping trade); James Gard and Anne Turner in 1784 and so on. There is a tombstone attached to the church wall in Forrabury churchyard commemorating Elizabeth, wife of Walter Guard who was buried on 18 October 1697, and the family business papers state the business was founded in 1640.

There is a William Gard and a Touchwicke Garde, churchwarden, in the protestation returns for Minster in 1642, and parish records show that a Walter Gard was commissioned to demolish the remaining walls of Minster priory in the same year. The original family name was LeGarde and it has been established that the Gard family building business goes back to the mid-seventeenth century.

William Bastard Gard, named after Abraham Bastard, a Cornish wrestler from St Teath.

The same Christian names make regular appearances throughout the generations, particulary William and Walter and more recently Philip. Walter

William and May Gard.

Eunice, Phyllis and Pamela Gard with their aunt Ethel in glasses.

Gard, a builder, was born in Boscastle in 1797. We have already seen that the early supporters of the Bible Christian movement were often Cornish wrestlers. Walter's son William Gard was born in 1820 and married Elizabeth, the daughter of one such wrestler, Abraham Bastard of St Teath, at the St Teath Bible Christian chapel on 31 July 1851. Their son Walter Bastard Gard was born in 1856 and they lived in their farmhouse at Sunny Corner. William was a mason and builder as well as a farmer, and he had a dairy business supplying milk around the village. William Bastard Gard died in 1944 and his sons William Philip and Walter took over the family business after the war. William Philip's son Walter was indentured into the business in 1954. William Philip and his wife May lived at the coachman's house of Melbourne House. They had five children, Walter, Phyllis, Mary, Eunice and Pamela. Walter spent 40 years in the business until his retirement in 1993. He has always been an active member of the village, playing in the band since it was re-formed in 1947 and going on to play with St Gennys' band. He has been a parish councillor for many years and a member of the LSA and Coastguard. His sisters Eunice, Mary and Phyllis also live in the village in 2004 and Pamela, who married Michael Ward the son of Ward's store owners, lives in Portugal.

Returning to Dunn Street where Slip Road joins Old Road and New Road, and as the street starts to run downhill towards the Wellington Hotel and Bridge, we find what was once known as Post Office Lane or Oxen Road. On the right-hand side we find a terrace of three houses just before Jordan Terrace. The first of the three cottages was Ivy Cottage, where Mrs Mugford took in visitors in the 1930s and in the 1950s and '60s Barclays Bank had a sub-branch. Next was Glen View and finally Trevalver. Trevalver was the home of the Ferrett family.

The Ferretts came to Boscastle from Egloskerry. Henry Ferrett and his wife Mary, née Cowling, had five children – Jane, Henry, Richard, Mary and William. Richard, who was born in 1789, married Jane Olver. They had two children, Mary Ann (1839) who married John Spettigue and Henry (1835) who married Rachel Frayne on 5 April 1866. In his lifetime Henry worked as a labourer and wagoner, and had a grocery store at Treneglos. It was Henry and Rachel who came to Boscastle. They had nine children – Rachel, Ada Jane (1883), Emily Grace (1880), Jane (1867), Alec, Ellen Louise (1886), Gertrude and Mary Ann (1871) who was born at Providence House in High Street and became a servant at Corentin in the 1890s. Henry and Rachel's other son was William Henry Ferrett. He was born on 15 January 1865 and was known as 'Waggoner Bill'. He married into one of the established Boscastle families when he married Lilian Honey on 31 December 1892. Lily, as she was known, was the daughter of Emma Teresa and Charles Burdon Honey. Bill and Lily lived at Brooklets and had eight children, one of whom was Sidney Honey Ferrett, who was born in 1898 and grew up to become a railway fireman. He married Dorothy Ellen Hill on 4 April 1922. Dorothy Jane Ferrett, who was known as Doll, married Victor Richard Beasley on 12 December 1928. Alan George Ferrett married Doris Monica Rogers on 20 December 1923 and his brother William

Beth Ferrett with her mother Hilda Saltern and daughter Jennifer.

Linda Ferrett, Margaret Brown and Ann Ferrett.

Jennifer, David and John Ferrett in the doorway of Trevalver.

Jim Ferrett is pictured centre front with some of his comrades in India in 1944.

Graham, Alan, David and Richard Ferrett.

Alan and Fred Ferrett (standing), *Jim and Art* (seated).

married Doris' sister Violet May Rogers on 21 October 1922. Arthur married Doris Osbourne. Frederick John married Belinda Metherell on 7 June 1934 and Frank James, who was known as Jim, married Beth Saltern on 17 April 1937. There was one other son, Charles Henry Ferrett, who was born on 26 January 1899. Charlie, as he was known, was a stretcher-bearer with the 8th Battalion the Somerset Light Infantry. He had originally enlisted, like so many other local young men, with the Duke of Cornwall's Light Infantry and was given the service number 38111. Stretcher-bearers comprised some of the highest casualties in the First World War, and Charlie was no exception. He was seriously wounded in September 1918 on the Western Front. At first it was thought he might recover and Bill and Lily got permission to visit him in France, where he had been for eight months. A few days after their return they received the news that he had died aged 19 from gunshot wounds at No. 12 General Hospital, Rouen on 20 September. 29357 Private C.H. Ferrett is buried at the St Sever military cemetery near Rouen.

When William Ferrett and Violet Rogers were married in 1922, Violet placed her bouquet of white carnations and chrysanthemums on the war memorial in memory of her youngest brother.

On return from their honeymoon William and Violet were met by the Town Band, of whom William was a member. They were presented with a pair of stag-handled carvers in a velvet-and-silk-lined case with the band's wishes for every happiness in the future. William and Violet had three children – Charles who married Edna Curtis, Margaret Joan who married Tony Fry and William Roger who is known as Roger. He married Marion Rose Andrews whose family came from Buckland Brewer.

Jim and Beth Ferrett had nine children – Jennifer who married Phil Smith, David who married Jean Goodman, John who married Margaret Webbs, Alan who married Marita Ebbers, Richard who married Sue Sawyer, Graham who married Margaret Coath, Ann who married Barry Saunter, Linda who is married to Roland Buckett and Angela who married Bill Pooley. Jim and Beth brought the family up at Trevalver where they lived for 40 years before moving to Langfords Meadow. As a young man, Jim was a member of the Territorial Army and just before the outbreak of the Second World War he was called up. He started military life in the Duke of Cornwall's Light Infantry, transferring into the Anti-Tank Reconnaissance Corps. He sailed to the Far East in the troopship *Dominion Monarch* and, having arrived in Burma, his unit was disbanded and Jim found himself part of Brigadier Orde Wingate's famous Chindits. Their job was to enter the jungle behind Japanese lines and sabotage the bridges and railway systems. Jim was promoted to Quartermaster-Sergeant and later became a paratrooper in the Indian Airborne Division. He made

Postman Noel Joyce blowing the hunting horn. On his right is Fun Philp.

Jordan Vale Post Office with posties Tom Martin from Camelford (seated) *and Bill Hockin.*

several drops over enemy territory before taking the safer job of recruitment officer. Following the war Jim worked at the Wellington Hotel and at Ward's stores. He spent the last ten years of his working life at the Spar shop in Camelford. Throughout his life Jim played a full part in village activities. He spent 25 years in the Coastguard where he was Auxiliary-in-Charge of a crew of 20 men. The crew kept rough-weather watch from the lookout tower at Willapark. After Jim had suffered a heart attack in 1989 he was taken to Derriford Hospital by air ambulance. He attributed his recovery to their quick response and spent the rest of his life helping to raise funds for the First Air Ambulance.

Jim's wife Beth was the daughter of Jack and Hilda Saltern and was born in Camelford. They lived at Hodges Ground at the end of Dark Lane. She came to Boscastle in 1934 to work at the Post Office in Jordan Terrace. Beth died at the age of 87, less than a year after Jim. They had been married for over 65 years.

Further down the road is Jordan Terrace where Sue Scott has her hairdressers' in 2004. Previously this end of terrace had been the Post and Telegraph Office. In the days when Mrs Smith ran the Post Office at No. 1 a young Eric Nicholls was living at No. 3. His best friend was Stan Kinsman whose family lived at Jordan Mill. Stan was the son of Bill Kinsman and grandson of Daniel Kinsman. The two boys used to push his small barrow around the village selling vegetables that Bill had grown. There was a mill on this site in Norman times, built in 1234. It was just below the castle where the Jordan and Butts Water meet, giving a stronger head of water. When Percy Jones was renovating Jordan Mill in the 1970s he discovered a stone in the mill wall dated 1309. The stone is still there but has been rendered over.

There were only six mills recorded in Cornwall in the Domesday survey. In the thirteenth century the monks of Minster priory were permitted to grind their corn at Bottreaux Mill. At the Launceston Assizes in 1306 William de Botreaux (VI) recovered a water-mill from Cecilia de Haccombe, Stephen de Haccombe and others, who claimed it was part of Worthefala. Other mills in the area are the one beside the Wellington Hotel which is fed by a leat from the Valency, one at New Mills, one at Anderton and an ancient one at Halamelin. The names Valency and Halamelin may originate from the Celtic language, 'Melyn-ty' meaning 'millhouse' becoming 'Valency'. 'Halamelin' means 'mill (melin) on the moor (hal)'. The Wellington mill had two water-wheels, one on either side. It was last used during the Second World War.

Before the First World War the Wellington mill was worked by women who carried grain sacks that would weigh up to two hundredweight. At harvest time women and children were permitted to gather grain left beside the hedges and paths after the main harvest. The grain they gathered was put into paper sacks and taken to the mill, where it would be ground for them. The houses beside the mill were once used by the manor as housing for the mill workers.

The Old or Oxen Road continues northwards down the hill from Jordan Mill to the Wellington Hotel, passing allotments once known as Frogapit gardens, on past Frogapits and Marine Terrace. Some of Boscastle's best-known local families lived at Marine Terrace during the twentieth century, including the Sandercocks, Frys and Beards. Jack Beard married Annie Fuge in 1934. Annie was the daughter of John Walter Fuge and his wife Gertrude who lived at Island Cottages. John had been a coachman before the First World War and he died fighting with the Duke of Cornwall's Light Infantry. In October 1920 Gertrude married again, this time to a carter, William Kinsman, the son of Daniel Kinsman. He was living in Dunn Street at the time.

Annie and Jack Beard's neighbours Fred and Joan Sandercock married in 1927 and their first home together was at Hill Cottage, where their first children were born. They later moved to Marine Terrace where Fred had been brought up from the age of three. Fred and Joan had three children, John, Rodney and Barbara, all of whom grew up at Marine Terrace. Joan was a talented musician and worked for Dr Watson and then for 28 years for Dr and Mrs Weir. She continued working until she was 80 years old.

Fred was born in Boscastle in 1915. His father William was a fish merchant and sold fish from a pony and trap. On leaving school Fred went to work for Cornwall County Council and remained with them until he retired 40 years later. He loved singing and would join in the sing-alongs at the Wellington where he met his wife Joan. During the Second World War Fred served in the DCLI. He landed in Normandy on D-Day and narrowly escaped death on what became known as Cornwall Hill. The 5th Battalion (Territorial Army) landed in Normandy with the 43rd (Wessex Division) on 23 June 1944, and within three days was engaged in fierce fighting in the difficult Bocage country of Normandy. Among their many heroic actions the Battle of Hill 112 stands out. Fred was one of so many local men who served with the DCLI.

Marine Terrace was built by the Board of Trade for the forerunners of the Coastguard Service. Riding Officers were the oldest branch of the Preventative Service. They patrolled from the shore and were established in 1698. By 1713 troops were being stationed along the coast specifically to assist the Customs Officers. A Preventative Water Guard was set up in 1809 – it was a sea-going force with the aim of combating smuggling in the background of the Napoleonic Wars. It was feared that smugglers were actually involved in the passing of information from spies operating in London. Smugglers had to penetrate a triple barrier of the Revenue cruisers, the Preventative Water Guard and the Riding Officers patrolling the coastline. Men of the Boscastle Preventative Water Guard in the 1830s included Chief Officer James Scott, John Jermyn, Peter Davies, John Bowden, William Wedge, Thomas Bennett, Ephraim Trevorrow, Benjamin Day and Henry Hicks. The men of the Preventative Service were housed in the village in the Preventative Houses. Theirs was a dangerous occupation and the sea took its toll. In one instance on 12 January 1822 one of their boats was returning to Boscastle from Bude in a strong north-easterly gale with a boisterous sea running, when she upset in sight of people watching on the cliffs at St Gennys. The crew of five were lost, four of whom left families.

Following the Napoleonic Wars there was a surplus of naval ships and men and they were transferred to 'coast watching' duties to boost the prevention of smuggling. They were not yet involved in life saving but were a uniformed branch of the Royal Navy. Until dedicated housing was built for them they were lodged with local families. There was such a preventative presence in Boscastle in 1820. They were involved in an incident on the night of 11 December 1820. Samson Woodcock and his men, stationed at Boscastle, were on duty in the preventative boat and, whilst on patrol, they went ashore at Millook and found between 400–500 tubs of foreign spirits which had been stashed there. They beached their boat and waited on guard. The smugglers' cutter arrived and two waiting armed boats were sent out after her. They and the cutter exchanged fire. The smugglers came ashore and attacked Sampson Woodcock and his men who were outnumbered, and the smugglers succeeded in carrying off their booty together with the preventative boat. The Commissioners of His Majesty's Customs was obliged to offer a reward of £200 for information leading to the conviction of the smugglers. The smugglers' cutter was described as having 16 black ports, eight on each side, black bulwarks painted with a broad yellow stripe on the side and narrow black streak above, red counter with a yellow moulding, dark gaff topsail, dark foresail, white jib, running bowsprit and topsail yard across. The reward was never paid nor the smugglers caught but rumour suggested they were Frenchmen from the port of Roscoff.

In 1820 several Royal Navy ships were engaged specifically in the prevention of smuggling. In 1822 the Preventative Water Guard, Revenue Cruisers of the Inland Revenue and Riding Officers were combined to form the Coastguard. This enabled the service to become more efficient and their duties and prize money were formalised to combine the duties of the three separate units, but still this did not officially include a specific life-saving role. Prize money was paid out to the men involved in particular rescues. For example, after the wreck of the Swedish brigantine *William* at Crackington Haven the Coastguard log recorded:

Received from Board of Trade £7.0.0d and paid Wm Moyse £2.0.0., to H. Rogers £2.0.0., J. Piper £1.0.0., J. Greenwood and R. Goodman £1.0.0., for rescuing the mate of the William, *also by Board of Trade orders handed the purse and contents £2.2.5d to Hodge who found it on the beach at Crackington at time of wreck and delivered same to Coastguard-15 March 1894. Received from LSA 15 a cheque for £21.8.9d for Coastguard and volunteers for services at wreck of* William.

In the early 1840s Boscastle had a Customs Officer in Patrick Crossman who married Ann Burke, a daughter of the captain of the schooner *Briton's Queen*. There was also a coast waiter in William Powell, who at one time was being monitored for an alcohol problem and whilst he was in Boscastle his wife and seven children remained in Swansea. When the Duke of Cornwall was born the following year the Coastguard took part in the village celebrations. It was reported that they were immediately 'drawn out and a salute was fired'. The vessels in the harbour hoisted their colours and in the evening an enormous bonfire was lit.

The Coastguard station was fully established in Boscastle in 1844 and Marine Terrace housed the Coastguard Station Officer at the end next to the Wellington Hotel. Robert Fuzzard was the Commander Boatman at that time and he was one of the first to live in Marine Terrace, or Coastguard Cottages as they were then called. With him in the other cottages were John Tanner, Thomas Dangar and Ephraim Trevorrow. Elsewhere in the village were John Pike of the Inland Revenue and William Powell, a Customs Officer at the Custom House.

Robert Fuzzard, the Commander Boatman, played his part in the village not only in his role as a Coastguard but privately as well. He was responsible for carrying out work, at his own expense, to cut and excavate many of the footpaths to sites previously inaccessible on the cliffs. He also supplied and placed the seats on them to command the most picturesque views.

In 1845 the Coastguard became a naval reserve and was given training in coastal defence, paving the way for 3,000 of their men to serve in the Crimean War. The Coastguard boathouse was situated at the seaward end of the buildings that stood on the site where the youth hostel stands in 2004.

In February 1860 the brig *Principe Alberto* went ashore near Tremoutha – she was bound from Glasgow to Havanna with a cargo of manufactured goods. The crew of 12 Spaniards were taken off the wrecked vessel by Boscastle Coastguard using Dennetts rockets, a forerunner of the breeches buoy.

A volunteer crosses the harbour in the breeches bouy, 1898.

Men of the LSA prepare to fire the line which will carry the breeches bouy in 1898.

Luxon Pickard on duty at the coastguard lookout at Willapark.

Boscastle LSA team, 1950. Left to right, back row: *A. Olde, F. Scott, A. Biddick, C. Biddick, A. Biddick, F. Sandercock, W. Beer, George Clift;* middle row: *S. Mugford, S. Lawrence, L. Perry, W. Ferrett, J. Beard, E. Sleeman, P. Nicholls, E. Nicholls;* front row: *F. Sandercock, ?, R. Kernick, ?, J. Kinsman.*

An illustration of rocket apparatus being used to rescue the crew of a stricken vessel in 1911, taken from a postcard.

Boscastle Auxiliary Coastguard in 2003. Pictured are, left to right: *Les Siford (Station Officer), Graham King (Deputy Station Officer), Anthony Williams, Dan Roots, Dave Williams, Richard Alexander, Joe Mills, Tim Little.*

Harold Ward, Home Guard, 1940s.

By 1856 the Coastguard had come under the Admiralty. The wages of chief officers was £100 a year and for a chief boatman £36, at a time when village workers earned 8s. to 10s. a week. Their jobs included keeping watch for smugglers and ships in distress. They had charge of the breeches buoy life-saving apparatus which was supplied by the Board of Trade. The breeches buoy, or life-saving apparatus, was the invention of Cornishman Henry Trengrouse. It was light and portable and could be readily carried on to the cliffs. A rocket carried a line to the stricken vessel or from the vessel to shore. Its track was shown by a trail of fire making it visible in the dark. At one time almost every ship carried this apparatus and it was standard Board of Trade equipment from 1854. The Boscastle rocket and its breeches buoy was used until the 1980s. The line fired from shore to ship could be pulled aboard. This line carried a heavier rope which, when tethered, would carry the canvas 'breeches', which would carry a man to safety as it was pulled along the rope to shore.

By 1861 the Coastguard Cottages were lived in by four members of the team of Coastguards and William Selley was Chief Boatman-in-Charge. With him were Richard Nicholls (Boatman), Richard Ching (Commissioned Boatman) and John Pascoe Sharrock (one of the coastguards who served in the Crimea and a Commissioned Boatman), and living elsewhere in the village were Ephraim Trevorrow (Boatman) and John Tanner (Chief Boatman). At about this time Henry Ellis became a coastguard in Boscastle. He had joined the Royal Navy at the age of 13 in 1841 as a boy 2nd class. He had progressed five ranks to leading seaman before transferring to Boscastle in 1857. He later transferred to Bude and Porthcawl and died in 1898 at the age of 69.

The year 1866 saw pensions introduced for coastguards and as well as its serving coastguards Boscastle had two pensioners in 1871 – John Tanner and Ephraim Trevorrow, who had remained in the village after retirement.

The Coastguard Cottages at Marine Terrace were eventually replaced by a new larger station on the Tintagel Road at Cambeak which had a lookout at its northern end to supplement the Willapark lookout. There were better quarters for the men's families and a yard where they mustered before attending duties. It was built after the Admiralty confirmed in 1870 that the Coastguard duties were (for the first time) for life-saving purposes. New Coastguard stations were built around the country until there were 533 of them. The Boscastle station was closed in 1933. Those serving at the time of closure, like Coastguard Henry J. Godfrey, were transferred to other full-time stations.

Boscastle's Life-Saving Apparatus, or LSA, was station number 29. It was part of Holyhead District and came under Padstow Division. It was housed in a small stone shed on the south bank of the river at Bridge which was rented from the manor at a cost of £2 per year in the 1890s. It held the wagon, new in 1888, which carried the rocket apparatus. Horses, usually six, were hired in the event of an emergency and the coastguards were assisted by a band of volunteers. In December 1900 it consisted of six members of the Coastguard and 17 volunteers approved by the Board of Trade, and it was described as the 'Brigade'. The volunteers were trained alongside the regular men and were encouraged to better their skills by regular line-throwing or throwing-the-lead contests and the award of long-service medals which were given for 20 years of unbroken service. Visitors would often visit, especially to see an LSA drill, and it was not unknown for a lady visitor to Boscastle to be rescued from the 'wreck' in the breeches buoy amidst great enthusiasm. These drills took place every three months.

Newspaper accounts of the time describe the methods of rescue used and the dangerous conditions these men had to work in. When the *Iota* of Naples was wrecked in 1893 she was sailing under her master Vincenza Mazzella from Cardiff for Trinidad. She came ashore under Great Lye Rock at Tintagel. Her crew tried to leap for the rocks but two fell into the sea and were crushed under the barque's bilges and 14-year-old Cantanese Domenica was swept away. The Boscastle Brigade under the command of Henry Hughill were called out when the signal gun was fired from the Life-Saving House. Within a few minutes the men assembled, the horses were attached to the wagon and the Brigade headed westward until the *Iota* was sighted driving towards Bossiney Cove. The Brigade made for the spot and fired their rocket. The Italians did not understand how the rocket worked and the language difficulties meant they couldn't be given instruction and so three men, Hughill, Hambly a local quarryman, and Glanville, climbed over the rocks in the teeth of the gale and boarded the ship. They succeeded in rescuing the Italian captain, mate and seven crew.

Just a few weeks later the Boscastle Brigade was in action again, this time at Crackington Haven where the Swedish brigantine *Welm* had driven ashore. The signal was given for the Brigade to assemble. Six horses, supplied by Mr Brendon of the Wellington Hotel, were harnessed to the wagon and, with Mr Cory Scott as driver, they set off. Much praise was given to Cory Scott for the way he handled a team of horses and it is testament to his skill that he was given this job with the Brigade. This time the Brigade were not successful. By the time they arrived all but one of the crew had perished.

In 1898 a new rocket house was built on the opposite bank of the river at a cost of £143. It was used until the 1980s when a garage for the modern Land Rover rescue vehicle was built near Harbour Cottage with a room for training above the storage area.

Giving help to those in peril on the sea has been a long tradition in Boscastle as it has in the rest of Cornwall and around the coast of Britain. Tales of wrecking have very little basis in fact and although they make a ripping good yarn it is difficult to imagine families, whose menfolk made a hard and dangerous living at sea, being involved in deliberately taking the lives of other seafarers. Although Boscastle merchant, Thomas Rickard Avery, was described as a wrecker, as we have seen he was not involved in the act of wrecking but in the legitimate salvage of wrecks. The coast here is littered with wrecks from the nineteenth century alone. From Tintagel to Crackington Haven they include the *Iota* (1893), *Jessie Logan* (1843), *Gazelle* (1899), *Bottreaux Castle* (1879), *Londos* (1891), *Cassandra* (1841), *Sarah* (1843), *Adulpho Marie* (1877), *J.B.C.* (1866), *Canadian* (1842), *Prince Alberto* (1850), *Pendarves* (1829), *Edwin* (1817), *William* (1894), *Eugenie* (1865), *Nugget* (1859), *Trio* (1859) and *Blossom* (1869).

Headstones in Forrabury churchyard pay tribute to the men who lost their lives at sea. One such man was the master of the brigantine *Gazelle*. In April 1899 the *Gazelle*, of Boulogne, under master Amede Kerforcen, was sailing from Llanelly for St Valery. A gale drove her ashore under Pentargon cliffs. When the brigade arrived they fired the rocket but the sailor recovering it fell overboard. Captain Kerforcen had blood pouring down his bearded face and was supported at the wheel by a young sailor. A wave broke over the stern washing the captain overboard, leaving the lad jammed under the wreckage of the wheel. The coastguards had to descend the cliffs by ladders and then an 80-foot rope on to the badly listing deck. Coastguard Charles Hambly was twice engulfed by the huge seas. Eventually the men were rescued and they climbed the ladders up the cliffs to safety. Captain Kerforcen's body was recovered three days later.

Great respect has always been given to those whose lives have been lost at sea and to the men involved in saving lives. At the funerals of men in the Coastguard service, both serving or retired, the coffin would be draped with the Union Jack and often accompanied by bearers in full naval uniform. Flags at the Coastguard station and the church would be flown at half-mast.

In addition to their peacetime duties the Coastguard service had a wartime role. Ships were sunk by torpedoes in the First and Second World Wars. The remains of a German E-boat came ashore near Crackington Haven. During the wars Coastguard duties had added urgency. Auxiliary Coastguard William (Bill) Kinsman wrote a poem about the Boscastle Coastguard in the Second World War, in which he refers to local men John Scoble and Jack Downing and to wartime doctor Lucas Hillier. It reads as follows:

Pentargon O Pentargon a rough and rugged spot
In winter time it is too cold
And summer time too hot
Now the lookout hut at Rusey
Stands on much higher ground
You can view the sea for miles and miles
If you only look around.
The dawn patrol on Strangles beach
Trudges through the leaking sand
To see if there is anything
That's dangerous to man.
Twas on a frosty morning
Poor Scoble he fell down
And Downing came upon the scene
And brought him to the town.
The doctor met him at the bridge
And administered a pill
And pumped in oxygen and stuff
To help him up the hill.
The poor old chap is better now
And fit again for war
He could manage it much better
If he only had a car.
But the war is drawing to a close
And some are feeling ill
To get the pick and shovel out
Will be a bitter pill.
But the Labour Exchange
Is still intact
So there is no need to worry
If they once get there
They will not care
To start work in a hurry.

The wartime Auxiliary Coastguard stood on duty in a temporary hut at Rusey above Pentargon. On 13 April 1941 Bill Kinsman and Arthur Nicholls were on duty when a Heinkell 111 German aircraft was attacked during its action against a British Merchant convoy off Newquay. It crashed into the sea off Boscastle at 9p.m. At midnight the crew landed on the beach at Pentargon in their inflatable survival craft and were captured by Bill and Arthur who were on patrol. They marched the prisoners to the Millhouse tearooms to await the arrival of the Camelford police. PC Brown and the Home Guard arrived and took charge of the prisoners whilst awaiting the arrival of the police. The men were handcuffed and taken by the Army to the Infantry Training Centre of the DCLI, Bodmin. The inflatable raft was taken to a local airfield for examination as it was the first parachute raft seen. Mrs Dorothy Stock, proprietor of the Wellington Hotel and Millhouse tearooms, showed sympathy to the airmen, despite the actions of some of the evacuee women who spat at them and tried to punch them. Mrs Stock's own son John, an RAF bomber pilot, was missing at that time. He was picked up by a North Sea trawler for the third time before he finally went missing and was reported killed in action in August 1942. She knew perhaps how families at home in Germany would worry about their own sons.

It was not only seamen who lost their lives off this area of treacherous coast. In 1851 Mary Elizabeth Harris of Clapham, Surrey was washed off rocks when bathing, as was Thomas Reed Harris of London in 1874. Thomas Cotton Mellish and his sister, Amy Adeleide of London, were drowned in 1893 in the harbour and Hugh Anstead lost his life trying to save them. Two students, Eliza Cummins and Beatrice Pinks of Moorfield Training College, London, lost their lives while bathing in 1915. In 1911 Hermon Canson died after falling from the cliff at Pentargon. In January 1923 two lady visitors to Boscastle, Misses Browne and Franklyn, went to Pentargon to bathe. Going down the footpath Miss Browne slipped and fell 50 feet on to a ledge and in trying to get back slipped a further 20 feet on to the rocks below. Miss Franklyn went to the Boscastle Coastguard station for help. Coastguardsmen Robinson and Puddefoot were lowered to the rocks below to give first aid. Miss Browne, who was a medical student from London, was taken to hospital with a fractured arm.

Strangers to this part of the country are often unaware of how dangerous the sea and coast can be. Today the role of the Coastguard, although different, is just as vital. The number of men required is less but the level of training is high. Twenty-first-century volunteers learn about pollution and all aspects of rescue together with first aid and resuscitation methods. The Coastguard is part of the 999 emergency service alongside the police, fire and ambulance services, a fact we are occasionally reminded of when we hear with relief the sounds of their vehicle siren as they travel to the site of the latest incident. They work together with teams from Port Isaac and Bude and have the advantage of a modern vehicle and a link with the helicopter rescue service, but in the end, in a difficult and dangerous situation, it is the bravery of the man on the spot that counts.

In 2004, carrying on the tradition of life-saving, the Auxiliary Coastguard of the Boscastle Company are led by Station Officer Les Siford who took over from Mac Reynolds in 1999. Les has served in the Coastguard for 15 years. He is the son of Harbour Master Fred Siford who was also a Coastguard member. There are eight members of the Boscastle Company: Les Siford (Station Officer), Graham King (Deputy Station Officer), Anthony Williams, Dan Roots, Dave Williams, Richard Alexander, Joe Mills and Tim Little. They continue a long and brave tradition of which we are all rightly proud.

Postman delivering mail in Dunn Street in 1902.

On the cliffs overlooking Meachard Rock is one of the seats provided by Coastguard Fuzzard in the 1850s.

Above: *Boscastle LSA team manoeuvre the Life Saving Apparatus over the lower bridge in 1898.*

Left: *Arthur Olde was a member of the British Legion, Coastguard Service, Men's Club, Parish Council and a steward at the Methodist chapel.*

SUBSCRIBERS

Mr and Mrs D. Adams, Oldbury, West Midlands
Mrs D.P. Adams (née Mugford)
Mr and Mrs J. Adams, Boscastle, Cornwall
Canon J.M. Ayling, formerly of Boscastle
Les Baker, Tintagel, Cornwall
Mrs B. Ball, Bruton, Somerset
Babs Ball (née Fry), Plymouth, Devon
Shirley and Arthur Bannister, Boscastle
Bernadette Barkley, Calgary, Canada
Ruth Barkwill
Jenny and Martin Barnes, Suffolk
Cyril Bath, Feniton (strong family links in Boscastle)
Mervyn Beard, Tregadillett, Launceston
N. John Beasley, born Boscastle 1926
Brian R. Beer, Plymouth, Devon
Peter and Diane Bentall, Boscastle
Debbie Beszant, Boscastle, Cornwall
Arthur G.H. Biddick, late of Boscastle
Mr and Mrs H.M. Biddick, Boscastle, Cornwall
Mr K. Biddick, Tregadillett, Launceston, Cornwall
Stuart Biddick, Boscastle
Wendy A. Bircher (née Brewer)
Elizabeth A. Bowering, Boscastle, Cornwall
Jim and Diane Bradford, St Albans, Hertfordshire
Jonathan Bradley and Harriet Knight, Tamarisk Cottage, Boscastle
Derek Bright, Boscastle, Cornwall
V. Bright
Vernon Bright
Paul Broadhurst, The Bridge, Boscastle
Mr T.C. and Mrs L.A. Brockman, Boscastle, Cornwall
Joanne Brooker, Boscastle, Cornwall
Elin Brooks, Redditch, Worcestershire
Louise and Andrew Brown
Priscilla Brown
Stuart and Jenny Brown,
Sally, David, Philip, Stephen and Christopher Burley, St Day, Cornwall
K.J. Burrow, Bucks Cross, Devon
Elizabeth M. Callaway, St Tudy
Jim and Jane Castling, Valency House
Alan and Sue Champion, Boscastle, Cornwall
Bob and Jill Clark, Boscastle, Cornwall
Barbara Coltman, Boscastle, Cornwall
Mr and Mrs Cooper, The Bottreaux Hotel, Boscastle
David T. Couch, North Baddesley, Hampshire
David and Di Cray, Boscastle, Cornwall
Samantha Cray, Southampton, Hampshire
Anne and Aubrey Cronin
Sue and John Davis, Boscastle, Cornwall
Pat Day, Boscastle, Cornwall
Marigold and John Dewfall, Milborne Port, Somerset
John Hawker Dinham, Krugersdorp, South Africa
Graham and Alison Dodson, Old Brig Inn
Jean and David Eagles
Sandra Eyles (née Fry), Wellington, Somerset
Peter Fanshawe, Welltown Manor, Boscastle
Pearl M.G. Fearnley
Alan L. Ferrett
David and Jean Ferrett
Miss Elaine Marie Ferrett, Delabole, Cornwall
Graham Ferrett, Cheshire
Mr John Ferrett, New Zealand
Michael Alan Ferrett, formerly of Dunn Street, Boscastle
Roger Ferrett
Sue and Richard Ferrett, Delabole, North Cornwall
Peter Fleming, Woodford
Graham, Jane, Sebastian, Benedict Flood, Fairfield, Boscastle
David and Valerie Flower, Tintagel
Debbie Foster, Solihull, West Midlands
Frazer Freeman, Essex
Raymond Gale, Falmouth
W.M. Gard
Betty Godwin, Sydney, Australia
Kerriann Godwin, Pencliffe, Boscastle, Cornwall
Ian and Jane Gourley, Boscastle, Cornwall
Mrs K. Gray, Dalwood, Axminster, Devon
Ian Grimes, St Teath, Cornwall
Jackie Gynn, born and raised in Boscastle
Mrs Jackie Haddy (Treleaven Family), Tredorn Farm
Charles and Jean Hancock, Hayle, Cornwall
Delia and Sam Hancock, Paradise Farm, Boscastle
Peter Hancock, born in Boscastle
Royston J. Hancock, Boscastle, Cornwall
Sarah Hancock, Elm Cottage, Boscastle
Sheila M. Hancock, Boscastle, Cornwall
Roy and Valerie Harvey, Oxford
Judith Headon, Trevalga, Boscastle
Ann Heard, Camelford
Derek Hicks, Delabole, Cornwall
Jeremy J. Hicks, Boscastle, Cornwall
D.A. and A.J. Higgs and Family, Boscastle, Cornwall
Philip Higgs, Menzies Creek, Victoria 3159, Australia
Mike and Helen Hinton, Aldwick, West Sussex

Mr and Mrs M.S. Hircock, Boscastle, Cornwall
Pauline Hodge, formerly of Boscastle
Cynthia Holt, for Peter Holt (deceased)
Ann and Graham Honey, St Austell
Nigel J. Honey, Bodmin, Cornwall
J.A. and N.A. Hopkins, Boscastle, Cornwall
Gillian and Andy Howell, Crackington Haven, Cornwall
James T. Hughes, Boscastle, Cornwall
Rosalind, Keith and Matthew Ireland, Boscastle
Mr and Mrs R. and N. Irving-Little, Boscastle Pottery
Elizabeth and Tony Jackson, Plymouth
Miss Miriam James, Trehane Farm, Trevalga
Doug and Bridget Johnson, Boscastle
Keith and Esme Jones, Boscastle, Cornwall
C.R. Jose, Boscastle, Cornwall
S.J. Jose, Boscastle, Cornwall
Dudley H.J. Kernick, Solihull, UK
Maxwell Kernick, Solihull, West Midlands
Doreen L. Kilpatrick (née Mugford), Victoria, B.C., Canada
Graham King, Boscastle
James and Gladys Kinsman, Boscastle, Cornwall
John and Joan Kinsman, Boscastle
Peter James Kinsman, Boscastle, Cornwall
Deborah Langevin, Calgary, Canada
Les and Hazel Lee, Epsom, Surrey
Brian Le Messurier, Exeter, Devon
Richard B.P. Leschallas, Eastbourne, Sussex
Norman and Mary Lilly, Perran-Ar-Worthal, Cornwall
Pat Ling, Tremore Valley, Cornwall
Rob and Teresa Lloyd, Boscastle, Cornwall
Trevor and Celia Lloyd, Boscastle, Cornwall
Mr and Mrs G.W. Long, Bridgwater, Somerset
Fran and Reuben Long, Scorrier, Cornwall
Elizabeth E. Lugg (née Gard), Forrabury, Boscastle, Cornwall. 26.1.22.
Mr Stephen Macdonald-Brown BSc MRSC, Boscastle
Muriel J. Mason (née Beard), Tresparrett, Camelford
Ray Mason, Blisland, Bodmin
John Maughan, Boscastle Busker
Mr Clive A.J. May, Watford, Hertfordshire
Mr Julian May, Wallingford, Oxon
Malcolm McCarthy, Padstow
John and Bonnie McKenzie, Boscastle, Cornwall
Sarah J. Melton (née Couch), Tintagel, Cornwall
Mike and Kate Metcalfe
Cdr Joe Mills, St Day, Cornwall
H. and L. Mills
Simon Mills, Melton, Victoria, Australia
Nina A. Mitchell, Par, Cornwall
Mrs E.M. Molesworth, Paradise, Boscastle
Peggy and John Molesworth, Boscastle, Cornwall
Carol and Aage Møller, Plummers Plain, West Sussex
Andrea and Alisa Moore, Northampton
Ian and Janice Moore, Northampton
David Morgan, Marhamchurch, Cornwall
Terry and Bill Moule, Cheshunt, Hertfordshire
Julie Muscutt, Harbour Terrace, Boscastle, Cornwall
The Museum of Witchcraft, Boscastle
Rachel Nancekivell, Lesnewth
David and Joy Nash, Falmouth
Martin Nash, Trethevy, Cornwall
Arthur and Mary Nicholls, Senwood, Boscastle, Cornwall
Joan and Eric Nicholls, Wilmar, Boscastle
Nicholas Nicholls, Boscastle, Cornwall
Nicky and Maria Nicholls, Trelawney, Boscastle
Stephen and Cheryl Nicholls, Trerosewell, Boscastle
Stephen W. Nicholls, Boscastle, Cornwall
Ian Olde, Luton, Bedfordshire
Iris J. Olde (née Hockin), Boscastle, Cornwall
Pat Olde, Aylesbury, Buckinghamshire
Catherine E. Parsons, Boscastle, Cornwall
Frank and Annette Parsons, Boscastle
Alan and Juanita Partridge, Boscastle, Cornwall
Major General John Pearn AM RFD, Brisbane, Australia
S. Pearson, Melbourn, Royston, Hertfordshire
Margaret H. Perry, Boscastle, Cornwall
William and Phyllis Perry, Boscastle
Charles and Judith Pettit, Shenington, Oxfordshire
Monica Pickard, Boscastle, North Cornwall
Wal and Beryl Picton, formerly of Boscastle
Renate Ploger, Boscastle
Anne and Adrian Prescott, Lower Meadows House, Boscastle
The Family of the late May Prout (née Gard), Australia
Dave and Beti Richards, Peterborough, Cambridgeshire
Mr and Mrs A. Rigby-Jones, Cornwall
Richard and Odette Rigby-Jones, Boscastle, Cornwall
Chris and Ann Rodda, Boscastle
John Rogers, formerly of Boscastle
Christine Roshanzamir (née Nicholls), Gillingham, Kent
Graham and Susan Rush, Boscastle, Cornwall
Joanne Safhill, Boscastle, Cornwall
Ann Saunter, Launceston, Cornwall
Sue Scott, Boscastle, Cornwall
Mr and Mrs C. Searle, St Juliot, Boscastle
Joan Seldon, Boscastle, Cornwall
Mrs Patricia Shearwood-Wood, Boscastle, Cornwall
Rod Shepherd and Mary Wright, Treforda Water, Boscastle
Geoff and Jan Showell, Boscastle, Cornwall

June and Fred Siford, Boscastle Harbour
Gloria A.R. Smale, Calgary, Canada
John Smale, Calgary, Canada
Mr Christopher Smith, Bristol
Jennifer Smith (née Ferrett)
Derek C. Stedman, Falmouth
Fiona Steeds, Boscastle, Cornwall
Ruth Stephens, Essex
Richard Strugnell, Christchurch, Dorset
June E. Swanson, Boscastle
Kathryn Swiston, Calgary, Canada
Jennifer Symons, Boscastle, Cornwall
Robina Symons, now Teague, Crackington Haven
Moira Tangye, Newquay, Cornwall
Chris W. Taylor, Alresford, Essex
Cynthia and Stephen Taylor, Gwel An Mor, Boscastle
D.M. and M.J. Taylor, Camelford
S.M. Taylor, Camelford
John and Denise Tillinghast, Boscastle, Cornwall
Pam Torster, Newnham, Launceston, Tasmania
Sonjia Tremain, Tintagel
Michael R. Turner, Boscastle, Cornwall
Jean Valadon, Malaga, Spain
John and Shirley Wakelin, Boscastle, Cornwall
John F.W. Walling, Newton Abbot, Devon
Michael and Pamela Ward, Portugal
E. and M. Warwick, Boscastle, Cornwall
C. and E. Webb, Boscastle, Cornwall
Michael Webber, Launceston
Simon Webster, Highbank Road, Lewes, East Sussex
Trixie Webster (née Webber), grandaughter of Richard Webber
Dr and Mrs D. Weir, Boscastle, Cornwall
Sally Whitaker, christened at Forrabury
P. White, Crackington Haven
Pamela G. White (née Hancock), Hayle, Cornwall
C.N. Wiblin, Shrewton, Wiltshire
Kathleen P. Wightman, Sherborne, Dorset
Derek Wivell
Derek M. Wood, Boscastle, Cornwall
Tony and Wendy Wood, Corentin, Boscastle
Lee Zwicker, Victoria, B.C., Canada

Community Histories

The Book of Addiscombe • Canning and Clyde Road Residents Association and Friends
The Book of Addiscombe, Vol. II • Canning and Clyde Road Residents Association and Friends
The Book of Axminster with Kilmington • Les Berry and Gerald Gosling
The Book of Bampton • Caroline Seward
The Book of Barnstaple • Avril Stone
The Book of Barnstaple, Vol. II • Avril Stone
The Book of The Bedwyns • Bedwyn History Society
The Book of Bickington • Stuart Hands
Blandford Forum: A Millennium Portrait • Blandford Forum Town Council
The Book of Bramford • Bramford Local History Group
The Book of Breage & Germoe • Stephen Polglase
The Book of Bridestowe • D. Richard Cann
The Book of Bridport • Rodney Legg
The Book of Brixham • Frank Pearce
The Book of Buckfastleigh • Sandra Coleman
The Book of Buckland Monachorum & Yelverton • Pauline Hamilton-Leggett
The Book of Carharrack • Carharrack Old Cornwall Society
The Book of Carshalton • Stella Wilks and Gordon Rookledge
The Parish Book of Cerne Abbas • Vivian and Patricia Vale
The Book of Chagford • Iain Rice
The Book of Chapel-en-le-Frith • Mike Smith
The Book of Chittlehamholt with Warkleigh & Satterleigh • Richard Lethbridge
The Book of Chittlehampton • Various
The Book of Colney Heath • Bryan Lilley
The Book of Constantine • Moore and Trethowan
The Book of Cornwood and Lutton • Compiled by the People of the Parish
The Book of Creech St Michael • June Small
The Book of Cullompton • Compiled by the People of the Parish
The Book of Dawlish • Frank Pearce
The Book of Dulverton, Brushford, Bury & Exebridge • Dulverton and District Civic Society
The Book of Dunster • Hilary Binding
The Book of Edale • Gordon Miller
The Ellacombe Book • Sydney R. Langmead
The Book of Exmouth • W.H. Pascoe
The Book of Grampound with Creed • Bane and Oliver
The Book of Hayling Island & Langstone • Peter Rogers
The Book of Helston • Jenkin with Carter
The Book of Hemyock • Clist and Dracott
The Book of Herne Hill • Patricia Jenkyns
The Book of Hethersett • Hethersett Society Research Group
The Book of High Bickington • Avril Stone
The Book of Ilsington • Dick Wills
The Book of Kingskerswell • Carsewella Local History Group
The Book of Lamerton • Ann Cole and Friends
Lanner, A Cornish Mining Parish • Sharron Schwartz and Roger Parker
The Book of Leigh & Bransford • Malcolm Scott
The Book of Litcham with Lexham & Mileham • Litcham Historical and Amenity Society
The Book of Loddiswell • Loddiswell Parish History Group
The New Book of Lostwithiel • Barbara Fraser
The Book of Lulworth • Rodney Legg
The Book of Lustleigh • Joe Crowdy
The Book of Lyme Regis • Rodney Legg
The Book of Manaton • Compiled by the People of the Parish
The Book of Markyate • Markyate Local History Society
The Book of Mawnan • Mawnan Local History Group
The Book of Meavy • Pauline Hemery
The Book of Minehead with Alcombe • Binding and Stevens
The Book of Morchard Bishop • Jeff Kingaby
The Book of Newdigate • John Callcut
The Book of Nidderdale • Nidderdale Museum Society
The Book of Northlew with Ashbury • Northlew History Group
The Book of North Newton • J.C. and K.C. Robins
The Book of North Tawton • Baker, Hoare and Shields
The Book of Nynehead • Nynehead & District History Society
The Book of Okehampton • Roy and Ursula Radford
The Book of Paignton • Frank Pearce
The Book of Penge, Anerley & Crystal Palace • Peter Abbott
The Book of Peter Tavy with Cudlipptown • Peter Tavy Heritage Group
The Book of Pimperne • Jean Coull

The Book of Plymtree • Tony Eames
The Book of Porlock • Dennis Corner
Postbridge – The Heart of Dartmoor • Reg Bellamy
The Book of Priddy • Albert Thompson
The Book of Princetown • Dr Gardner-Thorpe
The Book of Rattery • By the People of the Parish
The Book of St Day • Joseph Mills and Paul Annear
The Book of Sampford Courtenay with Honeychurch • Stephanie Pouya
The Book of Sculthorpe • Gary Windeler
The Book of Seaton • Ted Gosling
The Book of Sidmouth • Ted Gosling and Sheila Luxton
The Book of Silverton • Silverton Local History Society
The Book of South Molton • Jonathan Edmunds
The Book of South Stoke with Midford • Edited by Robert Parfitt
South Tawton & South Zeal with Sticklepath • Roy and Ursula Radford
The Book of Sparkwell with Hemerdon & Lee Mill • Pam James
The Book of Staverton • Pete Lavis
The Book of Stithians • Stithians Parish History Group
The Book of Stogumber, Monksilver, Nettlecombe & Elworthy • Maurice and Joyce Chidgey
The Book of Studland • Rodney Legg
The Book of Swanage • Rodney Legg
The Book of Tavistock • Gerry Woodcock
The Book of Thorley • Sylvia McDonald and Bill Hardy
The Book of Torbay • Frank Pearce
The Book of Watchet • Compiled by David Banks
The Book of West Huntspill • By the People of the Parish
Widecombe-in-the-Moor • Stephen Woods
Widecombe – Uncle Tom Cobley & All • Stephen Woods
The Book of Williton • Michael Williams
The Book of Witheridge • Peter and Freda Tout and John Usmar
The Book of Withycombe • Chris Boyles
Woodbury: The Twentieth Century Revisited • Roger Stokes
The Book of Woolmer Green • Compiled by the People of the Parish

For details of any of the above titles or if you are interested in writing your own history, please contact: Commissioning Editor, Community Histories, Halsgrove House, Lower Moor Way, Tiverton Business Park, Tiverton, Devon EX16 6SS, England;
email: katyc@halsgrove.com